Scotland

Board

Self-Catering

Caravans & Camping 441

Wales

Board

Self-Catering

Caravans & Camping 486

Ireland

Caravans & Camping

©MAPS IN MINUTES™ / Collins Bartholomew (2009)

© FHG Guides Ltd, 2011
ISBN 978-1-85055-435-6

Typeset by FHG Guides Ltd, Paisley.
Printed and bound in China by Imago.

Distribution. Book Trade: ORCA Book Services, Stanley House,
3 Fleets Lane, Poole, Dorset BH15 3AJ
(Tel: 01202 665432; Fax: 01202 666219)
e-mail: mail@orcabookservices.co.uk
Published by FHG Guides Ltd., Abbey Mill Business Centre,
Seedhill, Paisley PA1 ITJ (Tel: 0141-887 0428 Fax: 0141-889 7204).
e-mail: admin@fhguides.co.uk

500 Great Places to Stay in Britain is published by FHG Guides Ltd,
part of Kuperard Group.

Cover design: FHG Guides
Cover Picture: Padstow, Cornwall, courtesy of Cutkive Wood Holiday Lodges (page 213).

symbols

 Totally non-smoking   Pets Welcome

 Children Welcome   **SB** Short Breaks

 Suitable for Disabled Guests   Licensed

Cornwall

Cornwall, with the longest stretch of coastline in the UK, has become a major centre for watersports, whether sailing, surfing, windsurfing, water-skiing, diving in the clear waters to explore historic wrecks or enjoying a family beach holiday. There are busy fishing towns like Looe, Padstow, and traditional villages such as Polperro, with plenty of inns and restaurants where you can sample the fresh catch. There are gardens at Mount Edgcumbe and the Lost Garden of Heligan, as well as a wide choice of National Trust properties including Lanhydrock. The magnificent coast is ideal for birdwatchers, artists and photographers, while Bodmin Moor, one of Cornwall's 12 Areas of Outstanding Natural Beauty, is well worth a visit.

Bude

Hampton Manor

This six-bedroom country house hotel offers high quality accommodation, food and service in a beautiful setting in the Tamar valley which borders Devon and Cornwall. We are within easy reach of north and south coasts, the Eden Project, many interesting gardens and National Trust properties, and a good variety of challenging walks on Bodmin Moor and Dartmoor.

It's an ideal place to 'get away from it all' – and be spoilt!

B&B from £35pp
3-night break DB&B from £130pp.

Alston, Near Callington PL17 8LX • Tel: 01579 370494
e-mail: hamptonmanor@supanet.com • www.hamptonmanor.co.uk

Higher Trezion
Tresinney, Advent,
Camelford PL32 9QW
Tel: 01840 213761

Edge of Bodmin Moor

Are you looking for peace and relaxation? Come and stay on our small sheep farm and unwind in a unique setting off the beaten track. An ideal base for walking, or touring around Cornwall. Just 1½ miles from the A39 Atlantic Highway. Enjoy a day out on Bodmin Moor, or at the Eden Project, cycle the Camel Trail, walk the Coastal Paths, surf at Polzeath, Bude or Newquay, or visit one of the many golf clubs. The family, including our dog and cats, offer a relaxing atmosphere and warm welcome. One kingsize/twin and one double on ground floor; one kingsize/twin upstairs, all en suite. Start your day with an old fashioned 'farmhouse' breakfast, juices and cereals, sausage, bacon and hogs pudding etc, all cooked on the Aga, lots of home-made bread, fresh eggs, fruit and yogurt, tea and coffee. Wi-Fi available.

Dogs by arrangement. Good pubs and restaurants nearby.

e-mail: higher.trezion@btinternet.com • www.highertrezion.co.uk

Falmouth, Fowey, Launceston

SB

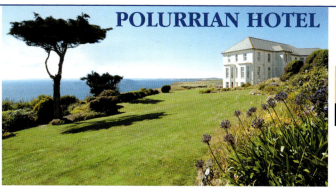

Mawgan Porth

Mevagissey, Mullion

Mrs Dawn Rundle, Lancallan Farm, Mevagissey, St Austell PL26 6EW
Tel & Fax: 01726 842284
e-mail: dawn@lancallan.fsnet.co.uk
www.lancallanfarm.co.uk

SB

Lancallan is a large 17th century farmhouse on a working 700-acre dairy and beef farm in a beautiful rural setting, one mile from Mevagissey. We are close to Heligan Gardens, lovely coastal walks and sandy beaches, and are well situated for day trips throughout Cornwall. Also six to eight miles from the Eden Project (20 minutes' drive). Enjoy a traditional farmhouse breakfast in a warm and friendly atmosphere.

The farmhouse comprises three bedrooms to let, two are double en suite and the third is a family room with one double and one single bed with a private bathroom. All bedrooms have a colour TV, tea and coffee making facilities, a hairdryer, towels and toiletries. There is a separate dining room for guests, and a relaxing lounge.

Terms and brochure available on request. SAE please.

Newquay

Newquay

Please note...

All the information in this book is given in good faith in the belief that it is correct.
However, the publishers cannot guarantee the facts given in these pages, neither are they responsible for changes in policy, ownership or terms that may take place after the date of going to press. Readers should always satisfy themselves that the facilities they require are available and that the terms, if quoted, still apply.

Penzance, Polperro, Port Isaac,

T'Gallants *Guest House*
St Austell • Cornwall

Overlooking the historic Charlestown Harbour near St Austell, T'Gallants Guest House offers superior Bed and Breakfast accommodation in seven tastefully decorated bedrooms, including a four-poster. All accommodation is non-smoking. An ideal base for visiting St Austell, mid-Cornwall including Mevagissey, Fowey, and the Roseland Peninsula.

6 Charlestown Road, Charlestown, St Austell, Cornwall PL25 3NJ • Tel: 01726 70203
• E-mail: enquiries@tgallants.co.uk • www.tgallants.co.uk
Self-catering Cottage also available.

Nanscawen Manor House
Prideaux Road, Luxulyan Valley, Near St Blazey
Cornwall PL24 2SR
Tel: 01726 814488 / 07811 022423

Dating from the 14thC, the Manor House offers four luxurious bedrooms, all south-facing with views of the garden towards the beautiful Luxulyan valley. A full English breakfast is served in the Victorian conservatory. Sample the locally smoked salmon and freshly baked croissants. Relax in the pool or the hot tub at the end of an enjoyable day's sightseeing. Totally non-smoking.

keith@nanscawen.com • www.nanscawen.com

Rosecare Villa Farm Holidays • North Cornwall

Situated on the stunning North Cornwall Coast in an Area of Outstanding Natural Beauty this family-run Bed and Breakfast is halfway between the turning to Boscastle and Crackington Haven.
Three bedrooms in converted barns surrounding a central courtyard. All rooms en suite with television and tea making facilities. Disabled access ranging from M1 to M3. Children welcome in family room with free hire of cots and highchairs. Non-smoking. Ample private car parking. 500yds from the National Cycle Network.

SB

Rosecare Villa Farm
Wainhouse Corner, St Gennys
Nr Bude, Cornwall EX23 0BG
Tel: 01840-230474
info@northcornwallholidays.com
www.northcornwallholidays.com

---

symbols

   Totally non-smoking

   Children Welcome

   Suitable for Disabled Guests

 Pets Welcome

SB *Short Breaks available*

Licensed

Dalswinton House

St. Mawgan-in-Pydar, Cornwall TR8 4EZ. Tel: 01637 860385
www.dalswinton.com • dalswintonhouse@btconnect.com

HOLIDAYS FOR DOGS AND THEIR OWNERS

Overlooking the village of St Mawgan, Dalswinton House stands in 10 acres of gardens and meadowland midway between Padstow and Newquay with distant views to the sea at dog-friendly Mawgan Porth.

- Dogs free of charge and allowed everywhere except the restaurant
- 8 acre meadow for dog exercise. Nearby local walks. Beach 1.5 miles
- Heated outdoor pool (May-Sep). Off-street car parking
- All rooms en suite with tea/coffee fac., digital TV and clock radios
- Wi-Fi access in public rooms and all bedrooms (except the lodge)
- Residents' bar and restaurant serving breakfast and dinner
- Bed and breakfast from £46 per person per night
- Weekly rates available and special offers in Mar/Apr/May/Oct
- Self-catering lodge sleeps 3 adults
- Easy access to Padstow, Eden Project, Newquay Airport & Coastal Path
- Dog-friendly self-catering near Falmouth

Regret no children under 16
Maximum 3 dogs per room at proprietor's discretion

Bampton

Devon

Think of moorland, and Devon immediately comes to mind. A county of contrasts, to the north are the wild moors of the Exmoor National Park, fringed by dramatic cliffs and combes, golden beaches and picturesque harbours, with busy market towns and sleepy villages near the coast. For family holidays, one of the best known of the many Blue Flag beaches on the north coast is at Woolacombe, with three miles of sand and a choice of holiday parks. Ilfracombe, originally a Victorian resort, with an annual Victorian festival, provides all kinds of family entertainment. An experience not to be missed is the cliff railway between the pretty little port of Lynmouth and its twin village of Lynton high on the cliff, with a backdrop of dramatic gorges or combes.

Fairwater Head Hotel
3 Star Accommodation at Sensible Prices

 ★★★ *75%*

Located in the tranquil Devon countryside and close to Lyme Regis, this beautiful Edwardian Country House Hotel has all you need for a peaceful and relaxing holiday.

Dogs Most Welcome and Free of Charge
Countryside location with panoramic views • *AA Rosette Restaurant*

The Fairwater Head Hotel
Hawkchurch, Near Axminster, Devon EX13 5TX
Tel: 01297 678349 • Fax: 01297 678459
e-mail: stay@fairwaterheadhotel.co.uk
www.fairwaterheadhotel.co.uk

Elizabethan Manor House in secluded gardens, surrounded by rolling countryside. Run by family for 40 years. Friendly and relaxing atmosphere.
One mile from local pub serving excellent food.
Easy access to coast and moor and Marwood Hill Gardens.
All bedrooms are large and face South, overlooking the valley.
One four-poster, one double and one twin.
All en suite with colour TV, tea/coffee making facilities and central heating in rooms.

Bed and Breakfast from £30pppn, two or more nights from £27pppn.

LEE HOUSE
**Marwood, Barnstaple, Devon
EX31 4DZ ·
Tel: 01271 374345**

Near Barnstaple • Farmhouse B&B

SB

Mrs J. Ley,
West Barton,
Alverdiscott, Near Barnstaple,
Devon EX31 3PT
Tel: 01271 858230

B&B £25pppn. Reduced rates for children under 12; weekly terms on request.

Our family working farm of 240 acres, with a pedigree herd of suckler cows and sheep, is situated in a small rural village between Barnstaple and Torrington, the Tarka Trail and Rosemoor Gardens. Six miles to the nearest beaches. Double room en suite, twin bedroom also available.
Guest lounge with TV and tea/coffee making facilities.
Good farmhouse cooking. £25 pppn.
Ample parking • No pets • Non-smoking

HAXTON DOWN FARM
Bratton Fleming, Barnstaple EX32 7JL
Tel: 01598 710275

Traditional country living on a working farm set in spectacular surroundings, close to the coast, Exmoor and so many places to visit you will be spoilt for choice. This 17th-19th century farmhouse offers comfort, charm and warmth to make a relaxing base. En suite rooms with TV, tea making facilities, radio, hairdryer etc. Guest lounge with TV, DVD and CD player, and cosy wood burner for cooler evenings. Dining room with separate tables with wide choice of breakfast and dinner dishes. There is a varied selection of inns and restaurants in the area. Whatever your holiday tastes, North Devon has a lot to offer. Open mid April to mid November.

Children and pets welcome. Parking.

B & B from £25 to £27.50pppn, Evening Meal from £12.

e-mail: haxtondownfarm@btconnect.com
www.haxton-down-farm-holidays.co.uk

Graham and Liz White, **Bulworthy Cottage**, Stony Cross, Alverdiscott, Near Bideford EX39 4PY
Tel: 01271 858441

Once three 17th century miner's cottages, Bulworthy has been sympathetically renovated to modern standards whilst retaining many original features. Our twin and double guest rooms both offer en suite accommodation, with central heating, colour TV, and many other extras. Relax in the garden with views across the countryside to Exmoor. Standing in quiet countryside, Bulworthy is within easy reach of the moors, Tarka Trail, South West Coastal Path, Rosemoor and numerous National Trust properties. We offer a choice of breakfasts and evening meals, using home grown and local produce. A selection of wines and beers to complement your evening meal is available.

B&B from £32pppn.

e-mail: bulworthy@aol.com • www.bulworthycottage.co.uk

Yeoldon House Hotel

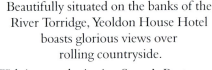

Beautifully situated on the banks of the River Torridge, Yeoldon House Hotel boasts glorious views over rolling countryside.

With its award winning Soyer's Restaurant, this Country House Hotel is the perfect North Devon holiday destination.

The house has ten bedrooms (three of these can be converted into twins). Each room has everything you need for a relaxing and comfortable stay, including hair dryers, irons and ironing boards, modem telephones and flat screen, digital televisions. Four-poster and garden view rooms are available.

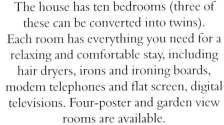

Proprietors Brian and Jennifer Steele seek to create a peaceful and welcoming atmosphere where comfort is a priority and excellent service the norm.

**Yeoldon House Hotel
Durrant Lane, Northam, Bideford,
Devon EX39 2RL
Telephone: 01237 474400
E-mail: yeoldonhouse@aol.com
www.yeoldonhousehotel.co.uk**

The Mount, Northdown Road, Bideford EX39 3LP Tel: 01237 473748

A warm welcome awaits you at The Mount in the historic riverside town of Bideford. This small, interesting Georgian building is full of character and charm and is set in its own semi-walled garden, with a beautiful Copper Beech, making it a peaceful haven so close to the town. Within five minutes easy walking, you can be in the centre of the Old Town, with its narrow streets, quay, medieval bridge and park. The Mount is also an ideal centre for exploring the coast, countryside, towns and villages of North Devon. The quiet, restful bedrooms, (single, double, twin and family) are all en suite. Tea and coffee making facilities are available. All rooms have TV. Non-smoking.
Bed and Breakfast £35 to £40 per person per night.
Golfing breaks – discounted green fees
e-mail: andrew@themountbideford.co.uk
www.themountbideford.co.uk

AA ★★★★ Guest House
HIGHLY COMMENDED

Silver SILVER AWARD

West Titchberry Farm

Tel & Fax: 01237 441287

Situated on the rugged North Devon coast, West Titchberry is a traditionally run working stock farm, half a mile from Hartland Point.

The South West Coastal Path crosses the farm making it an ideal base for walkers. Pick ups and kit transfers available. Long term parking on site

The three guest rooms comprise an en suite family room; one double and one twin room, with wash basins. All rooms have colour TV, radio, hairdryer, tea/coffee making facilities; bathroom/toilet and separate shower room on the same floor, plus a downstairs toilet. Outside, guests may take advantage of a sheltered walled garden. Sorry, no pets.
Hartland village is 3 miles away, Clovelly 6 miles, Bideford and Westward Ho! 16 miles and Bude 18 miles.

• *B&B from £24–£30pppn* • *Evening meal £14*
• *Children welcome at reduced rates for under 11s*
• *Open all year except Christmas*

Mrs Yvonne Heard, West Titchberry Farm, Hartland Point, Near Bideford EX39 6AU

Dartmoor

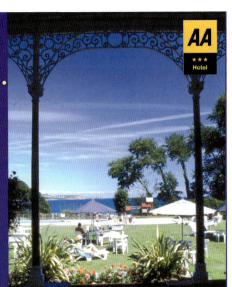

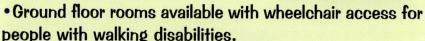

Exeter

Standing in four acres of mature subtropical gardens, overlooking two miles of sandy beach, yet within easy reach of Dartmoor and Exeter, Devoncourt provides an ideal base for a family holiday.

BEDROOMS: The accommodation is in 54 single, double or family rooms, all with private bathroom, colour TV, tea and coffee making facilities and telephone.

LEISURE: Swimming pool, sauna, steam room, whirlpool spa, solarium and fitness centre, snooker room, hair and beauty salon. For those who prefer to be out of doors there is a tennis court, croquet lawn, attractive outdoor heated pool, 18 hole putting green and golf practice area, all within the grounds.

DINING: Brasserie 16 operate the attractive lounge bar and restaurant overlooking the fabulous gardens, with fantastic sea views from the large picture windows. Children's menus and vegetarian options available.

DEVONCOURT Douglas Avenue, Exmouth, Devon EX8 2EX
Tel: 01395 272277 • Fax: 01395 269315
e-mail: enquiries@devoncourt.com • www.devoncourthotel.com

Staghunters Inn
Brendon, Exmoor EX35 6PS

SB

*Bargain rates, Log fires, Real Ales, Choice Wines
Come once and you'll want to return.*

- Friendly, family-run inn on the banks of the East Lyn river, in the picturesque Lorna Doone Valley.
- The inn features beautiful landscaped gardens, riverside beer garden, log fires, real ales and fine wines.
- Meals are available in the cosy bar and are homemade, using fresh local produce.
- 12 en suite bedrooms with central heating, tea/coffee making facilities, TV.
- Ideal location for walking, riding, fishing and easy access to moorland and coastline.
- Ample car parking. Open all year. Terms on request.

e-mail: stay@staghunters.com
www.staghunters.com
Tel: 01598 741222
Fax: 01598 741352

Owners: The Wyburn Family

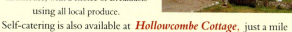

SB

Hillside House

Situated on the East Lyn River at Lynmouth, in a perfect position to explore an abundance of coastal, riverside and woodland scenery. Hillside House is ideally suited to the needs of walkers or those of a less strenuous disposition. Double, twin or single rooms are available, each has a TV, hair-dryer, tea/coffee making facilities and either en suite or private bath/shower room. We offer a four-course breakfast in our dining-room where a large selection of books and magazines are available. Well behaved dogs are welcome. Packed lunches on request. Kit transfer can be arranged. Non-smoking.

22 Watersmeet Road, Lynmouth, Devon EX35 6EP
Tel: 01598 753836
e-mail: info@hillside-lynmouth.co.uk
www.hillside-lynmouth.co.uk

BRENDON HOUSE
Brendon, Lynton, Devon EX35 6PS
Tel: 01598 741206
e-mail: brendonhouse4u@aol.com
www.brendonhouse4u.com

Brendon House is a licensed country guesthouse with five well appointed en suite bedrooms with colour TV and tea/coffee making facilities. There is a residents' lounge with log fire in the winter months, and an award-winning restaurant serving local food and game and home grown seasonal vegetables from the garden.

Sitting in almost an acre of mature gardens, Brendon House provides the ideal location to just relax and unwind or as a base from which to explore the beautiful countryside, walks and views of the Exmoor National Park and the rugged North Devon coast.

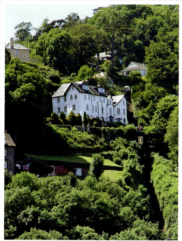

The North Cliff Hotel, standing in its own grounds, has some of the finest views of the North Devon coastline. It is in a peaceful position some 500 feet above sea level overlooking Lynmouth Bay, and a 200 metre walk to Lynton. With car parking facilities on the forecourt, the hotel is an ideal base for exploring the coastline and Exmoor National Park, whether it is your annual holiday or off-season break.

The rooms boast some of the best sea views in Lynton; bedrooms are individually decorated and are en suite. All bedrooms have colour television and facilities for making your favourite beverage.

We can accommodate family gatherings or walking parties as there are 7 doubles, 2 twins, 1 single and 4 family rooms (which can be used as twins or doubles).

We have a licensed bar available for a drink after a hard day of walking or an aperitif before dinner in our restaurant, which has magnificent sea and coastal views.

Children of all ages and pets are very welcome.

Local activities include walking, riding, tennis, and putting. The famous water-powered Cliff Railway linking Lynton and Lynmouth passes within a few feet of the hotel and is accessed via the stepped garden.

SB

North Cliff Hotel
North Walk, Lynton, North Devon EX35 6HJ

Tel: 01598 752357
e-mail: holidays@northcliffhotel.co.uk
www.northcliffhotel.co.uk

Lynton

Blue Ball Inn
formerly The Exmoor Sandpiper Inn

is a romantic Coaching Inn dating in part back to the 13th century, with low ceilings, blackened beams, stone fireplaces and a timeless atmosphere of unspoilt old world charm. Offering visitors great food and drink, a warm welcome and a high standard of accommodation.

The inn is set in an imposing position on a hilltop on Exmoor in North Devon, a few hundred yards from the sea, and high above the twin villages of Lynmouth and Lynton, in an area of oustanding beauty.

The spectacular scenery and endless views attract visitors and hikers from all over the world.

We have 16 en suite bedrooms, comfortable sofas in the bar and lounge areas, and five fireplaces, including a 13th century inglenook. Our extensive menus include local produce wherever possible, such as locally reared meat, amd locally caught game and fish, like Lynmouth Bay lobster; specials are featured daily. We also have a great choice of good wines, available by the bottle or the glass, and a selection of locally brewed beers, some produced specially for us.

Stay with us to relax, or to follow one of the seven circular walks through stunning countryside that start from the Inn. Horse riding for experienced riders or complete novices can be

arranged. Plenty of parking. Dogs (no charge), children and walkers are very welcome!

Blue Ball Inn formerly The Exmoor Sandpiper Inn
Countisbury, Lynmouth, Devon EX35 6NE
01598 741263
www.BlueBallinn.com • www.exmoorsandpiper.com

Coombe Farm
Countisbury, Lynton, Devon EX35 6NF

SB

A warm welcome awaits you at our 17thC farmhouse which is on a working farm within the Exmoor National Park. There are 5 comfortable guest bedrooms to choose from. An extensive breakfast is served in the dining room with its old beams and inglenook fireplace. The surrounding area is one of outstanding natural beauty and has many attractions. A perfect place for walkers, with nearby trout and sea fishing and riding stables.

Tel: 01598 741236 • e-mail: robert.pile@btconnect.com
www.brendonvalley.co.uk/coombe_farm.htm

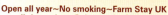

Great Sloncombe Farm
Moretonhampstead Devon TQ13 8QF
Tel: 01647 440595

Share the magic of Dartmoor all year round while staying in our lovely 13th century farmhouse full of interesting historical features. A working mixed farm set amongst peaceful meadows and woodland abundant in wild flowers and animals, including badgers, foxes, deer and buzzards. A welcoming and informal place to relax and explore the moors and Devon countryside. Comfortable double and twin rooms with en suite facilities, TV, central heating and coffee/tea making facilities. Delicious Devonshire breakfasts with new baked bread.

Open all year~No smoking~Farm Stay UK
e-mail: hmerchant@sloncombe.freeserve.co.uk • www.greatsloncombefarm.co.uk

---

Peace and Tranquillity are easily found at

SB

A delightful 16th century Devon longhouse in the beautiful Otter Valley

Fluxton Farm

Occupying a sheltered position just south of Ottery St Mary, and only 4 miles from the sea at Sidmouth. We are no longer a working farm, but keep ducks and chickens and have lots of cats. We have 7 bedrooms, all en suite, and two charming sitting rooms. Our beamed dining room has a large open fireplace and separate tables, where a full English breakfast is served.

The house stands in peaceful, lawned gardens with a small trout stream flowing through.

As well as peace and quiet, we offer a warm welcome and an easy-going atmosphere.

• Children over 8 only.
• Pets welcome
(not in public rooms)

AA ★★

Fluxton Farm, Ottery St Mary
Devon EX11 1RJ
Tel: 01404 812818 • Fax: 01404 814843
Proprietor Ann Forth • www.fluxtonfarm.co.uk

Mortehoe

The Smugglers Rest is a family-run business situated in the pretty stone-built village of Mortehoe surrounded by beautiful countryside and within walking distance of the beaches and coves of the North Devon coast.

The luxury accommodation ranges from twin rooms through to the family suites. All rooms are en suite and have tea & coffee making facilities.

Treat yourselves and your pets to beautiful coastal walks and golden beaches, before you sample our delicious home-cooked meals, real ales and warm, year round hospitality.

The Smugglers Rest

**North Morte Road, Mortehoe,
North Devon EX34 7DR
Tel/Fax: 01271 870891
info@smugglersmortehoe.co.uk
www.smugglersmortehoe.co.uk**

SB

SB

Paignton, Plymouth

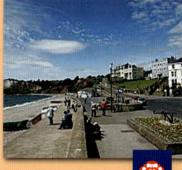

FHG Guides publish a large range of well-known accommodation guides. We will be happy to send you details or you can use the order form at the back of this book.

Sidmouth, Torquay

Welcome

Located on a quiet tree-lined road overlooking its own secluded gardens and pool, the Riviera Lodge Hotel offers a range of facilities and services to make your stay both pleasant and relaxing.

Enjoy a drink in the spacious colonial-style bar, soak up the Riviera sunshine in the sun lounge or catch a glimpse of the bay from the terrace.

Our established garden can be enjoyed all year round with its terrace, patio and lawned area providing the perfect place to sit and relax. The heated swimming pool is open from late May to September.

The hotel offers a full restaurant service and an exceptional full breakfast is included in all room tariffs.

Three levels of en suite accommodation are offered, Standard, Standard Plus and Premium. For that extra special stay, why not book one of our Premium rooms. Our large Premium rooms are equipped with Flat Screen TVs, CD/DVD players and offer the additional comfort of a sitting area and Mini Bar service. All bedrooms are non-smoking.

The hotel has a large car park which is free of charge for residents and we are located just a short walk from the seafront, harbour, shops and Riviera Conference Centre.

The Riviera Lodge Hotel
26 Croft Road, Torquay TQ2 5UE
Tel: 01803 209309 • e-mail: stay@rivieralodgehotel.co.uk
www.rivieralodgehotel.co.uk

Bournemouth

Dorset

Denewood is a smart, friendly family hotel, ideally situated to take advantage of the Bournemouth beaches and the new surf reef which are only 500 yards away, the popular Boscombe shopping centre and the famous Opera House. The hotel has a Health and Beauty salon offering a wide range of pampering treatments. For the business traveller there is a complete set of office facilities, plus internet access points.

B&B from £22.50-£30. Special weekly rates available and Short Break discounts

All 12 of our bedrooms, which are divided over 2 floors, are individually decorated and have a range of amenities such as a desk and chair, en suite facilities, tea and coffee making equipment and a television.

DENEWOOD HOTEL
40 Sea Road, Bournemouth BH5 1BQ
Tel: 01202 309913 • Fax: 01202 391155
www.denewood.co.uk

AA
Associate
Guest
Accommodation

★★★
GUEST
ACCOMMODATION

Dorset has plenty to offer for an outdoor break. The spectacular cliffs of the Jurassic Coast, a World Heritage Site, form a major attraction for fossil hunters, particularly in the area around Charmouth and Lyme Regis. There are resorts to suit everyone, from traditional, busy Bournemouth with 10 kilometres of sandy beach and a wide choice of entertainment, shopping and dining, to the quieter seaside towns of Seatown, Mudeford and Barton-on-Sea, and Charmouth with its shingle beach. Lulworth Cove is one of several picturesque little harbours, and Weymouth, Lyme Regis and West Bay provide ideal facilities for sailing holidays. With almost half the county included in Areas of Outstanding Natural Beauty, walking enthusiasts have a choice of both coast and country, from cliff paths above the sea to rolling countryside, the Avon and Stour Valleys and fringes of the New Forest inland.

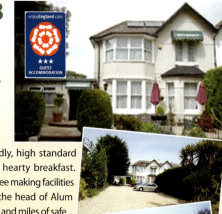

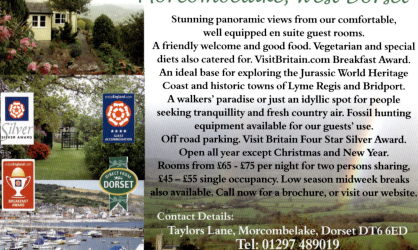

Bridport

SB

Westwood House

29 High West Street, Dorchester DT1 1UP
01305 268018 • www.westwoodhouse.co.uk
reservations@westwoodhouse.co.uk

SB

Personally run by owners, Tom and Demelza Stevens, Westwood House offers comfortable, informal, non-smoking accommodation.
Each bedroom has digital TV, complimentary wi-fi, and tea/coffee making.
Breakfast is served in the light and airy conservatory.

A variety of pubs, restaurants and cafes are just a short stroll away.
The lovely market town of Dorchester has many places of historical interest, and is an ideal base for exploring the Dorset coast and countryside.

Portland, Sherborne

symbols

 Totally non-smoking

 Children Welcome

 Suitable for Disabled Guests

 Pets Welcome

SB *Short Breaks available*

 Licensed

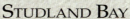

STUDLAND BAY

A peaceful oasis and wonderful atmosphere
where families matter

~

Easy access to three miles of golden beach
Outdoor pool (level deck), golf and tennis for all ages
Health Spa with plunge pool and sauna

~

Connecting rooms for families with children
Separate younger children's restaurant
Playroom and fabulous Adventure Playground

~

Open Easter - end November. Dogs also welcome

STUDLAND BAY
DORSET
BH19 3AH
01929 · 450450
info@knollhouse.co.uk
www.knollhouse.co.uk

ONLY
2 HOURS
FROM
HEATHROW

SB

Our beautiful listed farm house is ideally positioned in the glorious county of Dorset where many beauty spots are just waiting to be explored. Comfortable, well equipped and sleeping up to 5, we also serve a full English breakfast with various choices.

Contact Jill & Brian Miller, Lower Fifehead Farmhouse
Fifehead St Quinton, Sturminster Newton
Dorset DT10 2AP • Tel/Fax: 01258 817335
E-mail: lowerfifeheadfarm@googlemail.com

SB

Luckford Wood Farmhouse
Church Street, East Stoke
Wareham, Dorset BH20 6AW

In the heart of Dorset countryside, warm welcome, very peaceful. Recently refurbished, all en suite, free Wi-Fi. Extensive classical farmhouse breakfast served in the dining room, conservatory (or garden). Ideal for cyclists, walkers, beach lovers and golfers. Tank Museum, Monkey World, Lulworth nearby. B&B from £30pppn, open all year. Caravan and camping available and storage.

Tel: 01929 463098 • Mobile: 07888 719002 / 07737 742615
e-mail: luckfordleisure@hotmail.co.uk
www.luckfordleisure.co.uk

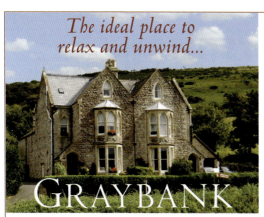

The ideal place to relax and unwind...

GRAYBANK

Lisa and Clive Orchard,
Graybank Bed and Breakfast,
Main Road, West Lulworth BH20 5RL
Tel: 01929 400256
e-mail: lisa@graybank.co.uk
www.graybank.co.uk

Children aged 12 and over welcome. We do not accept pets.
B&B from £40 per person per night.

SB

Built in 1871, Graybank is set in the picturesque village of West Lulworth, a beautiful and quiet location just a short walk from the spectacular Lulworth Cove and the World Heritage Coastline.

Four double en suite guest rooms and one twin guest room. All rooms have flat screen TV with FreeSat, and tea/coffee making facilities.

Full breakfast menu with vegetarian options. Good choice of pubs, cafes and restaurants within walking distance.

Free parking for all guests. Strictly non-smoking throughout. Open all year, whatever the weather!

Bristol

Gloucestershire

Just to the north of Bath, Gloucestershire forms the major part of the Cotswolds Area of Outstanding Natural Beauty, with gently rolling hills, sleepy villages and market towns full of character, ideal for a relaxing break whatever the season. There are gardens to visit, country pubs, antique shops, cathedrals and castles, as well as all kinds of outdoor activities, from 4x4 off-road driving to all the watersports on offer at the Cotswold Water Park, in the south east corner of the county. The Forest of Dean is another area well worth visiting for the wide variety of spring flowers and amazing autumn colours in the ancient woodlands.

Cheltenham

Chipping Campden

SB

A warm and friendly welcome awaits you at our completely refurbished 15th century Grade II Listed farmhouse, in the heart of this beautiful village.

Spacious beamed rooms, inglenook fireplace in dining room where a full English breakfast is served. Large private car park at rear.
All bedrooms are en suite and have coffee/tea making facilities, TV, radio and hairdryer.

Accommodation comprises two double, two twin and one family suite consisting of a single and a double room en suite.

Sorry no pets allowed in the house.

Non-smoking. No children under 12.

Terms per night: from £65 per double-bedded suite, 2 persons sharing. More than two nights from £60. Family room for 3 persons sharing £90.

Veronica Stanley,
Home Farm House,
Ebrington, Chipping Campden
GL55 6NL
Tel & Fax: 01386 593309
willstanley@farmersweekly.net
www.homefarminthecotswolds.co.uk

ETC ★★★★

Honeybourne Lane, Mickleton, Chipping Campden, Gloucestershire GL55 6PU

Tel: 01386 438890
Fax: 01386 438113
enquiries@brymbo.com
www.brymbo.com

A warm and welcoming farm building conversion with large garden in beautiful Cotswold countryside, ideal for walking and touring.

All rooms are on the ground floor, with full central heating.
The comfortable bedrooms all have colour TV and tea/coffee making facilities.
Sitting room with open log fire. Breakfast room. Children and dogs welcome.
Two double, two twin, one family. Bathrooms: three en suite, two private or shared.
Parking. Brochure available. Credit Cards accepted.
Bed and Breakfast: single £35 to £50; double £55 to £75; family from £85.

Close to Stratford-upon-Avon, Broadway, Chipping Campden and with easy access to Oxford and Cheltenham.

SB

Tel: 01452 840224

Quality all ground floor accommodation. "Kilmorie" is Grade II Listed (c1848) within conservation area in a lovely part of Gloucestershire. Mostly en suite, double, twin, family or single bedrooms, all having tea tray, colour digital TV, radio. Very comfortable guests' lounge, traditional home cooking is served in the separate diningroom overlooking large garden. Perhaps walk waymarked farmland footpaths which start here. Children may "help" with our pony, and "free range" hens. Rural yet perfectly situated to visit Cotswolds, Royal Forest of Dean, Wye Valley and Malvern Hills. Children over five years welcome. Hartpury College 3 miles. Ample parking.

Bed and full English Breakfast from £26 per person

S.J. Barnfield, "Kilmorie Smallholding", Gloucester Road, Corse, Staunton, Gloucester GL19 3RQ
e-mail: sheila-barnfield@supanet.com; Mobile 07840 702218

SB

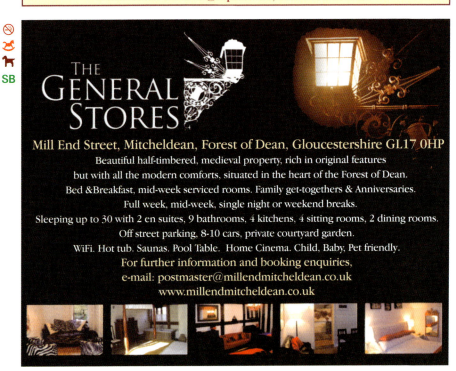

THE
GENERAL STORES

Mill End Street, Mitcheldean, Forest of Dean, Gloucestershire GL17 0HP

Beautiful half-timbered, medieval property, rich in original features
but with all the modern comforts, situated in the heart of the Forest of Dean.
Bed &Breakfast, mid-week serviced rooms. Family get-togethers & Anniversaries.
Full week, mid-week, single night or weekend breaks.
Sleeping up to 30 with 2 en suites, 9 bathrooms, 4 kitchens, 4 sitting rooms, 2 dining rooms.
Off street parking, 8-10 cars, private courtyard garden.
WiFi. Hot tub. Saunas. Pool Table. Home Cinema. Child, Baby, Pet friendly.
For further information and booking enquiries,
e-mail: postmaster@millendmitcheldean.co.uk
www.millendmitcheldean.co.uk

SB

Bed and Full English Breakfast from £25 (reductions for children)

A traditional farmhouse with spectacular views of Cotswold countryside. Quiet location one mile from Stow. Ideally situated for exploring all Cotswold villages including Bourton-on-the-Water, Broadway, Burford and Chipping Campden. Within easy reach of Cheltenham, Oxford and Stratford-upon-Avon; also places of interest such as Blenheim Palace, Warwick Castle and many National Trust houses and gardens. Family, twin and double bedrooms; mostly en suite. TV, tea tray and hairdryer in all rooms. Relaxing guest lounge/dining room with Free Wi-Fi. Excellent pub food five minutes' walk away. Children welcome. Open all year.

Robert Smith and Julie-Anne, Corsham Field Farmhouse,
Bledington Road, Stow-on-the-Wold GL54 1JH • 01451 831750 • Fax: 01451 832247
e-mail: farmhouse@corshamfield.co.uk • www.corshamfield.co.uk

Upper Hasfield, Winchcombe

Ashbrittle, Bath

Somerset

SB

On Devon/Somerset borders, 230 acre family-run farm with cattle, sheep, poultry and horses. Ideal for walking, touring Exmoor, Quantocks, both coasts and many National Trust properties. Pleasant farmhouse, tastefully modernised but with olde worlde charm, inglenook fireplaces and antique furniture, set in large gardens with lawns and flower beds in peaceful, scenic countryside. Two family bedrooms with private facilities and tea/coffee making. Large lounge, separate dining room offering guests every comfort. Noted for relaxed, friendly atmosphere and good home-cooking.

Bed and Breakfast from £28; Dinner £14 per person.
Reductions for children.

Tel: 01398 361296
lowerwestcott@aol.com
www.lowerwestcottfarm.co.uk

Mrs Ann Heard, Lower Westcott Farm, Ashbrittle, Wellington Somerset TA21 0HZ

The Kennard is an original Georgian townhouse, carefully maintained and restored and offering all the modern features which are now expected: en suite rooms with showers, telephones with data port, wireless internet connection, flat screen TV and beverage trays. The original Georgian kitchen, now a delightful breakfast room, is the setting for a full choice of English or Continental breakfasts. For those arriving by car, free residents' parking permits will be provided. No Smoking. Children over 8 years of age are most welcome. Terms on request.

The Kennard
11 Henrietta Street, Bath BA2 6LL
• Tel: 01225 310472 •

Email: reception@kennard.co.uk
www.kennard.co.uk

Winsbere House

Attractive private house set in pretty gardens on the edge of Dulverton, 10 minute walk from the centre and a short drive to Tarr Steps and the moors. Comfortable, tastefully decorated rooms with lovely country views and a friendly informal atmosphere. One double, one twin, both en suite, plus one double/single with private bathroom. Superb full English breakfast.

Cyclists welcome. Route Three West Country Way on doorstep. Ample private parking and lock-up cycle shed.

No dogs • Non-smoking • Children welcome aged 8 or over. • Excellent location for touring Exmoor, West Somerset and North Devon.

Open all year (except Christmas and New Year). Terms: £28 to £35pppn (single from £30).

Mrs M. Rawle, Winsbere House, Dulverton, Exmoor, Somerset TA22 9HU (01398 323278).
e-mail: info@winsbere.co.uk
www.winsbere.co.uk

SB

Bruneton House
Brompton Regis
Exmoor National Park
TA22 9NN

Built around 1625 for a wealthy landowner, Bruneton House offers spacious accommodation in three comfortable, south-facing bedrooms, each individually designed and equipped to the highest standards, with beverage facilities and a radio. There is a separate TV lounge overlooking a pretty cottage garden and the stunning Pulham Valley.

A full English breakfast is included in the nightly rate, and evening meals are available by arrangement, using fresh local produce whenever possible. Meal times are flexible and special diets can be catered for.

Brompton Regis nestles on the southern edge of Exmoor National Park, within easy reach of the north and south Devon coasts, where you will find beautiful beaches, fishing villages, and countless attractions for all the family. Set in some of the most beautiful countryside in the British Isles, Bruneton House is an ideal base for rambling, riding, twitching and fishing.

AA Red Star for Quality
(5 years running)
Tariff: from £26-£30pppn
Children under 12 half price.

For further information contact Mrs Jennifer Stringer Tel: 01398 371224 or e-mail: brunetonhouse@hotmail.com

Wells

SB

Modern farmhouse accommodation on a family-run working farm. Comfortable family home in beautiful gardens with views of Somerset Levels and Mendips. Quiet location, off the beaten track in lovely countryside. Breakfast room for sole use of guests. Full English breakfast. Meals available at local pub five minutes' walk away. En suite rooms with fridge, hairdryer, tea/coffee making facilities, shaver point, colour TV and central heating. Non-smoking.

Terms £30pppn,
reduced rates
for 3 nights
or more.

Mrs Sheila Stott:

Lana Farmhouse

**Hollow Farm, Westbury-sub-Mendip,
Near Wells, Somerset BA5 1HH
Tel: 01749 870635
jstott123@btinternet.com**

Wiltshire

**Longwater Farm
Guest House
Erlestoke, Devizes
SN10 5UE**

Tel & Fax: 01380 830095

Welcome to Longwater. We offer good old-fashioned hospitality but with all the comfort and facilities of a modern home. Explore the beautiful cities of Bath and Salisbury, enjoy coarse fishing in our tranquil lake, play golf on the adjacent 18-hole course, or simply relax in our gardens or conservatory overlooking our picturesque lakes and parkland. Traditional farmhouse breakfast; local inns offer excellent dinners. All rooms en suite with tea/coffee facilities, fridge, TV, radio. Twin and double rooms and family room (children over 5 years); ground floor rooms. Wheelchair-friendly. Pets welcome. Brochure on request. Terms: Single Rooms from £38, Double/twin from £55 and Family from £65.

SB

For the greatest concentration of prehistoric sites in Europe, visit Wiltshire. Most famous is the World Heritage Site, Stonehenge, on Salisbury Plain, dating back at least five thousand years, and with evidence of even earlier work.

Salisbury is the most well known centre in south Wiltshire, with its famous medieval cathedral, as well as individual shops in a historic setting. There is also the safari park at Longleat, farm parks, and stately homes and beautiful gardens to visit in the countryside, where there are also plenty of opportunities for walking and cycling.

Malmesbury

London (Central & Greater)

Big Ben and the Houses of Parliament from the London Eye

London has everything to offer! With a range of accommodation at prices to suit every pocket, it's easy to spend a weekend here or take a longer break. Among the most popular places for visitors are the museums and art galleries. The National Gallery houses one of the largest collections in the world, while the Tate Modern concentrates on the work of artists from the beginning of the 20th century. Except for some special exhibitions, entry to both is free, and this also applies to the Natural History Museum, where a new Darwin Centre has opened and the Victoria and Albert Museum, with such a wide range of exhibits of art and design from different cultures. Smaller, more specialised museums exist too, including the Old Operating Theatre and Herb Garret, a real operating theatre dating from 1821, and the Movieum of London, the film museum where you have the opportunity to shoot your own film, and to see props used in Superman and other favourite films.

The Athena

110-114 SUSSEX GARDENS, HYDE PARK, LONDON W2 1UA

Tel: 0207 706 3866; Fax: 0207 262 6143

E-Mail: athena@stavrouhotels.co.uk www.stavrouhotels.co.uk

TREAT YOURSELVES TO A QUALITY HOTEL AT AFFORDABLE PRICES

The Athena is a newly completed family run hotel in a restored Victorian building. Professionally designed, including a lift to all floors and exquisitely decorated, we offer our clientele the ambience and warm hospitality necessary for a relaxing and enjoyable stay. Ideally located in a beautiful tree-lined avenue, extremely well-positioned for sightseeing London's famous sights and shops; Hyde Park, Madame Tussaud's, Oxford Street, Marble Arch, Knightsbridge, Buckingham Palace and many more are all within walking distance.

Travel connections to all over London are excellent, with Paddington and Lancaster Gate Stations, Heathrow Express, A2 Airbus and buses minutes away.
Our tastefully decorated bedrooms have en suite bath/shower rooms, satellite colour TV, bedside telephones, tea/coffee making facilities. Hairdryers, trouser press, laundry and ironing facilities available on request. Car parking available.

Stavrou Hotels is a family-run group of hotels.
We offer quality and convenience at affordable rates.
A VERY WARM WELCOME AWAITS YOU.

Single Rooms from £50-£89
Double/Twin Rooms from £64-£99
Triple & Family Rooms from £25 per person
All prices include full English breakfast plus VAT.

Our hotels accept all major Credit cards, but some charges may apply.

Windsor

Berkshire

SB

- Town centre location.
- Licensed bar and steam room.
- High quality accommodation at guest house prices.
- All rooms have en suite bathrooms, TV, tea/coffee making facilities, radio alarms, hairdryers, free wi-fi and internet.
- Heathrow Airport 25 minutes by car.
- Convenient for Legoland and trains to London.

Clarence Hotel
9 Clarence Road, Windsor, Berkshire SL4 5AE
Tel: 01753 864436 • Fax: 01753 857060
e-mail: clarence.hotel@btconnect.com • www.clarence-hotel.co.uk

Whatever your interests, whether in the countryside or the town, Berkshire has much to offer. In the east of the county, just a short train ride away from central London, is Windsor Castle, the largest inhabited castle in the world. Racegoers will find plenty of action in Berkshire, with both Ascot and Royal Windsor in the east, and Newbury to the west, where you can also take a tour of the stables at Lambourn and watch the early morning gallops.

Terms quoted in this publication may be subject to increase if rises in costs necessitate

Buckinghamshire

Poletrees Farm

This working family farm provides spacious, comfortable 4 Star Bed & Breakfast ground floor accommodation for couples and individuals, whether on an overnight visit or longer.
• Non-smoking • En suite bedrooms in 4 cottages with colour TV and tea/coffee tray

The Burnwode Jubilee Way cuts through the farm, and there are many places of historic interest in the area.

Ludgershall Road, Brill, Near Aylesbury, Bucks HP18 9TZ • Tel & Fax: 01844 238276

For deposits and booking please phone or fax
www.country-accom.co.uk/poletrees-farm

SB

Only half an hour from London, the rolling hills and wooded valleys of the Buckinghamshire countryside provide a wonderful contrast to city life. Enjoy the bluebells in spring and the autumn colours of the woodland while following the innumerable footpaths, bridleways and National Trails that cross the county, looking at the local flora and fauna on the way.

There are fascinating historic towns and villages, including West Wycombe, owned by the National Trust, which also has many other interesting properties in the area. These include the stunning gardens at Cliveden, former home of the Astors and focus of the early twentieth century social scene. Shoppers will want to visit the complex at High Wycombe or for more specialised outlets, Amersham, the Georgian market town of Marlow, or Stony Stratford. Outdoors or in, there's plenty of choice in Buckinghamshire.

Visit the FHG website
www.holidayguides.com
for details of the wide choice of accommodation featured in the full range of FHG titles

Lyndhurst

Hampshire

The Crown Hotel, New Forest

The Crown Hotel, High Street, Lyndhurst, Hampshire SO43 7NF
Tel: 023 8028 2922 • Fax: 023 8028 2751
e-mail: reception@crownhotel-lyndhurst.co.uk
www.crownhotel-lyndhurst.co.uk

AA
★★★
HOTEL

Tired of the same old walks? Enjoy forest, heath and the
beach whilst staying at The Crown Hotel.

38 en suite rooms, all individual and
recently refurbished.

Our Chef of thirty years, Stephen
Greenhalgh, delights us with his
imaginative menus using local
produce wherever possible.
Dine in our newly opened
brasserie, or *al fresco* overlooking
the water feature garden.

Dogs are welcome to bring
their well-behaved owners!

Whether you prefer an active break or a quiet country holiday, Hampshire offers plenty of choices. There are gardens and country parks, historic houses and wildlife parks, museums and castles, and with its location on the Channel coast, all the activities associated with the seaside. Shopping and nightlife, the Historic Dockyard with HMS Victory and the spectacular views of the surrounding area from the Spinnaker Tower, taller even than the London Eye, make Portsmouth well worth a visit. There's plenty to do outdoors in Hampshire. Walking, cycling and horse riding on the heathland and ancient woodlands of the New Forest National Park, and for more thrills, paragliding and hang gliding at the Queen Elizabeth Country Park on the South Downs.

Bramble Hill Hotel

Bramshaw, New Forest, Hampshire SO43 7JG
Telephone: 023 80 813165 • www.bramblehill.co.uk

Peacefully located in tranquil surroundings, this country house hotel is only three miles from Junction 1 of the M27 and is set in ancient woodland with 30 acres of glades, lawns and shrubbery to enjoy. Ideal for country walks and horse riding. A short drive from many places of interest including Salisbury, Stonehenge, Winchester and Beaulieu. All bedrooms have en suite bathrooms and some have antique four-poster beds. Lounge and snooker room. A warm friendly welcome and good home cooked breakfast assured.

Weekly terms, daily rates — please phone for details.

AA ★★★★ Guest House   # Little Forest Lodge   **AA** ★★★★ Guest House

Poulner Hill, Ringwood, Hampshire BH24 3HS

A warm welcome to you and your pets at this charming Edwardian house set in two acres of woodland. The six en suite bedrooms are pleasantly decorated and equipped with thoughtful extras. Both the attractive wood-panelled dining room and the delightful lounge, with bar and wood-burning fire, overlook the gardens.
The Lodge is in an ideal location for exploring the ancient New Forest, historic Wessex, and the nearby sandy beaches. All well behaved dogs welcome.

Tel: 01425 478848 • Fax: 01425 473564

Southampton, Sway

Isle of Wight

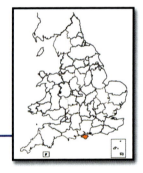

All kinds of watersports are available along the coast, but of course the Isle of Wight, only a short ferry ride away from the mainland, is the ultimate destination, with award-winning beaches, water sports centres, seakayaking, diving, sailing and windsurfing. For land-based activities there are over 500 miles of interconnected footpaths, historic castles, dinosaur museums, theme parks and activity centres, while the resorts like Sandown, Shanklin, Ryde and Ventnor offer all that is associated with a traditional seaside holiday. There is a thriving arts community, and of course two internationally renowned music festivals held every year. Something for everyone!

Chale, Totland

Ashford

Kent

Bolden's Wood Fiddling Lane, Stowting, Near Ashford, Kent TN25 6AP

Between Ashford/Folkestone. Friendly atmosphere – modern accommodation (one double, one single) on our Smallholding, set in unspoilt countryside. No smoking throughout. Full English breakfast. Country pubs (meals)

nearby. Children love the old-fashioned farmyard, free range chickens, friendly sheep and... Llamas, Alpacas and Rheas. Treat yourself to a Llama-led Picnic Trek to our private secluded woodland and downland and enjoy watching the bird life, rabbits, foxes, badgers and occasionally deer. Easy access to Channel Tunnel and Ferry Ports.

Bed and Breakfast £28.00 per person.
Contact: Jim and Alison Taylor

Tel: 01303 812011   **e-mail: StayoverNight@aol.com**

Kent, a county of gentle, rolling downland, long known as the 'Garden of England', provides opportunities for all kinds of outdoor pursuits. The North Downs Way makes its way through an Area of Outstanding Natural Beauty stretching from Kent through Sussex to Surrey, starting at Dover, including a loop to Canterbury along the Pilgrim's Way. In the White Cliffs area there are a number of heritage walks and trails to follow, while a stay in the downland villages offers an excellent opportunity to explore the many local paths. Gardening enthusiasts can wander through the series of gardens at Sissinghurst Castle or visit Scotney Castle near Tunbridge Wells. With easy access from London, the shingle and sandy beaches, many of which have been awarded a Blue Flag, have long been an attraction. Traditional resorts like Deal and Ramsgate, Margate and Herne Bay have plenty to offer for a family holiday.

Please note...

All the information in this book is given in good faith in the belief that it is correct. However, the publishers cannot guarantee the facts given in these pages, neither are they responsible for changes in policy, ownership or terms that may take place after the date of going to press. Readers should always satisfy themselves that the facilities they require are available and that the terms, if quoted, still apply.

Tunbridge Wells

Manor Court Farm • Bed and Breakfast

Manor Court Farm Bed & Breakfast is offered in a spacious, listed Georgian farmhouse on a 350-acre family farm.

We aim to create a warm and friendly atmosphere so guests can relax and enjoy the farm and the surrounding lovely countryside of Kent and Sussex.

One double and two twin rooms are available throughout the year and are tastefully and comfortably furnished to a high standard. Each room has hot and cold water, tea making facilities, TV and wonderful views of the gardens and surrounding countryside. Our spacious bedrooms are complemented by two large bathroom/shower rooms, exclusively for guests use.

A lounge/sitting room with an open fire, television, and DVD and video players is available

Rates: from £28 per person per night.
Reduced rate for children. Babies free.

**Mrs Julia Soyke, Manor Court Farm
Ashurst, Tunbridge Wells, Kent TN3 9TB
Telephone: 01892 740279
E-mail: jsoyke@jsoyke.freeserve.co.uk
www.manorcourtfarm.co.uk**

Oxfordshire

Oxford, the 'city of dreaming spires', has attracted visitors for centuries, and in contrast to lively city life, the Oxfordshire countryside is ideal for a relaxing break. Stretching from Oxford to the Cotswolds, the mysterious Vale of the White Horse is named after the oldest chalk figure in Britain, dating back over 3000 years. Open downland is covered by a network of footpaths connecting up with the ancient Ridgeway Trail and the riverside walks of the Thames Path, or try fishing or boating on the River Thames. The historic market towns like Abingdon and Wantage make good shopping destinations, or visit the pretty villages, stopping for lunch in one of the many traditional English pubs. Follow the village trail at Kidlington, the largest village in England, or visit the nature reserve at Adderbury Lakes, there's always something different to do.

COTSWOLD
Wildlife Park and Gardens

- ADVENTURE PLAYGROUND
- CHILDREN'S FARMYARD
- CAFETERIA • PICNIC AREAS
- NARROW GAUGE RAILWAY (runs Apr-Oct)
- Open All Year from 10am

Info. Hotline: 01993 823006
www.cotswoldwildlifepark.co.uk

Burford, Oxon OX18 4JP (Mid way between Oxford & Cheltenham)

Oxford, Wallingford

symbols

 Totally non-smoking

 Children Welcome

 Suitable for Disabled Guests

 Pets Welcome

SB *Short Breaks available*

Licensed

Surrey

Battle

East Sussex

The Powder Mills is a privately owned 18thC Listed country house hotel in 150 acres of beautiful parklands, woods and lakes, adjoining the famous battlefield of 1066. Once a famous gunpowder mill, it has been skilfully converted into a fascinating country hotel. The Orangery Restaurant, with its marble floor, Greek statues and huge windows looking out onto the terrace and pool, has been awarded an AA Rosette for fine dining. There is a range of 40 individually decorated en suite bedrooms and Junior Suites, many with 4-poster beds. The Pavilion is a delightful conference centre, accommodating up to 200 persons, situated away from the main hotel with its own parking facilities, and suitable also for concerts, events and weddings. The Powder Mills is open to non-residents every day for luncheon, light lunches and dinner.

Powder Mills Hotel & The Orangery Restaurant
Powdermill Lane, Battle TN33 0SP • Tel: 01424 775511
www.powdermillshotel.com • e-mail: powdc@aol.com

West and East Sussex share with neighbouring Kent an attractive coastline with cliffs and sandy beaches, and the countryside of the High Weald and the North Downs. There are endless possibilities for outdoor pursuits – walking, cycling, horse riding, golf, and if you're looking for something more adventurous, hang gliding and paragliding! Don't forget the castles, like Bodiam, near Hastings, now restored and run by the National Trust, and the historic ruins at Pevensey and Lewes, or Arundel, one of England's most important stately homes, in West Sussex. If you're looking for beaches, the 100 miles of coast offer something for everyone, whether your preference is for action-packed family fun or a quiet, remote spot. The best known resort is Brighton, with its pebble beach, classic pier, Royal Pavilion and Regency architecture. For a shopping day out visit the designer shops, art galleries and antique shops, or for something different, shop in The Lanes, there's so much to choose from.

Paskins
town house

Distinctive, different, comfortable

PASKINS is a small, green hotel that has found its own way. It's a sort of eclectic, environmentally friendly hotel with nice and sometimes amusing rooms, and brilliant breakfasts. You arrive at the Art Nouveau reception to be shown to one of the 19 slightly out of the ordinary rooms, each individual in design, perhaps a little quirky, but not at the expense of being comfortable. For example, one room has a genuine Victorian brass bed with several mattresses, just as Queen Victoria's did, which enabled her to sleep higher than all her subjects. Having been welcomed royally, you will sleep like a monarch, and come down to a regal spread at breakfast, prepared with mainly organic, fair trade or locally sourced produce. The Art Deco breakfast room continues the charming theme of the hotel, and has a menu of celebrated choice, including a variety of imaginative vegetarian and vegan dishes, some intriguing signature dishes, and a blackboard full of specials.

PASKINS TOWN HOUSE • 18/19 Charlotte Street, Brighton BN2 1AG
Tel: 01273 601203 • Fax: 01273 621973
www.paskins.co.uk • welcome@paskins.co.uk

Crowborough, Hailsham

Yew House
BED AND BREAKFAST

www.yewhouse.com

Yew House Bed & Breakfast is a detached property offering a good choice of well appointed bedrooms for the family holiday or business person. One four-poster en suite, one double en suite, one double with private bathroom, one single/twin with shower room. Located in the town of Crowborough, it is the ideal centre for visiting Ashdown Forest, the High Weald Area known for its Area of Outstanding Natural Beauty and National Trust Properties, not to mention Royal Tunbridge Wells (6 miles), Eastbourne (18 miles) and Brighton (20 miles). The local community of Jarvis Brook is within walking distance and has a good selection of shops and restaurants; railway station within walking distance. Bed and Breakfast is served, with evening meal and packed lunches available on request. Computer with WiFi for guests' use.

Yew House Bed & Breakfast, Crowborough Hill, Crowborough, East Sussex TN6 2EA
Tel: 01892 610522 or 07789 993982 • e-mail: yewhouse@yewhouse.com

Longleys
Farm Cottage

Situated in quiet private country lane one mile north of the market town of Hailsham with its excellent amenities including modern sports centre and leisure pool, surrounded by footpaths across open farmland. Ideal for country lovers. The coast at Eastbourne, South Downs, Ashdown Forest and 1066 country are all within easy access.

The non-smoking accommodation comprises one twin room, double room en suite; family room en suite and tea/coffee making facilities.

Bed and Breakfast from £30pp.

David and Jill Hook,
Harebeating Lane, Hailsham, East Sussex BN27 1ER
Tel & Fax: 01323 841227
www.longleysfarmcottage.co.uk

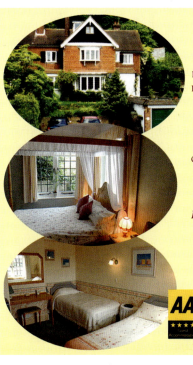
symbols

 Totally non-smoking

 Children Welcome

 Suitable for Disabled Guests

 Pets Welcome

SB *Short Breaks available*

 Licensed

Selsey

West Sussex

SB

ST ANDREWS LODGE

Chichester Road, Selsey, West Sussex PO20 0LX
Tel: 01243 606899 • Fax: 01243 607826

Welcome to St Andrews Lodge, the perfect place for a relaxing break. Situated in the small seaside town of Selsey and well located for Chichester and the South Downs; close to unspoilt beaches and 5 minutes from Pagham Harbour Nature Reserve. Enjoy our delicious breakfast and stay in one of our individually decorated rooms. All rooms have hospitality tray and ironing facilities. Fridges in some of the rooms. Some rooms open on to our large garden to allow your dog to stretch his legs. No charge for dogs but donation to local nature reserve welcome.

Licensed bar, wheelchair accessible room, large car park.

*Please apply for brochure and details
of our special winter offer.*

info@standrewslodge.co.uk
www.standrewslodge.co.uk

Cambridge

Cambridgeshire

- Within walking distance of city centre.
- Single, double/twin and family bedrooms, all en suite.
- All rooms with colour TV, hairdryer, tea/coffee making facilities, iron etc.
- Varied breakfast menu served in dining room overlooking picturesque garden.
- On-site parking; easy access to A14, M11, A10.

57 Arbury Road, Cambridge CB4 2JB
Tel: 01223 350086
www.victoria-guesthouse.co.uk
e-mail: victoriahouse@ntlworld.com

Victoria
Guest House

GUEST ACCOMMODATION

Cambridgeshire immediately brings to mind the ancient university city of Cambridge, lazy hours punting on the river past the imposing college buildings, students on bicycles, museums and bookshops. This cosmopolitan centre has so much to offer, with theatres, concerts varying from classical to jazz, an annual music festival, cinemas, botanic gardens, exciting shops and to round it all off, restaurants, pubs and cafes serving high quality food. In the surrounding countryside historic market towns, pretty villages and stately homes wait to be explored. Visit Ely with its magnificent cathedral and museum exhibiting the national collection of stained glass, antique shops and cafes. Spend a quiet break on the Fens, visiting the nature reserves with vast numbers of rare species which have long been of interest to botanists, including Charles Darwin. Elizabethan Burghley House and Elton Hall with its beautifully restored rose garden are among the stately homes and historic houses in the county, and there's a wide choice of art galleries to visit.

Clacton-on-Sea, Colchester

Essex

Earls Hall Farm
Clacton-on-Sea, Essex CO16 8BP
Tel: 01255 820458
Excellent base for the Essex Sunshine Coast.
Ideal for birdwatching, beaches, woodland walks and
exploring East Anglia. Non-smoking. Open all year.
Pets welcome by arrangement.

SB

Pond House Bed & Breakfast
Victorian farmhouse with one double (king-size) and one twin
room, both en suite. Guests' sitting room. Rates per night
from £60 double, from £40 single. VisitBritain
GOLD AWARD and BREAKFAST AWARD.

Pond Cottage Self Catering Holidays
Cosy cottage annexe, very well equipped, with full central
heating. Sleeps four in one king-size double and one
twin room, both en suite. Terms from £300-£490
per week. Short breaks available.

★★★★
FARM HOUSE

Contact Mrs Brenda Lord • e-mail: brenda_lord@farming.co.uk • www.earlshallfarm.info

★★★★
SELF CATERING

Rye Farm

This 17thC moated farmhouse enjoys a quiet location adjacent to
Abberton Reservoir, one of Europe's most important wildfowl havens.
Ideal for a relaxing break and a good base for exploring Colchester with
its castle and museums, Colchester Zoo, Mersea Island, Layer Marney
Towers, Beth Chatto Gardens, Maldon and Constable Country. 30
mins from the coast; 50 mins from Stansted Airport/Harwich Port.

*Three comfortable en suite rooms, with central heating, colour
TV/DVD, tea and coffee making facilities, fridge and hairdryer.
Substantial farmhouse breakfast. No smoking. No pets.
Children over 12 years only*

Rye Lane, Layer de la Haye, Colchester CO2 0JL
Tel: 01206 734350/07976 524276
e-mail: peterbunting@btconnect.com • www.ryefarm.org.uk

★★★★
FARMHOUSE

Seven Arches Farm

Georgian farmhouse set in large
garden close to the ancient town
of Colchester. The farm extends
to 100 acres and supports both
arable crops and cattle. Private
fishing rights on the River Colne,
which runs past the farmhouse.
This is a good location for visits to North Essex,
Dedham and the Stour Valley which have been
immortalised in the works of John Constable, the
landscape painter.

• Children and pets welcome.
• Open all year.
• Static caravan on caravan
  site also available.

SB

◆ Bed and Breakfast from £30
◆ Twin room £60
◆ Family room en suite

**Mrs Jill Tod, Seven Arches Farm,
Chitts Hill, Lexden, Colchester CO3 9SX
01206 574896**

Norfolk

THE OLD PUMP HOUSE

Holman Road, Aylsham, Norwich NR11 6BY
Tel: 01263 733789
theoldpumphouse@btconnect.com
www.theoldpumphouse.com

This comfortable 1750s house, owned by Marc James and Charles Kirkman, faces the old thatched pump and is a minute from Aylsham's church and historic marketplace.

It offers five bedrooms (including one four-poster and two family rooms) in a relaxed and elegant setting, with colour TV, tea/coffee making facilities, hairdryers and CD radio alarm clocks in all rooms. Wireless internet access in all rooms.

English breakfast with free-range eggs and local produce (or vegetarian breakfast) is served in the pine-shuttered sitting room overlooking the peaceful garden.

Aylsham is central for Norwich, the coast, the Broads, National Trust houses, steam railways and unspoilt countryside.

- Well behaved children and dogs welcome.
- Dinner by prior arrangement from October to May.
- Non-smoking.
- Off-road parking for six cars.
- *B&B from £75 single, £95 double.*

Great Yarmouth, Holt

Heacham

A Charming 16th Century Manor House

Located Between Hunstanton and Heacham on the beautiful West Norfolk Coast.

Luxury Accommodation
18 hole Golf Course Exquisite Cuisine Beautiful Gardens
Additional Cottages Wedding Receptions Coastline Sunsets

Open to non-residents, fine dining restaurant.
We look forward to welcoming you soon.

Heacham Manor Estate, Hunstanton Road, Heacham, West Norfolk. PE31 7JX
Tel: 01485 536 030   www.heacham-manor.co.uk

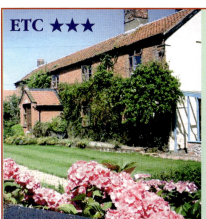

Woodgreen, Long Stratton
Norwich NR15 2RR

Greenacres Farmhouse

Period 17th century farmhouse on 30 acre common with ponds and natural wildlife, 10 miles south of Norwich (A140). The beamed sittingroom with inglenook fireplace invites you to relax. A large sunny dining room encourages you to enjoy a leisurely traditional breakfast. All en suite bedrooms (two double/twin) are tastefully furnished to complement the oak beams and period furniture, with tea/coffee facilities and TV. Full size snooker table and all-weather tennis court for guests' use. Jo is trained in therapeutic massage, pilates and reflexology and is able to offer this to guests who feel it would be of benefit. Come and enjoy the peace and tranquillity of our home.

Bed and Breakfast from £30. Reductions for two nights or more. Non-smoking.

Tel: 01508 530261 • www.abreakwithtradition.co.uk

SB

South Norfolk's Guest House • OAKBROOK HOUSE
The ideal base to explore East Anglia & The Norfolk Broads

Simon and Heather welcome you to this former village school, fully refurbished in 2005, with views over the quiet Tas Valley, south of Norwich. Oakbrook House is the ideal touring base for East Anglia for work or leisure, centrally situated in the region. Nine warm comfortable rooms of various sizes and prices to match individual budget and comfort, each with en suite wc and basin, colour TV, clock radio and hospitality tray, en suite or private shower. All diets catered for, central heating, smoke-free, pets by arrangement. Evening meals and daytime use of the facilities available.

Contact us for brochure. Long stay discounts. B&B from £19 pppn.

Oakbrook Guest House, Frith Way, Great Moulton, Norwich NR15 2HE
Tel: 01379 677359 • mobile: 07885 351212
e-mail: oakbrookhouse@btinternet.com • www.oakbrookhouse.co.uk

Wensum Guest House

225 Dereham Road, Norwich, Norfolk. NR2 3TF.

FOUR STAR • 18 SPACIOUS ROOMS • FREE CAR PARK
FREE WiFi • FREEVIEW TV • GOOD BREAKFAST BAR
HIGHLY RATED ON ALL REVIEW SITES

www.WensumGuestHouse.co.uk • 01603 621 069 (P)
info@WensumGuestHouse.co.uk • 01603 618 445 (F)

Stracey Hotel

*three star standard
excellent rates*

www.StraceyHotel.co.uk
info@StraceyHotel.co.uk
01603 628 093 (P)
01603 753 511 (F)

• 20 comfortable en suite rooms
• Free broadband & Freeview TV
• Express check-out/check-in
• Snug lounge and licensed bar
• Restaurant with award winning Chef

For a perfect stay in Norwich that's close to business centres, entertainment & the beautiful Riverside area. Very convenient for Norwich railway station. Please call or visit us online.

Wymondham

Suffolk

Bungay

Brandon House

HOTEL | RESTAURANT | BAR

Enjoy 3 Stars, Style & Georgian Splendour...

- 16 Large en-suite bedrooms
- Full breakfast included
- Highly regarded restaurant
- Comfortable Freehouse bar
- Close to Thetford & Mildenhall forests
- Lovely gardens and wood area
- Short walk from local railway
- Well located in central East Anglia on the Norfolk/Suffolk border

Welcome

Brandon House has a long standing history in hospitality one that assures our guests a welcoming atmosphere, and the very best facilities, service, food and drink.

call or book online...

Brandon House, High Street, Brandon, Suffolk. IP27 0AX.
www.BrandonHouse.co.uk | 01842 810 171

Framlingham, Hopton

SB

High House Farm
Cransford, Framlingham, Woodbridge IP13 9PD
Tel: 01728 663461
e-mail: b&b@highhousefarm.co.uk
www.highhousefarm.co.uk

Exposed oak beams • inglenook fireplaces • one double room, en suite and one large family room with double and twin beds and private adjacent bathroom • children's cots • high chairs • books • toys • outside play equipment • attractive semi-moated gardens • farm and woodland walks.
Explore the heart of rural Suffolk, local vineyards, Easton Farm Park, Framlingham and Orford Castles, Parham Air Museum, Saxtead Windmill, Minsmere, Snape Maltings, Woodland Trust and the Heritage Coast.
Bed and Breakfast from £30. Reductions for children.

Signposted on B1119, Fiddlers Hall is a 14th century, moated, oak-beamed farmhouse set in a beautiful and secluded position. It is two miles from Framlingham Castle, 20 minutes' drive from Aldeburgh, Snape Maltings, Woodbridge and Southwold.
A Grade II Listed building, it has lots of history and character.
The bedrooms are spacious; one has en suite shower room, the other has a private bathroom. Use of lounge and colour TV. Plenty of parking space. Lots of farm animals kept. Traditional farmhouse cooking. Bed and Breakfast terms from £75 per room.

Mrs Jennie Mann, Fiddlers Hall, Cransford, Near Framlingham, Woodbridge IP13 9PQ • 01728 663729 • www.fiddlershall.co.uk

SB

The Old Rectory is a Listed building dating from the 16th century, well situated to explore East Anglia, being on the Suffolk/Norfolk border. Bury St Edmunds is 12 miles away, the market town of Diss is 8. Cambridge, Ipswich and Norwich are within easy reach. The house is beautifully furnished and many period features add to the charm of this lovely stylish family home.
The luxurious bedrooms have en suite bathrooms.
Sarah and Bobby delight in entertaining guests in their beautifully restored home. A no smoking house.

Bobby & Sarah Llewellyn, The Old Rectory
Hopton, Suffolk IP22 2QX • Tel: 01953 688135
e-mail: llewellyn.hopton@btinternet.com
www.theoldrectoryhopton.com

• Continental/English breakfast • dinner available by arrangement
• licensed • children and pets welcome by arrangement
• closed Christmas, New Year and occasionally

Ashbourne

Derbyshire

For walking, climbing, mountain biking and caving visit Derbyshire. There are activities available at every level and courses to suit everyone. From the gently rolling farmland and National Forest in the south to the rugged demanding landscape of the Dark Peak in the north there are trails for cyclists and walkers to follow, many along old railway lines. Everyone can visit Poole's Cavern to see the best stalagmites and stalactites in Derbyshire (and discover the difference!), and the Blue John Cave at Castleton where this rare mineral is mined, and perhaps buy a sample of jewellery in one of the local shops. Buxton was a spa from Roman times, but the main attractions now are concerts, theatre and the annual literary and music festival. Concerts are held at Calke Abbey and at Chatsworth, the best known of the stately homes, with impressive interiors and magnificent gardens and grounds, and period dramas at Haddon Hall at Bakewell. Visit the market town of Chesterfield to see the church with the crooked spire, and for a step back in time go to Crich Tramway Village for a tram ride down a period street and on into the countryside.

BONEHILL FARM

01332 513553

This 120 acre mixed farm with Georgian farmhouse is set in peaceful rural surroundings, yet offers all the convenience of being only three miles west of Derby, on the A516 between Mickleover and Etwall. Within 10 miles there is a choice of historic houses to visit; Calke Abbey, Kedleston Hall, Sudbury Hall. Peak District 20 miles, Alton Towers 20 miles.

Accommodation in three bedrooms (one twin, one double en suite, one family room with en suite facilities), all with tea/coffee making facilities. Cot and high chair provided. Open all year. Croquet available. B&B per night: single from £30, double from £55.

A warm and friendly welcome awaits you.

Mrs Catherine Dicken, Bonehill Farm, Etwall Road, Mickleover DE3 0DN
e-mail: bonehillfarm@hotmail.com
www.bonehillfarm.co.uk

Graham and Julie Caesar
Windy Harbour Farm Hotel
WOODHEAD ROAD, GLOSSOP SK13 7QE
01457 853107

Situated in the heart of the Peak District on the B6105, approximately one mile from Glossop town centre and adjacent to the Pennine Way. All our bedrooms are en suite, with outstanding views of Woodhead and Snake Passes and the Longdendale Valley is an ideal location for all outdoor activities. A warm welcome awaits you in our licensed bar and restaurant serving a wide range of excellent home-made food.

Bed and Breakfast from £30 per night

symbols

Totally non-smoking	 *Pets Welcome*
Children Welcome	 **SB** *Short Breaks available*
Suitable for Disabled Guests	*Licensed*

Winster

Herefordshire

Hereford

SB

Ledbury

Set amidst the beautiful North Herefordshire countryside on a family-run stock and arable farm, this attractive 17th Century farmhouse offers a warm, friendly welcome. Within easy reach of the Welsh border country, Hereford, Leominster and Ludlow. Spacious and well appointed bedrooms with tea and coffee trays.

Guests' own bathroom and sitting room. Open all year except Christmas and New Year. This is a no smoking house.

Mrs Jenny Davies
Holgate Farm
Kingsland
Leominster HR6 9QS
Tel: 01568 708275

B&B £25 pppn, single room £30.
Reductions for children.

❖ Thatch Close Bed & Breakfast ❖
Llangrove
Ross-on-Wye HR9 6EL

Situated between the Black Mountains and the Wye Valley, with marvellous views from every angle, Thatch Close is the ideal location for a weekend break or a longer stay.

Secluded, peaceful, comfortable Georgian farmhouse, yet convenient for A40, M4 and M50. Our three lovely bedrooms, all en suite, have magnificent views over the unspoilt countryside. Relax in the visitors' lounge or sit in the shade of mature trees in our garden.

You may be greeted by our dog or free-flying parrot. Terms from £60 per room. Children and dogs are welcome. Please telephone or e-mail for brochure.

Mrs M.E. Drzymalski (01989 770300)
e-mail: info@thatchclose.co.uk • www.thatchclose.co.uk

Herefordshire, on the on the border with Wales, will appeal equally to outdoor lovers and enthusiasts for the arts, crafts and literature, as well as to all food lovers! There are endless opportunities for all kinds of outdoor activities, including white water canoeing through the steep-sided gorge at Symonds Yat, or longer, more gentle trips on the meandering sections of the River Wye. The Black and White Village Trail takes visitors through beautiful countryside to pretty little villages, each with its own individual characteristics and shops. Leominster specialises in antiques and fine art auctions, Ross-on-Wye in antiques and Ledbury, in the east, runs an annual poetry festival. The climate and fertile soil has resulted in wonderful local produce, particularly fruit and vegetables, beef and dairy products. All these are available to sample in restaurants, cafes and tearooms or to take home from farm shops as a reminder of the holiday.

Leicestershire & Rutland

RELAIS &
CHATEAUX.

FAYCE·QUE·VOUDRAS

HAMBLETON HALL

AA
★★★★
HOTEL

**Michelin
Star**

The county of Rutland is verdant, undulating, and largely unspoilt, making it an ideal place to spend a tranquil vacation. No better venue for such an excursion exists than this fine hotel, perched in the very centre of man-made Rutland Water.

The superb cuisine exhibits flair and refreshing originality, with the emphasis very much on seasonal, freshly sourced ingredients. Beautifully furnished in subtle shades, elegant and profoundly comfortable, with 17 individually and lavishly decorated bedrooms. Hambleton is within easy reach of numerous places of historic interest, wonderful gardens and antique shops. On-site tennis, outdoor heated swimming pool and croquet lawn, and within a short drive, horse riding, golf, sailing, fishing and boating.

Hambleton, Oakham, Rutland LE15 8TH

Tel: 01572 756991 • Fax: 01572 724721

hotel@hambletonhall.com • www.hambletonhall.com

Boston

Lincolnshire

An early 18th century Listed farmhouse with spacious en suite bedrooms and original beamed ceilings.

Enjoy a generous farmhouse breakfast using fresh local produce.

Centrally located for five 'Bomber Country' museums, championship golf at Woodhall Spa, antiques at Horncastle and local fishing. Historic pubs nearby serving excellent evening meals. Within easy reach of the east coast and the Lincolnshire Wolds.

• •One double and one twin bedroom• •
• •Central heating, tea and coffee facilities and colour TV• •

Open all year except Christmas • No smoking • Children welcome
B&B from £20pp.

SB

Mrs C. Whittington, High House Farm, Tumby Moorside, Near Coningsby, Boston PE22 7ST • Tel: 01526 345408
e-mail: HighHousefarm@aol.com
www.high-house-farm.co.uk

Coast or country, the choice is yours for a holiday in Lincolnshire. With award-winning beaches, miles of clean sand, theme parks, kite surfing, wake boarding and water skiing, there's action and excitement for everyone along the Fun Coast and at Cleethorpes on the Humber estuary. At Skegness, as well as all the fun on the beach, children will love watching the seals being fed at the seal sanctuary, and the exotic birds and butterflies flying overhead in the tropical house. Further north, at Cleethorpes with its wonderful beaches, take a ride on the Cleethorpes Coast Light Railway. Keen fishermen can always find a peaceful spot along the extensive network of rivers and canals and for golfers there's a wide variety and standard of courses, with the home of amateur golf in England at the National Golf Centre at Woodhall Spa. In Lincoln walk round the battlements at the Castle, explore the cobbled streets lined with medieval buildings and visit the imposing Gothic cathedral, one of the finest in Europe. Cruise on the Roman canal that flows through the city, shop at the boutiques, eat at the restaurants and cafes, and in the evening enjoy a concert or a visit to the theatre.

Gainsborough

The *Black Swan* Guest House

Tel: 01427 718878

- **9 EN-SUITE ROOMS**
- **FREE WIRELESS INTERNET ACCESS**
- **WARM AND FRIENDLY ATMOSPHERE**
- **PRIVATE COURTYARD PARKING**

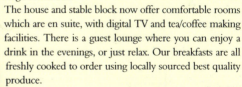

As resident proprietors, Judy and John Patrick offer a warm welcome at our delightfully converted former 18th century coaching inn. The property has been fully refurbished, using much of the original materials and retaining many original features.

The house and stable block now offer comfortable rooms which are en suite, with digital TV and tea/coffee making facilities. There is a guest lounge where you can enjoy a drink in the evenings, or just relax. Our breakfasts are all freshly cooked to order using locally sourced best quality produce.

The local area is steeped in history, from Roman times through to the old airfields of the Second World War, and the city of Lincoln is only 12 miles away, with its stunning cathedral and old city centre in the Bailgate area.

For those of you who need to keep in touch, wireless broadband is available.

We are a non-smoking establishment.

Single from £45, double/twin from £68.

21 High Street, Marton, Gainsborough, Lincs DN21 5AH
Tel: 01427 718878
info@blackswanguesthouse.co.uk
www.blackswanguesthouse.co.uk

SB

Baumber Park
Farmhouse B&B and Self Catering Cottage

Spacious elegant farmhouse of character in quiet parkland setting, on a mixed farm. Large colourful and inspiring plantsman's garden with extensive vistas and wildlife pond. Fine bedrooms with lovely views, period furniture, log fires and books. Central in the county and close to the Lincolnshire Wolds, this rolling countryside is little known, quite unspoilt, and ideal for walking, cycling or riding. Championship golf courses at Woodhall Spa. Well located for historic Lincoln, interesting market towns and many antique shops. Enjoy a relaxing break, excellent breakfasts, and a comfortable, homely atmosphere.
Two doubles, one twin, all en suite or private bathroom. Bed and Breakfast from £30.

Gathman's Cottage
Across the field, self-catering accommodation available in picturesque, 18th Century thatched cottage lovingly restored and with enough 'mod-cons', but retaining its great character. Surrounded by parkland and grazing cattle in summer; warm and cosy in winter, Lovely distant views, as far as Lincoln Cathedral. Three bedrooms –double and twin upstairs, small double downstairs. Private gardens and parking.
Short break from £200 or £300 weekly.

Mrs Clare Harrison, Baumber Park,
Baumber, Near Horncastle LN9 5NE
Tel: 01507 578235 • Fax: 01507 578417 • mobile: 07977 722776
e-mail: mail@baumberpark.com • www.baumberpark.com • www.gathmanscottage.co.uk

Redhurst B&B

Exchange the buzz of city traffic for the birdsong of the countryside whilst staying at Redhurst B&B, set in gardens and orchard in a small village nestling on the edge of the Lincolnshire Wolds. Ideal setting for visiting the many and varied attractions of Lincolnshire.
Two twin en suite (one ground floor), from £27 and £30 pppn.
One single with private facilities, from £27pn.
Open all year • Sorry no pets.
Non-smoking • Self-catering also available.

Mrs Vivienne Klockner, Redhurst,
Holton-cum-Beckering,
Market Rasen LN8 5NG
Tel/Fax: 01673 857927 • Mobile: 07804 636 858
www.RedhurstBAndB.co.uk
e-mail: Vivienne@RedhurstBAndB.co.uk

Bed & Breakfast at No. 19 West Street
Kings Cliffe, Near Stamford, Peterborough PE8 6XB
Tel: 01780 470365 • Fax: 01780 470623

A beautifully restored 500-year-old Listed stone house, reputedly one of King John's Hunting Lodges, situated in the heart of the stone village of Kings Cliffe on the edge of Rockingham Forest.

Both the double and the twin rooms have their own private bathrooms, and there is colour TV and a welcome tray in each. There is also a completely self-contained family suite, can be self catering. In the summer breakfast can be served on the terrace overlooking a beautiful walled garden. Off-street parking is behind secure gates.

Within 20 miles there are seven stately homes, including Burghley House famous for the Horse Trials, Rutland Water, and the beautiful old towns of Stamford and Oundle. Open all year.

A non-smoking house
Bed and Breakfast from £30 per person (2 sharing)
Proprietor: Jenny Dixon
e-mail: kjhl.dixon@gmail.com • www.kingjohnhuntinglodge.co.uk

Mrs S. Evans, Willow Farm, Thorpe Fendykes, Wainfleet, Skegness PE24 4QH
Tel: 01754 830316
e-mail: willowfarmhols@aol.com
www.willowfarmholidays.co.uk

In the heart of the Lincolnshire Fens, Willow Farm is a working smallholding with free range hens, goats, horses and ponies. Situated in a peaceful hamlet with abundant wildlife, ideal for a quiet retreat – yet only 15 minutes from the Skegness coast, shops, amusements and beaches. Also one-bedroom self-catering cottage available.

SB

Horse riding available

Bed and Breakfast is provided in comfortable en suite rooms from £25 per person per night, reductions for children (suppers and sandwiches can be provided in the evening on request). Rooms have tea and coffee making facilities and a colour TV and are accessible to disabled guests. Wifi access. Friendly hosts! Ring for brochure.

Woodhall Spa

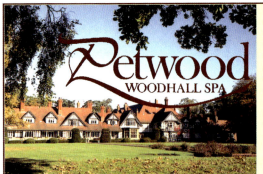

Stixwould Road,
Woodhall Spa LN10 6QG
Tel: 01526 352411
Fax: 01526 353473
reception@petwood.co.uk
www.petwood.co.uk

Originally built in the early 1900s The Petwood Hotel stands in 30 acres of mature woodland and gardens. During World War II, 617 Squadron, known as the "Dambusters", used the hotel as their Officers' Mess. Today it is a country house hotel of unique charm, offering a high standard of comfort and hospitality in elegant surroundings. All bedrooms are fully equipped to meet the needs of today's discerning guests, and the highly recommended Tennysons Restaurant offers the very best of English cuisine. There are ample leisure opportunities available locally as well as tranquil villages and historic market towns to explore.

AA ★★★

★★★ HOTEL

HOTEL • WEDDINGS • CONFERENCES • RESTAURANT

Kettering

Northamptonshire

ENJOY A HOLIDAY in our comfortable 17th century farmhouse with oak beams and inglenook fireplaces. Four-poster bed now available. Peaceful surroundings, large garden containing ancient circular dovecote. Dairy Farm is a working farm situated in a beautiful Northamptonshire village just off the A14, within easy reach of many places of interest or ideal for a restful holiday. Good farmhouse food and friendly atmosphere. Open all year, except Christmas.

B&B from £27 to £38 (children under 10 half price); Evening Meal £17.

SB

Mrs A. Clarke
Dairy Farm
Cranford St Andrew
Kettering NN14 4AQ
Tel: 01536 330273

Northamptonshire may appear a quiet, rural county, but it's very much a place for action and family fun. Everything you would expect to find in the countryside is here – walking, cycling, fishing, wildlife, beautiful villages and traditional inns and pubs. As well as all this there's sky diving, flying and gliding at Brackley or for a more gentle flight through the air, try hot air ballooning near Northampton. Motorsports enthusiasts will be more than satisfied, with stock car racing at the Northampton International Raceway, Santa Pod, the home of European Drag Racing and the Silverstone circuit. For shoppers, Northampton, the home of high quality footwear in Britain, is still a good place for bargains as well as bespoke shoes, and for some fun, why not visit at the time of the annual Balloon Festival? For a fun day out for everyone to end the holiday, Wicksteed Park at Kettering has all the family could want in events and entertainment.

Burton Joyce

Nottinghamshire

Willow House Bed and Breakfast

A period house (1857) in quiet village two minutes' walk from beautiful river bank, yet only five miles from City. Attractive, interesting accommodation with authentic Victorian ambience. En suite available. Bright, clean rooms with tea/coffee facilities, TV. Off-road parking. Porch for smokers. Ideally situated for Holme Pierrepont International Watersports Centre; golf; National Ice Centre; Trent Bridge (cricket); Sherwood Forest; Nottingham Racecourse; Shelford Pony Trials and the unspoiled historic town of Southwell with its Minster and Racecourse. Good local eating. Please phone first for directions.
Rates: From £26 per person per night.

**Mrs V. Baker, Willow House,
Burton Joyce NG14 5FD
Tel:0115 931 2070; Mob: 07816 347706
www.willowhousebedandbreakfast.co.uk**

Nottinghamshire's historic and literary connections make it a highly interesting area to spend a short break or longer holiday. Myth, legend and fact all play a part in the stories of Robin Hood, but visit Sherwood Forest, the hiding place of outlaws in medieval times, and make up your own mind from the evidence you find there. Whether you prefer taking part in sport or just enjoy watching, there's a great variety available. Watch cricket at Trent Bridge, horse racing at Nottingham and the all-weather course at Southwell, and ice hockey at Nottingham's National Ice Centre, or try ice skating yourself. There are golf courses from municipal and pay & play to championship standard, fishing in canals, lakes and fisheries, and everyone is welcome to play at the Nottingham Tennis Centre. The city of Nottingham is a wonderful place to shop, with designer outlets, independent shops and department stores, and don't miss the traditional Lace Market. At Mansfield visit the XplorActive environment gallery and the Making it! Discovery Centre, and at elegant Southwell, the very first workhouse for the poor, while the antiques fairs are a great attraction in Newark.

Elton

Shropshire

Church Stretton

If you're looking for a break from the pace of life today, but with plenty to do and see, and with a choice of superb food to round off your day, Shropshire is the place to visit. Visit the Shropshire Hills Discovery Centre at Craven Arms, where you can take a simulated balloon ride and meet the Shropshire mammoth. Stokesay Castle, the finest 13th century fortified manor house in England, is just one of over 30 castles in the county, as well as stately homes and all kinds of gardens, including Hawkstone Historic Park and Follies, a fairytale kingdom near Shrewsbury. At the Ironbridge Gorge museums, as well as learning all about the early inventions leading to the start of the Industrial Revolution, discover how all kinds of present-day objects work – and make it happen yourself.

Eccleshall

Staffordshire

Situated right in the middle of England, Staffordshire is a county of open spaces and ancient woodlands, exciting theme parks, stately homes and castles, miles of canals and the largest street-style skate park in Europe at Stoke-on-Trent. There are thrills and fun for every age group at the theme parks. As well as the heart-stopping rides, walk through the Ocean Tank Tunnel at Alton Towers to watch the sea creatures from all the world's oceans and make a big splash in the Waterpark. Take a look at life in the past at the complete working historic estate at Shugborough near Stafford, with working kitchens, dairy water mill and brewhouse. Out in the open heathland of Cannock Chase in the south there are well maintained paths and trails for all levels of mountain biking, bikes to hire and fishing pools at Rugely and walking and cycling trails at Hednesford, or follow the Chase Heritage Trail.

Kingsley

The Church Farm

Famous Alton Towers is just five and a half miles from our farm. The Churnet Valley, with steam railway, wildlife park, narrowboat trips, Nick Williams Pottery and a maze of footpaths, is a fifteen minute walk; truly a hidden paradise! The Potteries and Peak District are within eight miles. Having visited all of these, come and unwind in our spacious cottage garden or with a book by the log fire in winter. Enjoy our beautifully furnished period farmhouse built in 1700 with many thoughtful additions for your comfort. Breakfast menu using own and local produce. En suite bedrooms with TVs and beverage making facilities. Totally non-smoking. Tariff: Adults from £25.00, Single £30.00, children 12 years and under £12.50.

"AA BRITAIN'S BEST BED & BREAKFAST GUIDE."

Mrs Jane S. Clowes, The Church Farm,
Holt Lane, Kingsley, Stoke-on-Trent ST10 2BA • Tel: 01538 754759
e-mail: thechurchfarm@yahoo.co.uk
www.bandbatthechurchfarm.co.uk

Stratford-Upon-Avon

Warwickshire

Monks Barn Farm

**Shipston Road,
Stratford-upon-Avon,
Warwickshire CV37 8NA
Tel: 01789 293714**

SB

Monks Barn Farm is situated two miles south of Stratford on the A3400. Dating back to the 16th century, the farm lies along the banks of the River Stour. Now modernised, it still preserves the old character, and offers first-class amenities; some accommodation is separate from the main house. Ground floor rooms available. Pleasant riverside walks to the village of Clifford Chambers. Centrally situated for visiting Stratford, Warwick and the Cotswolds.

*Double/twin/family/single rooms, all en suite.
Children of all ages welcome. Non-smoking.*

B&B from £28-£30. Credit cards accepted.

ritameadows@btconnect.com • www.monksbarnfarm.co.uk

Think of Warwickshire, and Shakespeare and Stratford-on-Avon immediately come to mind. A great way to see round this interesting town of black and white, half-timbered buildings is to take a guided walking tour, or better still, hire a bike. A cruise on the river offers a more gentle approach to sightseeing, perhaps after an exhausting morning exploring the wonderful range of shops, and for something different, visit the Butterfly Farm. As well as Sir Basil Spence's Coventry Cathedral and two other churches designed by him, Coventry is home to Warwick Arts Centre, the largest in the Midlands, and there's an Art Trail to follow alongside Coventry Canal. The reconstructed Roman fort, the 16th century weaver's cottage and Coventry Transport Museum all illustrate different aspects of this city's development through the ages.

Forget-Me-Not Guest House

18 Evesham Place, Stratford-upon-Avon
Warwickshire CV37 6HT

Forget-Me-Not Guest House is a family-run establishment that offers immaculate en suite accommodation, delicious hearty breakfasts and a warm welcome right in the middle of Stratford upon Avon. A very enjoyable and unforgettable stay awaits you with Kate and John Morris. We are open all year round and are happy to accommodate you and your needs.

Forget-Me-Not offers 5 comfortable en suite rooms situated within 5 minutes' walking distance of the theatre and town centre - three double rooms, one twin, one luxury super king. Family rooms can be arranged. All bedrooms have colour television, tea and coffee making facilities. Iron and hair dryer are available on request. A babysitting service can be arranged if booked in advance. For your comfort, Forget-Me-Not is totally non-smoking.

Tel & Fax: 01789 204907
www.forgetmenotguesthouse.co.uk

Holly Tree Cottage

Birmingham Road, Pathlow, Stratford-upon-Avon CV37 0ES
Tel & Fax: 01789 204461

Period cottage dating from 17th Century, with antiques, paintings, collection of porcelain, fresh flowers, tasteful furnishings and friendly atmosphere. Picturesque gardens, orchard, paddock and pasture with wildlife and extensive views over open countryside. Situated 3 miles north of Stratford-upon-Avon towards Henley-in-Arden on A3400.

Rooms have television, radio/alarm, hospitality trays and hairdryers. Breakfasts are a speciality. Pubs and restaurants nearby.

Ideally located for Theatre, Shakespeare Country, Heart of England, Cotswolds, Warwick Castle, Blenheim Palace and National Trust Properties. Well situated for National Exhibition Centre, Birmingham and National Agricultural Centre, Stoneleigh.

Children welcome, pets by arrangement. Non-smoking.

Bed and Breakfast from £30 per person.

e-mail: john@hollytree-cottage.co.uk • www.hollytree-cottage.co.uk

Droitwich Spa

Worcestershire

Worcestershire, stretching south-east from the fringes of Birmingham, is a county of Georgian towns, Cotswold stone villages, Victorian spas, former industrial centres and wonderful walking country. Long distance trails cross the countryside in all directions, like the Geopark Way, over a hundred miles of rock over 700 million years old from Shropshire, to Gloucester. In the Malvern Hills choose between gentle and more strenuous exercise to appreciate the wonderful views of the surrounding countryside. If you're looking for a different kind of challenge, try mountain boarding in the hills near Malvern. Alternatively take a more restful look at the countryside by taking a ride on the Severn Valley Railway between Bromsgrove and Kidderminster. In Malvern there are festivals for music and the arts, and the Malvern Theatres For an unusual museum, go to the Avoncraft Museum of Historic Buildings at Bromsgrove, which houses the national collection of telephone kiosks, and of course there are country mansions and gardens to visit too.

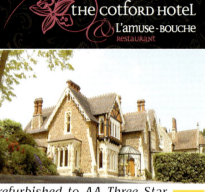

Malvern, Malvern Wells

SB

Pirton House Farm

Pirton, Worcester WR8 9EJ • Tel: 01905 820728

Set in tranquil countryside, this 19th century farmhouse offers an 'away from it all' break. Two double rooms with lovely views. Children welcome. Dogs and horses catered for. Lots of footpaths on the doorstep. Will take and collect to and from dog-friendly pub. Close to Malvern Showground. Free WiFi available.

e-mail: info@pirtonhousefarm.com • www.pirtonhousefarm.com

SB

MOSELEY FARM
BED AND BREAKFAST

Moseley Road, Hallow, Worcester WR2 6NL
Tel: 01905 641343

Spacious 17th Century former farmhouse with countryside views. Rural location four miles from Worcester City Centre, providing relaxed accommodation.

Room only or full English breakfast, from £25 per night. Large comfortable rooms - three family rooms (two en suite) and one standard twin. Colour Freeview TV, radio alarm clocks, tea/coffee making facilities and free wifi. Pets welcome at no additional charge

e-mail: moseleyfarmbandb@aol.com
www.moseleyfarmbandb.co.uk

symbols

	Totally non-smoking		*Pets Welcome*
	Children Welcome	**SB**	*Short Breaks available*
	Suitable for Disabled Guests		*Licensed*

Beverley, Bridlington

East Yorkshire

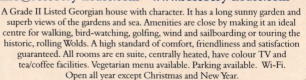

Bridlington, Kilnwick Percy

SB

THE TENNYSON
19 TENNYSON AVENUE, BRIDLINGTON YO15 2EU

Small, non-smoking, family guest house offering all usual amenities. Ground floor room available B&B from £25pppn. All rooms en suite. Located within easy walking distance of town centre, North Beach and cliff walks. Dogs £5 per dog per stay.

e-mail: dianew2@live.co.uk

Tel: 01262 604382 • www.thetennyson-brid.co.uk

Welcome to

PAWS - A - WHILE

★★★★
BED & BREAKFAST

When it is time for a break from the ordinary

A unique Bed and Breakfast for animal lovers and their companions. Pets and horses welcome.

Set in forty acres of parkland twixt York and Beverley.

Golf, Walking, Riding, Owl Watching. Brochure available.

Tel : 01759 301168 • Mobile: 07711 866869

e-mail: paws.a.while@lineone.net

www.pawsawhile.net • www.dickyphotos.com

Kilnwick Percy, Pocklington YO42 1UF

Coverdale, Glaisdale

North Yorkshire

Middle Farm

Peacefully situated 'traditonal' Dales
farmhouse, away from the madding crowd.

Two double rooms and one twin room, all
en suite, guests' own lounge, dining room in a
converted adjoining stable block.

Bed & Breakfast with optional Evening Meal. Home cooking. Pets and children welcome.

Off-road parking. Ideally positioned for walking and touring in the

beautiful Yorkshire Dales. Open all year.

Mrs Julie Clarke, Middle Farm,

Woodale, Coverdale, Leyburn,

North Yorkshire DL8 4TY

Tel: 01969 640271

e-mail: j-a-clarke@hotmail.co.uk

www.yorkshirenet.co.uk/stayat/middlefarm/index.htm

SB

SB

*Comfortable accommodation available in 16th century character
farmhouse in the beautiful Esk Valley, 9 miles from historic Whitby.*

One large family/double room sleeping up to four/five and one
family/double room en suite, sleeping up to three. Both rooms have
washbasins, colour TV and tea/coffee facilities. Guests' sitting/
diningroom with colour TV, and a conservatory. Cot and high chair
available. Full traditional farmhouse breakfast provided, or vegetarian
alternative available. Many historic towns, villages and places of interest to visit and nearby activities include
pony trekking and fishing. Camping facilities also available.

Hollins Farm
Glaisdale, Whitby, North Yorkshire YO21 2PZ

Tel: 01947 897516

Danby

Rowantree Farm

ROWANTREE FARM is a family-run dairy farm situated in the heart of the North York Moors. Ideal walking and mountain biking area, with panoramic moorland views. Coast easily accessible. Our non-smoking home comprises one family room and one twin-bedded room, with private bathroom and private shower room, also full central heating, beverage tray, CD clock radio and hairdryer. Relax in our residents' lounge with colour TV/video. Ample car parking.

- *Children welcome; cot and high chair available.*
- *Good home cooking (vegetarians catered for), served in our separate dining room.*
- *Packed lunches available.*
- *B&B from £27; Evening Meal by prior arrangement.*

Mrs L. Tindall, Rowantree Farm, Ainthorpe, Whitby YO21 2LE
Tel: 01287 660396 • e-mail: krbsatindall@aol.com
www.rowantreefarm.co.uk

Red House Farm

Listed Georgian farmhouse featured in "Houses of the North York Moors". Completely refurbished to the highest standards, retaining all original features. Bedrooms have bath/shower/toilet, central heating, TV and tea making facilities. Excellent walks straight from the doorstep. Friendly farm animals – a few cows, geese and pretty free-roaming hens. 1½ acres of gardens, sitting-out areas. Magnificent views. Interesting buildings – Listed barns now converted to 3 holiday cottages. Adult games room with snooker table. Eight miles from seaside/Whitby. Village pub within walking distance. Stabling available for horses/dogs. Non-smoking.

Tom and Sandra Spashett, Red House Farm, Glaisdale, Near Whitby YO21 2PZ • Tel & Fax: 01947 897242
e-mail: spashettredhouse@aol.com
www.redhousefarm.com

SB

Homely, comfortable, Christian accommodation. Spacious stone built bungalow in beautiful Nidderdale which is very central for touring the Yorkshire Dales; Pateley Bridge two miles, Harrogate 14 miles, Ripon nine miles. Museums, rocks, caves, fishing, bird watching, beautiful quiet walks, etc all nearby. En suite rooms (one twin, two double), TV. Private lounge. Tea making facilities available. Choice of breakfast. Evening meals available one mile away. Ample parking space on this working farm. Open Easter to end of October.

SB

Mrs C.E. Nelson, Nidderdale Lodge Farm, Fellbeck, Pateley Bridge, Harrogate HG3 5DR • Tel: 01423 711677

The city of York in North Yorkshire is full of attractions for the visitor. View it gently floating through the air on a balloon trip, or if you prefer to keep your feet on the ground take a walk round the ancient walls, to get a first glimpse of the compact urban centre dominated by the magnificent York Minster, the largest medieval Gothic cathedral in northern Europe. Have fun finding your way through the the Snickelways, the maze of hidden alleyways, and enjoy a morning – or longer – in the interesting independent little shops and boutiques as well as all the top high street stores. Outside the city the vast open stretches of the North York Moors and the Yorkshire Dales National Parks and the golden sandy beaches of the coast are perfect for an active holiday. Walking, riding, cycling, horse riding, or just enjoying the great outdoors, North Yorkshire provides an ideal destination.

The *Coppice*

A high standard of comfortable accommodation awaits you at The Coppice, with a reputation for excellent food and a warm friendly welcome. All rooms en suite with free Wi-Fi. Quietly located off Kings Road, five minutes' walk from the elegant shops and gardens of the town centre. Just three minutes' walk from the Conference Centre. Ideal location to explore the natural beauty of the Yorkshire Dales. Midway stop Edinburgh–London.

Bed and Breakfast from £45 single, £65 double, twin from £65, family room from £78. Two-course evening meal £15

9 Studley Road, Harrogate HG1 5JU
Tel: 01423 569626 • Fax: 01423 569005
e-mail: coppice@harrogate.com
www.guesthouseharrogate.com

Hawes

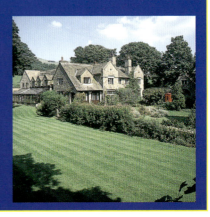

Helmsley

Barn Close Farm

BARN CLOSE FARM is nicely situated in the North York Moors National Park. This family farm in beautiful surroundings offers homely accommodation to holidaymakers all year round. Within easy reach of Rievaulx Abbey and many other places of interest, it is an ideal centre for touring this beautiful part of the country.

Highly commended for good food.

- Two double rooms, one en suite, with colour TV, hairdryer and tea/coffee making facilities

- TV lounge • Children welcome • Pets allowed

Pony trekking nearby • Good walking terrain • Private fishing

Bed and Breakfast from £28 to £40, Evening Dinner £18.

"WHICH?" RECOMMENDED.

"DAILY TELEGRAPH" RECOMMENDED.

Rievaulx, Helmsley, North Yorkshire YO62 5LH

Tel: 01439 798321 • *Mrs J. Milburn*

Helmsley

Helmsley is beautifully situated for touring the North York Moors National Park, East Coast, York, "Herriot" and "Heartbeat" country. There is a wealth of footpaths and bridleways to explore. A warm welcome awaits you in the comfortable relaxed atmosphere of this elegant Georgian town house just off the market square, overlooking All Saints Church to the front and Helmsley Castle to the rear.

All rooms are en suite, with tea/coffee making facilities, digital colour TV, radio alarm, hairdryer, central heating. Private gardens and car park. Highly recommended for good food. Bed and Breakfast from £28pppn. Please telephone, or write, for colour brochure.

As recommended by the *Which?* Good B&B Guide.

Stilworth House

1 Church Street, Helmsley YO62 5AD
Mrs C. Swift
Tel: 01439 771072 • *www.stilworth.co.uk*
e-mail: *carol@stilworth.co.uk*

VisitBritain ★★★★ Silver Award   *Laskill Grange • Near Helmsley*   AA ★★★★

Delightful country house is set in a one-acre garden which has a lake with ducks, swans, peacock and a visiting otter. All rooms lovingly cared for and well equipped. Four bedrooms are in beamed outbuildings and open onto a lawn. All rooms en suite. Generous cuisine using local fresh produce, and vegetarians catered for. Open all year. B&B from £28.50-£50. Also 7 luxury self-catering cottages with newly installed hot tubs.

Laskill Grange, Hawnby, Near Helmsley YO62 5NB
Contact Sue Smith • 01439 798268
e-mail: *laskillgrange@tiscali.co.uk* • *www.laskillgrange.co.uk*

---

symbols

 Totally non-smoking   *Pets Welcome*

 Children Welcome   **SB** *Short Breaks available*

 Suitable for Disabled Guests   *Licensed*

Kirkbymoorside, Leyburn

•Brickfields Farm•

Janet Trousdale
Kirkby Mills, Kirkbymoorside YO62 6NS
Tel: 01751 433074

Stylish, award-winning farmhouse B&B in rural North Yorkshire. Six light and airy guest rooms in the recently renovated Barn. Quality beds, comfortable seating areas with large sofa, flat screen TV, DVD, Freeview and well-stocked hospitality trays. Spacious en suite bathrooms feature walk-in "wet room" style showers, heated towel rails and "soft close" toilet seats. All rooms: ground floor, French doors opening to terrace, easily accessible for the less able guest, wholesome Yorkshire breakfasts. Wide range of restaurants and dining pubs locally. Brickfields Farm makes an ideal base for exloring North York Moors, Whitby and East coast, the local Abbeys, castles and stately homes.

Ample parking • No Smoking • No Children • No Pets.

B&B
from £47.50.
Open all year.

janet@brickfieldsfarm.co.uk
www.brickfieldsfarm.co.uk

THE OLD STAR
West Witton, Leyburn
DL8 4LU
Tel: 01969 622949
enquiries@theoldstar.com
www.theoldstar.com

Formerly a 17th century coaching inn, now a family-run guest house. You are always welcome at the Old Star.

The building still retains many original features. Comfortable lounge with oak beams and log fire. Bedrooms mostly en suite with central heating and tea/coffee making facilities.

Two good food pubs in village. In the heart of the Yorkshire Dales National Park we are ideally situated for walking and touring the Dales. Large car park. Open all year except Christmas.

En suite Bed and Breakfast from £27pppn.

★★★
GUEST
ACCOMMODATION

Malham • Miresfield Farm

- In beautiful gardens bordering village green and stream.
- Well known for excellent food.
- 11 bedrooms, all with private facilities.

Mr C. Sharp, Miresfield Farm, Malham, Skipton BD23 4DA • Tel: 01729 830414 www.miresfield-farm.com

- Full central heating.
- Two well furnished lounges and conservatory for guests' use.
- B&B from £32pppn.

Pickering

Banavie

is a large semi-detached house set in a quiet part of the picturesque village of Thornton-le-Dale, one of the prettiest villages in Yorkshire with its famous thatched cottage and bubbling stream flowing through the centre. We offer our guests a quiet night's sleep and rest away from the main road, yet only four minutes' walk from the village centre. One large double or twin bedroom and two double bedrooms, all tastefully decorated with en suite facilities, colour TV, hairdryer, shaver point etc. and tea/coffee making facilities. There is a large guest lounge, tea tray on arrival. A real Yorkshire breakfast is served in the dining room. Places to visit include Castle Howard, Eden Camp, North Yorkshire Moors Railway, Goathland ("Heartbeat"), York etc. There are three pubs, a bistro and a fish and chip shop for meals. Children and dogs welcome. Own keys. Car parking at back of house.

B&B from £29 pppn
• SAE please for brochure • Welcome To Excellence
• Hygiene Certificate held • No Smoking
Mrs Ella Bowes

BANAVIE, ROXBY ROAD, THORNTON-LE-DALE, PICKERING YO18 7SX
Tel: 01751 474616 • e-mail: info@banavie.uk.com • www.banavie.uk.com

Farfields Farm

Steve and Liz offer a warm welcome to this working farm, with a chance to relax and enjoy the peace and tranquillity within the magnificent National Park. A walkers' paradise, with spectacular views of the North York Moors Railway. Central for exploring the moors, Whitby and the Heritage Coast, and historic York. Very comfortable accommodation in five en suite rooms, two in the farmhouse and three in a lovely barn conversion adjacent. All rooms have colour TV and tea/coffee making facilities; one with small kitchenette. Lovely Yorkshire breakfasts using local produce wherever possible. Five minute stroll to local inn. Tariff £35-£50pppn.

Mrs E. Stead, Farfields Farm, Lockton, Pickering YO18 7NQ • Tel: 01751 460239
e-mail: stay@farfieldsfarm.co.uk
www.farfieldsfarm.co.uk

Pickering

ETC ★★★★

SB

One twin and one double en suite rooms, one single; all with tea/coffee making facilities and TV; alarm clock/radio and hairdryer also provided; diningroom; central heating.

Tangalwood

Roxby Road, Thornton-le-Dale, Pickering YO18 7TQ

Very clean and comfortable accommodation with good food. Situated in a quiet part of this picturesque village, which is in a good position for Moors, countryside, coast, North York Moors Railway, Flamingo Park Zoo and Dalby forest drives, mountain biking and walking. Good facilities for meals provided in the village. Open Easter to October for Bed and Breakfast from £30-£34pp. Private car park. Secure motorbike and cycle storage.

TELEPHONE: 01751 474688 • www.accommodation.uk.net/tangalwood

SB

Scarborough, Skipton

Please note...
All the information in this book is given in good faith in the belief that it is correct. However, the publishers cannot guarantee the facts given in these pages, neither are they responsible for changes in policy, ownership or terms that may take place after the date of going to press. Readers should always satisfy themselves that the facilities they require are available and that the terms, if quoted, still apply.

Town Pasture Farm

A warm welcome awaits on a 180- acre mixed farm in beautiful Boltby village, nestling in the valley below the Hambleton Hills, in the midst of Herriot country and on the edge of the North York Moors National Park. An 18th century stone-built farmhouse with full central heating, comfortable en suite bedrooms (one family, one twin) with original old oak beams, and tea/coffee facilities; spacious guests' lounge with colour TV. Good home cooking, hearty English breakfast. Ideal walking country and central for touring the Dales, York and East Coast. Pony trekking in village.

Children welcome • Pets welcome • B&B from £33 - £40

Mrs M. Fountain, Town Pasture Farm, Boltby, Thirsk YO7 2DY
Tel: 01845 537298 • www.townpasturefarm.co.uk

Ryedale House *Established 30 years*

SB

Exclusive to non-smokers, welcoming Yorkshire house of character at the foot of the moors, National Park. Three-and-a-half-miles from Whitby. Magnificent scenery, moors, dales, picturesque harbours, cliffs, beaches, scenic railways, superb walking. Highly commended, beautifully appointed rooms with private facilities, many extras. Guest lounge; breakfast room with views over Esk Valley. Large south-facing terrace and

landscaped gardens. Extensive traditional and vegetarian breakfast choice. Local inns and restaurants. Parking available, also public transport.

Mrs Pat Beale, Ryedale House, 156 Coach Road, Sleights, Near Whitby YO22 5EQ
Tel & Fax: 01947 810534 • www.ryedalehouse.co.uk

Bed and Breakfast: double £30-£32pppn, single £33pppn, minimum stay two nights. Weekly reductions all season. Monday-Friday 4 night offers available (not high season). Regret, no pets or children.

ALSO AVAILABLE: Character cottage in Whitby. Two apartments (ground and 1st floor); one double bedroom each, with fabulous panoramic views of harbour, sea and town. Adult non-smokers only, no pets. Prices from £195-£285 per week.
www.cliffhousewhitby.co.uk

York

ST GEORGE'S

6 St George's Place,
York YO24 1DR
Tel: 01904 625056
Fax: 01904 625009
e-mail: breakfastinyork@aol.com
www.stgeorgesyork.com

St George's is a small and friendly family-run Victorian residence in a quiet cul-de-sac by York's beautiful racecourse.

SB

- All rooms, one of which is on the ground floor, are en suite with tea/coffee tray and TV. • Non-smoking.
- Vegetarians options. • Private enclosed parking.
- The hotel is only a 10-minute walk from the City Walls and many places of historic interest.
- £65 per double or twin room

ST. GEORGE'S

WELLGARTH HOUSE

Wetherby Road, Rufforth, York YO23 3QB

Ideally situated in Rufforth (B1224), three miles from York, one mile from the ring road (A1237) and convenient for Park & Ride. All rooms are en suite and have tea and coffee making facilities and colour TV. Excellent local pub two minutes' walk away. Large private car park.
Bed & Breakfast from £30pppn.

TEL: 01904 738592
MOBILE: 07711 252577

A warm welcome awaits you at Wellgarth House

York

Church View B&B & Church View Cottages
Stockton-on-the-Forest, York YO32 9UP

This 200 year-old former farmhouse is located in a pretty village approximately 4 miles from York. All bedrooms are en suite and have been individually designed, including a romantic four-poster room and a large, ground floor family room. Cosy lounge with TV, video, and real log fire on chilly evenings. Breakfasts of your choice, made with local produce. Prices from £25pp.

Self-catering accommodation is available in three single-storey cottages sleeping 2-4, each tastefully decorated, with attractive furniture and fittings. Children welcome.

The Fox Inn, serving local ales, is just a stroll away; golf course to the rear. Ideal base for York, the North York Moors and the East Coast (approx. 30 minutes by bus).

Lynn & Alan Manners
tel: 01904 400403 • mobile: 07752 273371
e-mail: manners@87churchview.fsnet.co.uk • www.bandbyork.co.uk

---

The Cavalier
City Centre Accommodation

39 Monkgate, York, YO3 17PB　　Tel/Fax: 01904 636615

The Cavalier is an early Georgian Listed building, recently refurbished to provide very comfortable accommodation.
It is ideally located close to the city centre and yards from the ancient city walls and most of the historic sites.
Also convenient for touring North York Moors, Dales and East Coast resorts. Most rooms are en suite, and all have washbasins, colour TV, shaver points, radio alarms, and tea/coffee making facilities.
Hairdryer and ironing facilities are available on request.
Bed and full English breakfast with vegetarian options.
Amenities include sauna, pay phone, garage parking, full central heating. Full Fire Certificate • Open all year • Non-smoking
• Free wifi
Winter/Spring mini-breaks available, details on request.

39 Monkgate, York YO31 7PB
Tel & Fax: 01904 636615

www.cavalierhotel.co.uk

York

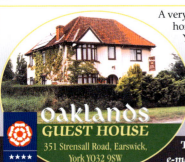

Nine miles north of York in the village of Huby in the Vale of York, the Motel is an ideal base for a couple of nights away to visit York (15 minutes to the nearest long-stay car park), or a longer stay to visit the East Coast of Yorkshire, the Dales, the Yorkshire Moors, Herriot Country, Harrogate and Ripon.

The Motel is situated behind the New Inn (a separate business) which, contrary to its name, is a 500-year old hostelry, originally an old coaching inn, and full of character. All rooms are en suite (singles, doubles, twin and family rooms), and have colour television and tea-making facilities. Good home cooking is served, including vegetarian meals, and a full English breakfast is a speciality.

THE NEW INN MOTEL
Main Street, Huby, York YO61 1HQ
Tel: 01347 810219

Pets are welcome (by arrangement)
Special breaks always available
Telephone for brochure

www.newinnmotel.co.uk
enquiries@newinnmotel.freeserve.co.uk

£35-£50 (single)
£60-£70 (double)
Special rates for
Short Breaks and
weekly rates

Highly Commended   AA ★★★ Guest Accommodation

Sheffield

South Yorkshire

SB

Padley Farm
Bed & Breakfast

Dungworth Green, Sheffield S6 6HE
Tel: 0114 2851427

Padley Farm is situated to the west of Sheffield in the quiet village of Dungworth, near the Dam Flask reservoir. Although in the countryside, we are only 10 minutes from the centre of Sheffield. All rooms have scenic views, en suite facilities and TV with DVD. Ground floor rooms have easy access from the courtyard. Visitors can enjoy hearty meals at local pubs. See our website for directions, local amenities and price lists.

www.padleyfarm.co.uk
aandlmbestall@btinternet.com

Not only does South Yorkshire have a considerable industrial heritage to offer, but its situation at the eastern gateway to the Peak District National Park makes it an ideal destination for anyone looking for an outdoor break. Have fun and learn at the same time at the Magna Science Adventure at Rotherham, where the interactive displays are based on the four elements, air, earth, fire and water, or for a day outdoors picnic in the peaceful grounds of the nearby historic Roche Abbey in the beautifully landscaped valley of Maltby Beck, while listening to the birdsong. As well as the abbey ruins, there are interesting churches and chapels to visit, and Doncaster has fine examples of Georgian architecture. Children will love getting really close to wild and farm animals from all over the world at the nearby Yorkshire Wildlife Park, or if the weather isn't so good, there's swimming, ice skating and a climbing wall at Doncaster Dome.

Cullingworth

West Yorkshire

If you are looking for a warm and comfortable environment in which to relax and enjoy your stay whilst visiting Yorkshire then The Manor will be perfect for you. This luxurious 5 Star Gold Award retreat offers a relaxing and refreshing base from which to explore some of the most beautiful countryside in Yorkshire. Lovingly restored, this 18th Century Manor House is enhanced by many original features. Ideally situated for exploring the rugged Pennine moorland or Bronte Country, the Yorkshire Dales and beyond.

SB

- Ample off-road car parking
- Centrally heated en suite rooms
- Welcome tray with homemade biscuits
- Top quality beds and linen
- Satellite TV with DVD player
- Wi-Fi Internet access
- Extensive DVD library
- Hairdryer, CD player & radio alarm clock
- Easy access to all major attractions
- Debit & credit cards accepted
- Private guest lounge
- Thick fluffy towels
- Extensive complimentary toiletries
- Iron & ironing board available
- Packed lunches available on request
- Hearty Yorkshire breakfast menu

The Manor Guest House
Sutton Drive, Cullingworth, Bradford BD13 5BQ
Tel: 01535 274374
e-mail: info@cullingworthmanor.co.uk
www.cullingworthmanor.co.uk

West Yorkshire is a mix of wild moorland and towns and cities with a long industrial heritage. Spend time in one of the many fascinating museums of past working life, then stride out over the moors, taking in the dramatic scenery, before a shopping spree or a wonderful afternoon tea. Leeds is the destination for a lively city break. Theatres, ballet, opera, festivals, restaurants, clubs, and of course, one of the best shopping experiences in the country, all are here to provide entertainment and a memorable stay. Visit the exclusive shops in the Victoria Quarter and find sought after brands in the new developments at The Light and Clarence Dock on the waterside. If all this is too much for some family members, Harewood House with its wonderful interior, gardens, and adventure playground is nearby, as well as the Yorkshire Planetarium.

The Bank House Hotel & Restaurant

11/13 Bank Street, Westgate, Wakefield WF1 1EH
Tel: 01924 368248 • Fax: 01924 363724
www.thebankhousehotelandrestaurant.com

We are a small family-run business with a warm and friendly welcome to all our guests. Our staff are always happy to help ensure your stay is a pleasant one. Our rooms are all en suite, with tea/coffee making facilities and Sky TV. All parties are welcome and are catered for.

We are two miles from the M1 and M62 and five miles from the A1. The main Westgate rail station and bus station are five minutes away. Our location is in the city centre, based near the Ridings shopping complex, the Theatre Royal Opera House, and all the popular Westgate nightlife. We have many local attractions nearby, which our staff will be happy to direct you to.

Beamish

Durham

SB

If you're looking for a few days' break somewhere different, why not go to Durham? Set between the North Pennines Area of Outstanding Natural Beauty and the Durham Heritage Coast on the meandering River Wear, the old medieval heart of the city of Durham with its cobbled streets is dominated by the cathedral and castle, a World Heritage Site, and a must for visitors. On the way back to the modern shopping centre, browse through individual boutiques and galleries in the alleys and vennels, and the stalls of the Victorian market, then enjoy a stroll along the riverside walks. Don't miss the wildflower meadows or the exotic trees and tropical glasshouses at Durham University Botanic Gardens, and just outside the city visit medieval Crook Hall with its English theme gardens and maze.

Frosterley in Weardale

SB

Northumberland

Alnmouth

SB

Westlea

Janice invites you to relax in the warm, friendly atmosphere of "Westlea", situated at the side of the Aln Estuary. It has an established reputation for providing a high standard of care and hospitality. Guests start the day with a hearty breakfast of numerous choices and in the evening a varied and appetising four-course traditional meal is prepared by chef son Paul, using local produce. All bedrooms are bright, comfortable and en suite with colour TVs, hot drinks facilities. Large visitors' lounge and dining room overlooking the estuary. Ideal for exploring castles, Farne Islands, Holy Island, Hadrian's Wall. Fishing, golf, pony trekking, etc within easy reach. Numerous Hospitality awards.

Private parking • Three bedrooms on ground floor • Children over 4 welcome

Janice Edwards, Westlea, 29 Riverside Road, Alnmouth, Northumberland NE66 2SD
Tel: 01665 830730
e-mail: ritaandray77@btinternet.com

BONDGATE HOUSE

The primary aim in our rooms is your comfort – a home from home. All our bedrooms have en suite shower rooms with cosy white bath sheets and a range of indulgent toiletries and soaps. The bedrooms all have the usual facilities such as central heating, colour TV, hairdryer and radio/alarm clock. A well-stocked hospitality tray provides tea and coffee, fresh milk, home-made biscuits or cake, and Anne's own blend of organic, herbal tea. Bedrooms are available either in the main house or in the coach house annexe, immediately behind the house.
We have twin-bedded and double rooms in the main house.

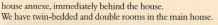

Bondgate House 20 Bondgate Without Alnwick, Northumberland NE66 1PN
Tel: 01665 602025 • e-mail: stay@bondgatehouse.co.uk • www.bondgatehouse.co.uk

14 Blakelaw Road, Alnwick NE66 1AZ

Rooftops

A friendly welcome awaits you at this award-winning Bed and Breakfast. The spacious en suite room has a double and single bed so can be let as double or twin; table and chairs and settee so you can relax and enjoy panoramic views over Alnwick, with the coast in the distance. The en suite bathrom is large, with bath and shower cubicle etc. Hospitality tray, basket of fruit and home-baked treats. *Alnwick is the perfect base to explore many attractions, castles and the spectacular coastline.*
From £30 pppn.
Tel: 01665 604201
www.visitnorthumberland.com/rooftops

Alnwick

Bamburgh

Set in six acres of mature wooded grounds,
Waren House has been reborn under the talented and loving
hands of owners, Anita and Peter Laverack,
and offers today's visitor a rare retreat for true relaxation,
along with a central point for venturing through the delights of
North Northumberland and the Scottish Borders.

Breakfast and dinner are served in the beautiful and romantic
dining room where food is presented with the utmost care.
Our cellar is stocked with a huge choice of reasonably priced
fine wines. All public rooms and bedrooms are non-smoking.

Relax in the gardens or in the comfortable lounge and adjacent library. For those seeking the
simple pleasures of walking - the sandy shore offers mile upon mile of beautiful scenery.

From this tranquil setting it is easy to find the treasures of the Heritage Coast, including the
magnificent castle at Bamburgh, just two miles away.

Waren Mill, Belford, Near Bamburgh, Northumberland NE70 7EE
Tel: 01668 214581 • Fax: 01668 214484
e-mail: enquiries@warenhousehotel.co.uk
www.warenhousehotel.co.uk

Situated one minute from Berwick-upon-Tweed's main thoroughfare, this hotel is surrounded by walls and ramparts built by Queen Elizabeth I to protect Berwick.

Accommodation consists of two family rooms, one double, one twin/triple and one single room (can sleep up to 14). All are en suite with colour TV, tea/coffee, central heating, hairdryer, trouser press and ironing facilities.

The Cobbled Yard Hotel

A wide range of attractions and activities are on offer with lots of beaches and picnic areas within easy walking distance. Ideal centre point for visits to Edinburgh and Newcastle. Private parking.
Restaurant and bar lounge. Vegetarians also catered for.

Fred and Lynda Miller, Cobbled Yard Hotel, 40 Walkergate, Berwick-upon-Tweed, Northumberland TD15 1DJ

Tel: 01289 308 407 • Fax: 01289 330 623
e-mail: enquiries@cobbledyardhotel.com
www.cobbledyardhotel.com

Situated in the heart of Crookham Village, this stone-built cottage offers the very best standards to guests. Quietly located in an estate village, Ivy Cottage provides a restful base to explore the wild and unspoilt beauty of North Northumberland just 5 miles from the Scottish Borders and Coldstream.
There is a choice of either twin or double bedded rooms; each room is individually decorated and has colour Freeview TV, tea making facilities and home-made biscuits. Both twin and double bedrooms have private bathroom, whilst the premier room is en suite. A sumptuous sitting room is available for guests' use, with a log-burning stove in winter, and there is a pretty garden to relax in. Terms from £35 pppn.

AA ★★★★★ Guest Accommodation

SB

Doreen Johnson, Ivy Cottage, 1 Croft Gardens, Crookham Village, Cornhill-on-Tweed TD12 4ST • 01890 820667
e-mail: stay@ivycottagecrookham.co.uk • www.ivycottagecrookham.co.uk

---

Hadrian Lodge is in a beautiful rural location overlooking lakes and set in open pasture bordered by pine forests. This former conversion of a stone-built hunting lodge offers comfortable, well furnished bed and breakfast accommodation. Hadrian Lodge provides a friendly social atmosphere with single, twin, double and family rooms with en suite bathrooms. Situated two miles from Hadrian's Wall and close to Roman forts of Vindolanda and Housesteads, it provides the ideal base for which to explore the beauty and history of the Northumberland National Park. A licensed bar and dining room host a varied menu of delicious home-cooked food.
Ample parking in our private grounds. Groups welcome.
Bed and Breakfast rates from £45 single, £65 double/twin.

Hadrian Lodge, North Road, Haydon Bridge NE47 6NF
Tel: 01434 6844867
e-mail: hadrian-lodge@btconnect.com
www.hadrianlodge.co.uk

Greenhead, Hadrian's Wall

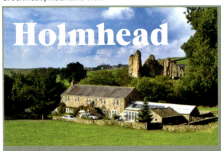

Standing directly on The Hadrian's Wall Path and Pennine Way, Holmhead is built with stones from Hadrian's Wall and stands on the foundations of this World Heritage Site.
Ideal for exploring Hadrian's Wall, the Lake District, Scottish Borders and North Pennines.

All bedrooms en suite. Beautiful country views.

Self-catering cottage sleeps four. Camping Barn also available.

**Holmhead Guest House
Hadrian's Wall
Greenhead
Northunberland CA8 7HY
Tel: 016977 47402
e-mail:
holmhead@forestbarn.com
www.bandbhadrianswall.com**

Bush Nook Guest House
Hadrian's Wall Country

Experience the wildness, freshness, culture and two millennia of history

Bush Nook Guest House is a traditional farmhouse situated within the wonderful Hadrian's Wall countryside, with panoramic views east to Northumberland National Park and Kielder Forest.

Comfortably furnished 4 star Bed and Breakfast accommodation, all bedrooms en suite, most with open beamed ceilings.

The area has excellent walking and cycling routes, offering open countryside, peacefulness, and fresh air. Easily accessible from both east and west.

Also available: superbly equipped 4 star self-catering holiday cottage in the Hay Barn, sleeping two people, with exceptional space and atmosphere. Sofa bed for an additional two people, ideal for a group or family unit for a cost effective holiday break.

*Rooms rates including breakfast from £35pppn • Special Breaks available – see website for details.
Quote FHG to receive discount*

**Bush Nook, Upper Denton, Gilsland CA8 7AF
Tel: 01697 747194 • info@bushnook.co.uk • www.bushnook.co.uk**

PETH HEAD •COTTAGE•

Bed & Breakfast in Hadrian's Wall Country

Welcome to our pretty rose-covered cottage dating from 1825 and located in the quiet hamlet of Juniper, 4 miles south of Hexham market town, Northumberland. An ideal base for visiting Hadrian's Wall, Durham Cathedral, Beamish Museum, Northumberland's Coast and Castles and the heather covered North Pennines.

We have 2 double en suite rooms with sunny south-facing aspects. Both rooms can be either double (super king-size) or twin-bedded rooms. Aga-cooked breakfasts. Private off-road parking available for your vehicle. Very quiet and peaceful countryside location. Non-smoking, sorry no pets.

Contact Joan Liddle, Peth Head Cottage, Bed and Breakfast, Juniper, Hexham, Northumberland NE47 0LA
Tel 01434 673 286 • E-mail info@peth-head-cottage.co.uk
www.peth-head-cottage.co.uk

Coach House Bed & Breakfast

Friendly, family-run B&B. We have two wonderfully cosy, well equipped, en suite rooms, the ground floor *Stable* and first floor *Hayloft* situated in our recently refurbished Coach House set in our large, well maintained gardens. Both rooms come fully equipped with TV, hospitality trays, en suite bathrooms. Great food. Stunning Hadrian's Wall Country. £35 per person per night.

Mrs C. Hall, Southview/Tavern House, Bardon Mill, Hexham, Northumberland NE47 7HZ • Tel: 01434 344779
E-mail: mail@bardonmillcoachhouse.co.uk • www.bardonmillcoachhouse.co.uk

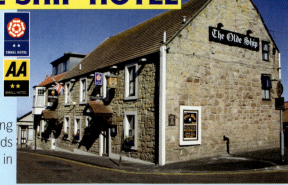

Regal House

Outstanding guest house/B&B accommodation on the Northumbrian Coast

Terry and Julie invite you to relax, unwind and enjoy the informal atmosphere of Regal House, an attractive, modern stone built property in a quiet location in Seahouses. Regal House is an ideal base from which to explore Northumberland, with The Farne Islands on the door step, Bamburgh Castle and Holy Island close by and attractions like Alnwick Garden and Berwick upon Tweed within easy reach. Comfortable en suite accommodation or room with private bathroom. Guests have the use of the dining room/lounge and access to the garden.

Wi-Fi. Ample parking. Families welcome. Non-smoking. No pets. Ideal for walkers, divers, bikers, twitchers, golfers.

10% off for club bookings. 3 for 2 nights fantastic winter breaks.

6 Regal Close, Seahouses NE68 7US
Tel: 01665 720008
e-mail: julieashford1@btinternet.com • www.regalhouse-seahouses.co.uk

LUXURY BED & BREAKFAST IN WARKWORTH

FAIRFIELD HOUSE

Fairfield House offers 5 star quality guest accommodation in an elegant Victorian house, quietly situated on the edge of the picturesque village of Warkworth, making it an ideal location for exploring the Alnwick District and Northumberland's stunning coastline, a designated Area of Outstanding Natural Beauty.

Fairfield House still retains many of its original Victorian features, including the fireplaces in the dining room and guest bedrooms, high corniced ceilings throughout and the restored conservatory through which you enter the house. Our tastefully decorated and furnished guest bedrooms all have spacious en suite bathrooms, and have been thoughtfully equipped to provide every comfort for your stay

The lovely terraced garden is south facing and borders on to fields and woodland - which attract other types of visitors such as a variety of birds, red squirrels, foxes and badgers!

Ms M. Lance, Fairfield House,
16 Station Road, Warkworth NE65 0XP
Tel: 01665 714455
E: mandy@fairfield-guesthouse.com
www.fairfield-guesthouse.com

Newcastle-Upon-Tyne

Tyne & Wear

Accessible with ease from both north and south, the new cosmopolitan city of Newcastle/ Gateshead in Tyne and Wear is a favourite destination for a short break. Shopping all day followed by a night out at one of the many bars, restaurants and clubs makes for an action-packed, lively weekend. For city centre shopping it takes a lot to beat Eldon Square and Northumberland Street in Newcastle and the elegant streets of nearby Grainger Town are the place to go for designer shopping. At the Metrocentre in Gateshead there are shops for all tastes and price levels, over 50 restaurants, cinema, and a brand new family entertainment area. Take a closer look at the Angel of the North, the 20 metre high statue that dominates the approach from the south or just wander through one of the parks or alongside the river to see the public artwork on view. Sample the fresh fish and chips in the bracing air of North Shields quay, or take a dip in the water at an award-winning beach at South Shields.

Cheshire

THE PHEASANT INN

Tucked in a peaceful corner of rural Cheshire, the 300-year-old Pheasant Inn at Higher Burwardsley stands atop the Peckforton Hills, with the most magnificent panoramic views of the Cheshire plains. Whether you come to drink, dine or unwind for a few days in one of our 12 en suite bedrooms, this atmospheric location will quickly have you under its spell. Freshly cooked wholesome food using local produce is on the menu, rewarded for its quality with a listing in the Michelin Good Pub Guide and Egon Ronay Guide. Delightful old sandstone buildings, open log fires, and the friendly, cosy atmosphere all add to the magic!

The Pheasant Inn
Higher Burwardsley, Tattenhall
Cheshire CH3 9PF
Tel: 01829 770434 • Fax: 01829 771097
e-mail: info@thepheasantinn.co.uk • www.thepheasantinn.co.uk

In Cheshire, just south of Manchester, combine a city break in historic Chester with a day or two at one of relaxing spas either in the city itself or in one of the luxury resorts in the rolling countryside. Time your visit to the historic Georgian mansion at Tatton Park to coincide with one of the wide choice of events held there throughout the year, including the annual RHS Flower Show. All the family will be fascinated by a visit to the giant Lovell Telescope at Jodrell Bank Visitor Centre near the old silk weaving town of Macclesfield or meeting the native animals and birdlife at the Cotebrook Shire Horse Centre. The walkways in nearby Delamere Forest provide pleasant and not too challenging walks, or hire a mountain bike to ride round the forest trails. Chester, with its wonderful array of Roman, medieval and Georgian buildings is a fascinating place to visit. Walk round the most complete example of city walls in the whole country, past the beautiful cathedral, before browsing through the wonderful range of shops, art galleries and museums.

Mitchell's of Chester Guest House
28 Hough Green, Chester CH4 8JQ
Tel: 01244 679004 • Fax: 01244 659567
e-mail: mitoches@dialstart.net
www.mitchellsofchester.com

This elegantly restored Victorian family home is set on the south side of Chester, on a bus route to the city centre.

Guest bedrooms have been furnished in period style, with fully equipped shower room and toilet, central heating, TV, refreshment tray and other thoughtful extras.

An extensive breakfast menu is served in the elegant dining room, and the guest lounge overlooks the well-maintained garden. Wi-Fi available.

The historic city of Chester is ideally placed for touring Wales and the many attractions of the North West of England.

Vicarage Lodge
11 Vicarage Road, Hoole, Chester CH2 3HZ

A late Victorian family-run guesthouse offering a warm welcome and peaceful stay. Situated in a quiet residential area just off the main Hoole Road, yet only one mile from the city centre. Double and twin rooms, en suite available.

All rooms have washbasins, central heating, hair dryers, shaver points, remote-control colour TV and tea/coffee facilities. Large selection of breakfast choices.
Private car park on premises.
Good-sized patio garden where guests can relax.

Bed and Breakfast from £25pp single, £45 twin/double. Weekly and winter terms available.

Tel: 01244 319533

Northwich

Ambleside

Cumbria

The region now known as Cumbria, in England's north west, has been attracting tourists since the end of the 17th century, and the number of visitors has been increasing ever since. The area is a walkers' paradise, and whether on foot, in a wheelchair or a pushchair there's a path and trail for everyone. There are magnificent views from the lakesides as well as from the hill and mountain tops, so whether you're following one of the 'Miles without Stiles' on relatively level, well laid tracks around the towns and villages, climbing in the Langdales or tackling Scafell Pike, the highest mountain in England, you won't miss out on all the Lake District has to offer.

Ambleside

Ambleside

CROYDEN HOUSE

Church Street, Ambleside LA22 0BU

Tel: 015394 32209

Croyden House is a non-smoking guest house situated on a quiet street just a minute's walk from the main bus stop and centre of Ambleside, a popular Lakeland village offering a wide range of shops, restaurants and inns catering for all tastes. The en suite rooms have colour TV, tea/ coffee making facilities; some have views of Loughrigg and Fairfield Horseshoe.

A generous home-cooked breakfast is served and special diets catered for by arrangement. Enjoy home baked scones and cakes, light lunches and afternoon teas in our adjacent Tea Rooms. Freshly made packed lunches by arrangement - home made cake included!

Guests have the use of a private car park.

B&B from £25 - £45 pppn.
Spring and Autumn Offers
Groups Welcome

ROTHAY MANOR
HOTEL & RESTAURANT

Independent, family-owned country house hotel in the heart of the Lake District, close to Ambleside and Windermere lake

Ideal base for walking, cycling, touring or just relaxing

Cumbria Tourism Awards 2010:
Finalist for 'Small Hotel of the Year' & 'Access For All'

Rothay Bridge, Ambleside, Cumbria, LA22 0EH
Tel: 015394 33605
hotel@rothaymanor.co.uk   www.rothaymanor.co.uk

*** AA   1 Red Rosette   *** VisitBritain   Silver Award
Good Food Guide for 41 years

Borrowdale, Bowness-on-Windermere, Broughton-in-Furness

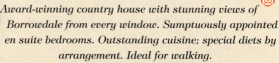
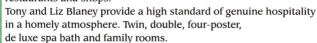

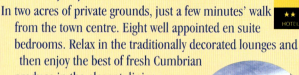

LAKE DISTRICT HOLIDAYS

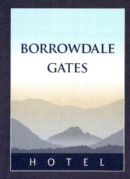

'Lakeland's most beautiful square mile'   A. Wainwright

Our country house hotel is the best-kept secret in the Borrowdale Valley, with log fires, wonderful Lakeland-inspired cooking and warm, comfortable bedrooms updated in classic, modern style – a real home-from-home, on the edge of the hamlet of Grange.

Surrounded by first-class fellwalking country and set in two acres of peaceful, wooded grounds, our Victorian country house is close to the shores of Derwentwater, with the many attractions of Keswick nearby.

Tel: 017687 77204   Borrowdale Gates Hotel
Email: hotel@borrowdale-gates.com   Grange-in-Borrowdale
Keswick, Cumbria
www.borrowdale-gates.com   CA12 5UQ

Keswick

Keswick

Windermere

New rooms, new dining experience, same fabulous location...

Nestling in a peaceful setting in the Gilpin Valley, The Wild Boar benefits from beautiful surrounding countryside, including its own private woodland for guests to enjoy, whilst exploring the rest of the National Park is easy with many other Lake District attractions close by.

New, individually designed bedrooms boast some unique features such as copper bath and log fires, as well as modern touches like iPod docking stations, flat screen TV's and DVD players providing even more creature comforts.

An exciting new Grill and Smokehouse with open kitchen and chef's table, a choice of real ales, guest beers, an extensive wine list and a range of over 50 whiskies.

Locally produced seasonal ingredients, a classic British hearty menu and an excellent ambience - which is famously The Wild Boar.

T 08458 504 604
thewildboarinn.co.uk

English Lakes
Hotels Resorts & Venues

Lancashire

EGERTON HOUSE HOTEL

RELAXED ELEGANCE

This beautiful Country House Hotel is privately owned
and set in three acres of stunning secluded gardens.
Egerton House is steeped in local history
and is the perfect location for any celebration.

Accommodation - 29 Individual Rooms
Conference - from 2 to 200 delegates
Weddings & Private Events - from 30 to 200 guests

The Dining Room provides a feast
of wholesome dishes using locally produced
products and is open for Dinner
Monday - Saturday and Sunday Lunch.

...relaxed elegance with that personal touch

Blackburn Road Egerton Bolton BL7 9PL Tel: 01204 307 171 Fax: 01204 593 030 Email: sales@egertonhouse-hotel.co.uk

www.egertonhouse-hotel.co.uk

Parr Hall Farm

ETC/AA ★★★★

Within an hour of the Lake District, Yorkshire Dales, Peak District, Chester and North Wales, Parr Hall Farm is an ideal base for touring the local area. Attractions nearby include Camelot Theme Park, Martin Mere, Southport, Blackpool and antiques at Bygone Times, Heskin Hall, Park Hall and Botany Bay. All rooms are en suite, with central heating. Good food nearby. Ground floor rooms. Off-road parking.

From M6 take A5209 for Parbold, then immediately take B5250 right turn for Eccleston. After five miles, Parr Lane is on the right, the house is first on the left.

B&B from £35 per person, reductions for children.

**Parr Hall Farm, Eccleston, Chorley PR7 5SL
01257 451917• Fax: 01257 453749
enquiries@parrhallfarm.com • www.parrhallfarm.com**

Rakefoot Farm

Chaigley, Near Clitheroe BB7 3LY
Tel: (Chipping) 01995 61332 or 07889 279063
Fax: 01995 61296 • e-mail: info@rakefootfarm.co.uk
website: www.rakefootfarm.co.uk

SB

Family farm in the beautiful countryside of the Ribble Valley in the peaceful Forest of Bowland, with panoramic views. Ideally placed for touring Coast, Dales and Lakes. 9 miles M6 Junction 31a. Superb walks, golf and horse riding nearby, or visit pretty villages and factory shops. Warm welcome whether on holiday or business, refreshments on arrival.

BED AND BREAKFAST or SELF-CATERING in 17th century farmhouse and traditional stone barn conversion. Wood-burning stoves, central heating, exposed beams and stonework. Most bedrooms en suite, some ground floor. Excellent home cooked meals service, pubs/restaurants nearby. Garden and patios. Dogs by arrangement. Laundry.

**B&B £25 - £35pppn sharing, £25 - £40pn single
S/C four properties (3 can be internally interlinked)
£111 - £695 per property per week. Short breaks available.**

Southport

Sandy Brook Farm

Farmhouse
Bed & Breakfast

Bed & Breakfast is offered in 6 en suite bedrooms, with TV and tea/coffee making facilities. Full English Breakfast, guests own sitting/ dining room. Special facilities for the disabled.

Please Contact:
Mrs Wendy Core, Sandy Brook Farm
52 Wyke Cop Road, Scarisbrick, Southport PR8 5LR
Tel: 01704 880337 • e-mail: sandybrookfarm@gmail.com
www.sandybrookfarm.co.uk

Generations of excited holiday-makers have visited Lancashire's coastal resorts, and amongst them Blackpool stands out as the star attraction. For seaside fun, amusements and entertainment it's difficult to beat, but the quieter resorts along the coast with traditional seaside attractions have their own appeal. For an outdoor break there are all kinds of activities from hot air ballooning to fishing on offer inland, from the lowland plain, along the winding valleys of the Ribble and the Lune, up into the Forest of Bowland and on to the moors of the western Pennines. There's fun for all ages in Blackpool, Britain's most popular resort, from the Big Wheel on Central Pier, the thrilling rides at the Pleasure Beach, and the Winter Gardens with award-winning shows, jazz and rock concerts, to the tropical sharks and reef fish at Sealife, the Sandcastle Waterpark, and a ride in a historic tram along the newly renovated Central Promenade, not forgetting sand, sea and donkey rides.

At Morecambe take part in the Catch the Wind Kite Festival held on the sands in July, just one of a number of events in the town each year. With the winds blowing in every direction conditions on this Irish Sea coast are perfect for kite-surfing, and instruction is available at Fleetwood, a family-orientated Victorian resort where the Fylde Folk Festival is held every September. Experience being locked in the dungeons at Lancaster Castle, on a visit to this historic centre with its cobbled streets and lively bars and restaurants. Preston, with everything from high street names to farmers' shops and markets, is the destination for shopping, as well as the National Museum of Football. Follow the Ribble Valley Food Trail to sample the wonderful produce on offer, and wherever you are look out for the panopticons, the modern sculpture installations in town and countryside.

SB

your cottage escape...

Cornwall | Devon | Somerset | Dorset

01237 459897

holidaycottages.co.uk

Cornwall

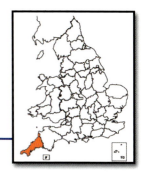

Cornwall, with the longest stretch of coastline in the UK, has become a major centre for watersports, whether sailing, surfing, windsurfing, water-skiing, diving in the clear waters to explore historic wrecks or enjoying a family beach holiday. There are busy fishing towns like Looe, Padstow, and traditional villages such as Polperro, with plenty of inns and restaurants where you can sample the fresh catch. There are gardens at Mount Edgcumbe and the Lost Garden of Heligan, as well as a wide choice of National Trust properties including Lanhydrock. The magnificent coast is ideal for birdwatchers, artists and photographers, while Bodmin Moor, one of Cornwall's 12 Areas of Outstanding Natural Beauty, is well worth a visit.

Bude, Crackington Haven

IVYLEAF BARTON SELF-CATERING COTTAGES are well equipped and sleep between 2 and 8 people. They are available all year round and some take pets by arrangement. Prices include bed linen and electricity.

All five cottages have both TV/video/DVD and CD/radio/ DAB players. Guests have the use of

an all-weather tennis court and the cottages are adjacent to a 9-hole golf course/driving range/mountain board slope.

The Cottages make an ideal safe location for families. Just 3 miles from Bude, they enjoy an elevated position with stunning views over both the coast towards Bude Bay and in the distance to Trevose Head and also the north Cornish countryside to Bodmin. The well known surfing beaches at Sandymouth Bay and Summerlease beach are both 10 minutes' drive away. *Details from Robert B. Barrett.*

Short breaks available all year excl. High Season & Bank Holidays

Ivyleaf Barton **HOLIDAY COTTAGES**

Ivyleaf Hill, Bude EX23 9LD • 01288 321237/07525 251773
e-mail: info@ivyleafbarton.co.uk • www.ivyleafbarton.co.uk

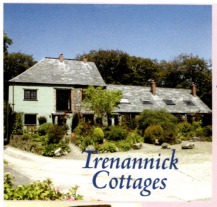

Trenannick Cottages

Five delightful cottages converted from 18th century farm buildings, standing at the end of a private, tree-lined drive, in a quiet rural setting. All cottages have small private gardens, and access to barbecue area, children's playing field, and small copse. Ideal touring base for North Cornish coast, two miles from A39, with Crackington Haven, Bude, and Boscastle all nearby.

SB

Accommodation varies from two to six persons per cottage, with wheelchair access in the Roundhouse.

Open throughout the year, with log fires for those colder evenings. Short Breaks available from £100. Pets welcome in certain cottages. Rates from £195 per week.

Lorraine Harrison, Trenannick Farmhouse, Warbstow, Launceston, Cornwall PL15 8RP
Tel: 01566 781443
e-mail: trenannick–1@tiscali.co.uk
www.trenannickcottages.co.uk

Crackington Haven, Falmouth

Coombe Cottages

Crackington Haven is a small unspoilt cove overlooked by 400 foot cliffs, with rock pools and a sandy beach at low tide – ideal for swimming or surfing.

Coombe Cottages are situated within this Area of Outstanding Natural Beauty, only 300 yards from the beach, coastal path or pub.

Little Coombe sleeps two, *Rivercoombe* sleeps four and both cottages have their own fenced gardens with picnic table and BBQ. Inside, they are well equipped and have open fires for those more chilly evenings.

Along the private drive there is a laundry room, and easy off-road parking is available outside each cottage.

Paul & Helen Seez, Coombe Cottages, Crackington Haven, Bude EX23 0JG
Tel: 01840 230664

SHASTA ANNEX

Shasta is an attractive detached bungalow, set in a lovely mature garden. The annex, together with its own entrance, is located at the side of the property, with off-road parking.

A short walk from Mawnan Smith, with 15th Century thatched pub, Italian restaurant, shops. Maenporth's sandy beach, the beautiful Helford river, tropical gardens are a short drive away. Ideal for coastal walking, Falmouth approx. four miles.

Kathy and Brian Terry, 'Shasta', Carwinion Road, Mawnan Smith, Falmouth, Cornwall TR11 5JD
Tel: 01326 250775
e-mail: katerry@btopenworld.com

Welcome pack on arrival. Terms from £250–£380 Brochure available.

SHASTA ANNEX
Self Catering Accommodation

Creekside Cottages offer a fine selection of individual water's edge, village and rural cottages, sleeping from 2-10, situated around the creeks of the Carrick Roads, near Falmouth, South Cornwall. Set in enchanting and picturesque positions, with many of the cottages offering panoramic creek views. Perfect locations for family holidays, all close to superb beaches, extensive sailing and boating facilities, Cornish gardens and excellent walks. The majority of the cottages are available throughout the year, and all offer peaceful, comfortable and fully equipped accommodation; most have open fires. Dogs welcome.

Just come and relax

For a colour brochure please phone
01326 375972
www.creeksidecottages.co.uk

SB

Fowey Harbour Cottages

We are a small Agency offering a selection of cottages and flats situated around the beautiful Fowey Harbour on the South Cornish Coast. Different properties accommodate from two to six persons and vary in their decor and facilities so that hopefully there will be something we can offer to suit anyone. All properties are registered with VisitBritain and are personally vetted by us.

Short Breaks and weekend bookings accepted subject to availability (mainly out of peak season but sometimes available at "last minute" in season).

Brochure and details from W. J. B. Hill & Son, 3 Fore Street, Fowey PL23 1AH
Tel: 01726 832211 • Fax: 01726 832901
e-mail: hillandson@talk21.com
www.foweyharbourcottages.co.uk

ETC ★★ – ★★★★

SB

St Anthony – Helford River

Enchanting creekside cottages in a timeless and tranquil hamlet. Springtime bluebell woods and hedgerows banked with primroses, reflections of multi-coloured sails off sandy beaches, the solitary blue flash of a Kingfisher in autumn, smoke grey herons and shining white egrets standing patiently by the shoreline all evoke the atmosphere of this truly beautiful corner of Cornwall.

- Stunning coastal and riverside walks
- Great country inns and local food
- Warm and comfortable with cosy log fires
- Our own sailing dinghies and fishing boats
- Moorings and easy launching
- National Trust and private gardens nearby
- Short breaks, open all year including Christmas

St Anthony Holidays, Manaccan, Helston, Cornwall TR12 6JW
Tel: 01326 231 357 • e-mail: info@stanthony.co.uk
www.StAnthony.co.uk

Forget-Me-Not Farm Holidays

Situated on Trefranck, our 340-acre family-run beef and sheep farm, in North Cornwall, on the edge of enchanting Bodmin Moor and six miles from the spectacular North Cornwall Heritage Coast. We offer all year round luxury, 4-star, self-catering acccommodation.

Forget-Me-Not Cottage can comfortably sleep 6 and is tastefully decorated and superbly equipped, with a real log fire and central heating. **The Old Wagon House** is a stylish barn conversion and sleeps 2, with a 4-poster bed – ideal for romantic breaks. Mobility rating. **The Stable** is an en suite twin annexe to the Old Wagon House. **Honeysuckle Cottage** sleeps 5. Lovely views of the moor; beautiful garden. Well equipped.
Meadowsweet Cottage (Okehampton, Devon) - barn conversion, sleeps 4, surrounded by own woodlands. Abundance of wildlife. Excellent for cycling and walking holidays.

Trefranck is within easy reach of the Eden Project, the Lost Gardens of Heligan, Padstow and the Camel Trail.

Visit Bude, Crackington Haven, Padstow, Tintagel & The Eden Project.

Trefranck Farm, St Clether, Launceston PL15 8QN
Mobile: 07790 453229
Tel: 01566 86284
e-mail: holidays@trefranck.co.uk
www.forget-me-not-farm-holidays.co.uk

Bamham Farm Cottages
Bamham Farm Cottages
Higher Bamham, Launceston PL15 9LD

Situated in beautiful countryside, the panoramic views from Higher Bamham across the Tamar valley to Dartmoor are superb. Our eight cottages were converted from the 18th century farmhouse and outbuildings and can accommodate between 2 and 6 people each or up to 37 for larger groups, celebrations and special occasions. The heated indoor swimming pool with dedicated paddling area (open all year) and new games room provide the perfect base for a family holiday. The farm is only one mile from Launceston town centre, historic capital of Cornwall, with all local conveniences and providing easy access to North Coast beaches and coastal villages, South Coast beaches and fishing ports, Bodmin Moor, Dartmoor National Park and the Eden Project. Many of the nearest North Coast and South Coast beaches are dog-friendly, details of which are provided on arrival. Flexible Short Breaks are available year round except during school holidays. The cottages are all well equipped and have VisitBritain 4-star rating.

A weekend in Cornwall has never been easier, we're only one mile from the A30 and 35 minutes from the M5.

Contact • Simon and Clare Hirsh • Tel: 01566 772141
e-mail:simon@bamhamfarm.co.uk • www.bamhamfarm.co.uk

Launceston, Liskeard

Hollyvagg Farmhouse

Part of cosy 17th century Listed Farmhouse in 80 acres of fields and woods. Working farm with sheep, geese, dogs and cats. Central to North and South coasts, Bodmin Moor, and the fabulous Eden Project. Golf and riding nearby. All modern conveniences. Sleeps 4. Also available luxury mobile home, sleeps 4, in idyllic private location.

Hollyvagg Farm
Lewannick, Launceston, Cornwall PL15 7QH
Mrs Anne Moore • 01566 782309
www.hollyvaggfarm.co.uk

Away from it all, yet close to everything

Get away from it all at Rosecraddoc Lodge, Liskeard, a well maintained, purpose-built holiday retreat on the edge of Bodmin Moor. Pub/restaurant on site, but NOT 'holiday camp' style. Ideally located for visiting attractions, including the Eden Project.

Liskeard 2 miles • Looe 9 miles • Plymouth 20 miles

Several well equipped and comfortable bungalows available, sleeping 4, 5 or 6. Everything you need including bed linen, etc. Available March-December. Weekly rates £130-£480. Discounts available.

Visit our website at **www.gotocornwall.info** or **Freephone 0800 458 3886** or **E-mail: rosecraddoc@uwclub.net**

symbols

 Totally non-smoking

 Children Welcome

 Suitable for Disabled Guests

 Pets Welcome

 SB *Short Breaks available*

 Licensed

Liskeard

Butterdon Mill Holiday Homes

SB

Idyllic rural site set in 2.5 acres
of mature gardens.
Two-bedroom detached bungalows sleeping
up to six. Games barn and children's play areas.
Ideal for touring coasts and moors of Cornwall and Devon.
Located 3 miles from Liskeard, 8 miles from Looe.
Discounts for Senior Citizens/couples Sept to June.
Children and pets welcome. Brochure available.

**Butterdon Mill Holiday Homes,
Merrymeet, Liskeard, Cornwall PL14 3LS
Tel: 01579 342636 • e-mail:butterdonmill@btconnect.com
www.bmhh.co.uk**

CUTKIVE WOOD HOLIDAY LODGES

Nestling in the heart of a peaceful family-owned country estate are six well-equipped comfortable
cedar-clad lodges. Set on the edge of ancient bluebell woods with lovely rural views, you can relax and
enjoy yourself in this tranquil and idyllic setting. Help with the animals, explore the woods and fields,
fun play area. So much for everyone to see and do – memorable beaches, wonderful coasts,
walk the moors, inspiring gardens and Eden, theme attractions, historic gems. Dogs welcome.
Ideally situated to enjoy coast and country holidays whatever the time of year.

**St Ive, Liskeard, Cornwall PL14 3ND • Tel: 01579 362216
www.cutkivewood.co.uk • e-mail: holidays@cutkivewood.co.uk**

Looe

Raven Rock and Spindrift

Contact: Mrs S. Gill,
Bodrigy, Plaidy,
Looe PL13 1LF
Tel: 01503 263122

• *Two bungalows adjacent to Plaidy Beach. Spindrift has en suite bedroom, sleeps two; Raven Rock has two bedrooms and sleeps four. Own parking spaces, central heating. Semi-detached bungalows are fully furnished, well equipped and have sea views. Set in peaceful surroundings at Plaidy. Open plan lounge-diner-kitchen. Colour TV. Patio garden. Electricity and gas included in rent. Pet by arrangement. Personally supervised.*

• *Looe is a fishing port with a variety of shops and restaurants and is only a few minutes by car or a 15 to 20 minute walk.*

• *Weekly terms: Spindrift from £270 to £370; Raven Rock from £315 to £480. Short breaks (three days minimum) before Easter and after end of October.*

TREWITH HOLIDAY COTTAGES
Self Catering Accommodation Open All Year

Paul & Barbie Higgins
Trewith, Duloe,
Near Liskeard
Cornwall
PL14 4PR

enjoyEngland.com
★★★★
SELF CATERING

Tel: 01503 262184
mobile: 07968 262184

Situated in a superb elevated position of outstanding natural beauty. Just 1½ miles from Looe. Choice of 4 refurbished cottages with 1-3 bedrooms. Fully-equipped and tastefully furnished with full central heating. Use of laundry room. Peaceful location with delightful walks. Many beaches, coves, fishing, shopping close by in Looe. Because of ponds young children need supervision. Well behaved dogs welcome.

e-mail: info@trewith.co.uk • www.trewith.co.uk

Padstow, Perranporth

GARDEN COTTAGE HOLIDAY FLATS

Holiday Accommodation in Constantine Bay - Cornwall's most relaxing holiday location

Constantine Bay, Padstow, Cornwall PL28 8JJ

Three beautifully appointed flats: *Tamarisk, Trevose View, and Treliza*, set in their own grounds with grassy lawns, ample parking and a barbecue and picnic area. All well equipped and situated just 200 yards from the golden sands of Constantine Beach. The area is full of opportunities for walking, cycling, water sports, and relaxation. Village shop half a mile from the flats, St. Merryn two miles away. At Trevose Golf Club there is also a swimming pool, tennis courts, 9-hole and championship 18-hole golf courses and all this is just at the end of Garden Cottage Flats' back field.

Liz and Russell Harris • Garden Cottage Holiday Flats
01841 520262 • www.gardencottageflats.co.uk • e-mail: liz@gardencottageflats.co.uk

Cradock Bungalow is in the centre of Perranporth and yet is secluded with a garden and parking. It is near the park, shops, pubs, restaurants and the magnificent sandy beach.

Sleeps 6-8 (can squeeze in some extras but only one bathroom and three bedrooms).

From £295-£695 per week.

Cradock

www.penkerris.co.uk
Contact: Gill-Carey - 01872 552262

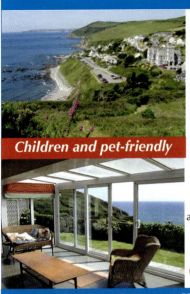

SB

St Ives

SB

SB

Cheriton Self-Catering, St Ives

In the centre of beautiful St Ives, four Apartments, sleep 2 to 5. Also three Fishermen's Cottages nearby (max 5 persons each). All well equipped, clean and comfortable. Inspected annually. Only 30 yards from harbour. Parking available. Very competitive rates. Short Breaks available October to May. Graded 3 or 4 stars.

Under the personal supervision of proprietors:

Mr & Mrs A. Luke, Cheriton Self-Catering, Cheriton House, Market Place, St Ives, Cornwall TR26 1RZ • Tel: 01736 795083

SB

CHAPEL COTTAGES • ST TUDY

Four traditional cottages, sleeping 2 to 5, in a quiet farming area. Ideal for the spectacular north coast, Bodmin Moor, and the Eden Project. Comfortable and well-equipped. Garden and private parking. Rental £175 to £475 per week. Also two cottages for couples at Hockadays, near Blisland - converted from a 17th century barn in a quiet farming hamlet. Rental £175 to £360 per week. Shop and pub/restaurant within walking distance. Regretfully, no pets. Brochure available.

Mrs M. Pestell, 'Hockadays', Tregenna, Blisland PL30 4QJ
Tel: 01208 850146
www.hockadays.co.uk

SB

Wadebridge

SB

Great Bodieve Farm Barns
Luxury Cottages in beautiful North Cornwall

Four spacious, luxury barns close to the Camel Estuary. Furnished and equipped to a very high standard. Wi-Fi. Most bedrooms en suite (king-size beds). Sleep 2-8. Excellent area for sandy beaches, spectacular cliff walks, golf, Camel Trail and surfing. One mile from Wadebridge towards Rock, Daymer and Polzeath.

**Contact: Thelma Riddle or Nancy Phillips,
Great Bodieve Farm Barns, Molesworth House,
Wadebridge, Cornwall PL27 7JE
enquiries@great-bodieve.co.uk
www.great-bodieve.co.uk
Tel: 01208 814916 • Fax: 01208 812713**

Devon

Think of moorland, and Devon immediately comes to mind. A county of contrasts, to the north are the wild moors of the Exmoor National Park, fringed by dramatic cliffs and combes, golden beaches and picturesque harbours, with busy market towns and sleepy villages near the coast. For family holidays, one of the best known of the many Blue Flag beaches on the north coast is at Woolacombe, with three miles of sand and a choice of holiday parks. Ilfracombe, originally a Victorian resort, with an annual Victorian festival, provides all kinds of family entertainment. An experience not to be missed is the cliff railway between the pretty little port of Lynmouth and its twin village of Lynton high on the cliff, with a backdrop of dramatic gorges or combes. In the centre of the county lies Dartmoor, with its wild open spaces, granite tors and spectacular moorland, rich in wildlife and ideal for walking, pony trekking and cycling.

SB

Wooder Manor

Widecombe-in-the-Moor, Near Ashburton TQ13 7TR

Cottages, converted coach house and stables nestled in the picturesque valley of Widecombe, surrounded by unspoilt woodland, moors and granite tors. Half-a-mile from village with post office, general stores, inn with dining room, church and National Trust Information Centre. Excellent centre for touring Devon with a variety of places to visit and exploring Dartmoor by foot or on horseback.

Accommodation is clean and well equipped with colour TV/DVD, central heating, laundry room. Children welcome. Large gardens and courtyard for easy parking. Open all year, so take advantage of off-season reduced rates. Short Breaks also available.
Two properties suitable for disabled visitors.
Brochure available.

Symondsdown Holiday Cottages

Tel: 01297 32385

SB

Symondsdown Cottages are situated in six acres of ground within an area of outstanding natural beauty. Our nearest beaches are only four miles away at Lyme Regis and Charmouth and the best of Dorset and Devon are within easy reach. We are fortunate to have many excellent pubs and restaurants in the local area offering a wide range of food. Horse riding, sailing, windsurfing, tennis, golf, fishing and swimming are available locally. There are wonderful country and coastal walks and a host of activities for families.

linen provided • cots and high chairs available • fully equipped kitchens • laundry room • table tennis
pets by arrangement (not during school holidays) • shops, pub etc half a mile • short breaks available
Woodbury Lane, Axminster EX13 5TL • www.symondsdownholidaycottages.co.uk

SB

Lea Hill

MEMBURY, AXMINSTER EX13 7AQ • 01404 881881

Tranquil location, wonderful scenery. Close to World Heritage Coast. Eight acres of grounds and gardens. Walks, footpaths, dog exercise field. Hot tub and barbecue. Comfortable, well equipped self-catering cottages with en suite bedrooms and own gardens. Lovely walks nearby.

Terms: £290-£435 (sleeps 2), £310-£560 (Sleeps 4).
e-mail: reception@leahill.co.uk
www.leahill.co.uk

Cider Room Cottage
Hasland Farm, Membury, Axminster.

This delightfully converted thatched cider barn, with exposed beams, adjoins main farmhouse overlooking the outstanding beauty of the orchards, pools and pastureland, and is ideally situated for touring Devon, Dorset and Somerset. Bathing, golf and tennis at Lyme Regis and many places of interest locally, including Wildlife Park, donkey sanctuary and Forde Abbey. Membury Village, with its post office and stores and church is one mile away. The accommodation is of the highest standard with the emphasis on comfort. Two double rooms; shower room and toilet; sitting/diningroom with colour TV; kitchen with electric cooker, microwave, washing machine, fridge. Linen supplied. Pets by arrangement. Car essential. Open all year. No smoking. **Terms from £250 to £390. Short Breaks available out of season £25pp.**

SAE, please, to **Mrs Pat Steele, Hasland Farm, Membury, Axminster EX13 7JF**
davidsteele887@btinternet.com
www.ciderroomcottage.com

Tel: 01404 881558

SB

An Exmoor Hideaway

Just below the hamlet of Martinhoe, these three lovely cottages, each accommodating 2 people, are completely secluded from the 21st century but still have all the comforts within.

SB

MARTINHOE CLEAVE COTTAGES

Overlooking the deep Heddon Valley, within the Exmoor National Park, they are close to some of the most beautiful and dramatic coastal scenery in Britain. Each cottage is equipped to a very high standard throughout and offers a perfect rural retreat for country-loving couples.

Open all year • Sleep 1-2

Martinhoe, Parracombe, Barnstaple, Devon EX31 4PZ • Tel: 01598 763313
e-mail: info@exmoorhideaway.co.uk
www.exmoorhideaway.co.uk

Barnstaple, Bigbury-on-Sea

Welcome to North Hill

deep in the rolling hills of Devon, a truly pastoral retreat

Carol Ann and Adrian Black, North Hill, Shirwell, Barnstaple EX31 4LG
Tel: 01271 850611
Mobile: 07834 806434
www.north-hill.co.uk

17th century farm buildings, sympathetically converted into cottages sleeping 2-6, with exposed beams, wood stoves and central heating. Set in 9 acres of pastures and gardens with a children's play area. Facilities include: indoor heated swimming pool, jacuzzi, sauna, all-weather tennis court and games room.

This area of North Devon offers some of the finest beaches in the country and the National Park of Exmoor offers thousands of acres of moorland to explore.

Terms from £195 to £935

SB

A delightful family working farm, situated on the coast, overlooking the sea and sandy beaches of Bigbury Bay. Farm adjoins golf course and River Avon. Lovely coastal walks. Ideal centre for South Hams and Dartmoor. The spacious wing (sleeps 2/6) comprises half of the farmhouse, and is completely self-contained. All rooms attractively furnished. Large, comfortable lounge overlooking the sea. There are three bedrooms: one family, one double and a bunk bed; two have washbasins. The kitchen/diner has a fridge/ freezer, electric cooker, microwave, washing machine and dishwasher. There is a nice garden, ideal for children. Sorry, no smoking. Reduction for two people staying in off peak weeks. Please write or telephone for a brochure. Jane Tucker.

e-mail: info@bigburyholidays.co.uk
www.bigburyholidays.co.uk
Tel: 01548 810267

Mount Folly Farm
Bigbury-on-Sea, Kingsbridge TQ7 4AR

SB

Brixham, Broadwoodwidger, Chulmleigh

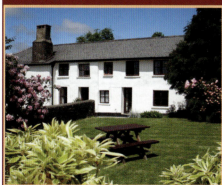

SB

BONEHAYNE FARM
COTTAGE: CARAVAN: BOARD
COLYTON, DEVON EX24 6SG

• Family 250 acre working farm • Competitive prices • Spectacular views

• Our two self-catering caravans are located on an exclusive site. Each on its own special area with stunning views over the enclosed garden and the Devon countryside.

• The farm cottage is full of character and adjoins Bonehayne farmhouse. South-facing with glorious views over the garden and the Devon countryside.

• Rooms are available for Bed and Breakfast in part of the farmhouse.

• Relax outside the cottage in the deckchairs provided.

• Four miles to the beach • Five minutes from Colyton

• Spacious lawns/gardens • Laundry room, BBQ, picnic tables

• Good trout fishing, woods to roam, walks

• Spacious enclosed lawn where children can play croquet and table tennis.

Mrs Gould • Tel: 01404 871396/871416
www.bonehayne.co.uk • e-mail: gould@bonehayne.co.uk

SB

Situated beside the village church, the cottages (sleep 4/5) have been tastefully renovated to maintain the old style of the barn. With panoramic views over the Coly valley, they provide a quiet holiday and offer many interesting walks. Riding stables and ancient monuments are within walking distance. Honiton Golf Course, swimming pool and bowling green are four miles away. Lyme Regis, Sidmouth and Exmouth plus many other quaint scenic coastal resorts and the Jurassic Coast are all within half an hour's drive; situated on the route of the East Devon (Foxglove) Way.

Each cottage has a modern kitchen complete with washing machine, dishwasher and microwave as well as a conventional cooker, comfortable lounge with colour TV and DVD/Digibox, two bedrooms, and bathroom with bath and shower. Central heating • Electricity by £1 meter • Bed linen supplied • Games room • Brochure on request.

Church Approach Cottages
Church Green, Farway, Colyton
Devon EX24 6EQ

For further details please contact: Sheila & Liz Lee
Tel: 01404 871383/871202
e-mail: lizlee@eclipse.co.uk • www.churchapproach.co.uk

SB

Rural tranquillity situated in Devonshire heartland. An ideal location for visiting moorlands, coasts, historic/heritage sites or attractions. All corners of Devon accessible. Just one mile from Crediton, convenient for shops, amenities, leisure centre, golf and restaurants. 8 miles away lies Exeter Cathedral City offering extensive activities. Stroll around our on-site estate lakes (carp and tench fishing) abundant with wildlife. Four 'cottage'-style apartments, three ground floor, all 4★ quality. Wheelchair accessible. Reasonably priced. Quaint local inns/restaurants/takeaways.

CREEDY MANOR
QUALITY
SELF-CATERING
ACCOMMODATION
Long Barn, Crediton, Devon EX17 4AB

Sandra & Stewart Turner • Tel: 01363 772684
• e-mail: info@creedymanor.com
• www.creedymanor.com

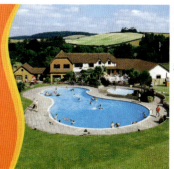

Hillcroft – Exmoor

Mrs M.E. Williams,
25 Jury Park,
South Molton,
North Devon
EX36 4DW
01769 579660

Hillcroft – Exmoor – Brayford Area

This bungalow is an ideal holiday centre, being near the moors and within easy reach of the coasts. Hillcroft is situated beside a quiet country road in the Exmoor National Park. Lovely walks, touring, pony trekking available locally or just relax and enjoy the glorious views. Lawn at front and back of bungalow.

3 double bedrooms and cot available • sittingroom, dining room • bathroom, toilet • kitchen with electric cooker • electricity metered • everything supplied except linen • Children welcome • Pets welcome • Available all year
From £100 to £250 weekly

SB

As far away from stress as it is possible to be!

High on a hillside with magnificent views of the lovely Otter Valley, Odle Farm is peacefully set within 10 acres of grounds in the Blackdown Hills, an Area of Outstanding Natural Beauty on the Devon/Somerset border. Clustered around a pretty courtyard, the farmhouse and barns have been sympathetically converted to create four supremely comfortable and beautifully furnished cottages, fully equipped to make your holiday a stress-free break away from the rest of the world ! *Wireless internet access is available on site.*

Odle Farm, New Road, Upottery, Near Honiton EX14 9QE
Tel: 01404 861105 • www.odlefarm.co.uk
e-mail: info@odlefarm.co.uk

• *All cottage residents have free use of the Hydrotherapy Spa/hot tub (Honeysuckle and Willow Cottages have their own private hot tubs).*
• *Wisteria, Rose and Jasmine Cottages contain the following:*
• Woodburner • 1st log basket free • DVD and video player • Washer/dryer
• 2nd TV in main bedroom • Fridge/freezer • Mini hi-fi • Microwave • Hairdryer
• Dishwasher • Underfloor heating • Linen and towels (except beach towels and cot linen)
• LCD TV in main lounge and Freeview • Cots and highchairs available • Double oven
• Barbecue and garden furniture
• Complimentary homemade cake, pint of milk and tea tray on arrival.

Hope Cove, Kingsbridge, Paignton

"West Ridge" bungalow stands on elevated ground above the small coastal town of Seaton. It has one-and-a-half-acres of lawns and gardens and enjoys wide panoramic views of the beautiful Axe Estuary and the sea. Close by are Lyme Regis, Beer and Branscombe. The Lyme Bay area is an excellent centre for touring, walking, sailing, fishing and golf. This comfortably furnished accommodation is ideally suited for up to four persons. A cot can be provided. Pets welcome. Available March to October, £195 to £525 weekly (fuel charges included). Full gas central heating. Digital TV. **SAE for brochure.**

Mrs E.P. Fox, "West Ridge",
Harepath Hill, Seaton
Devon EX12 2TA
Tel: 01297 22398
e-mail: fox@foxwestridge.co.uk
www.cottageguide.co.uk/westridge

SWEETCOMBE
Cottage Holidays

ATTRACTIVE, CAREFULLY SELECTED COASTAL COTTAGES, FARMHOUSES AND FLATS IN SIDMOUTH & EAST DEVON

All very well equipped.
Gardens, Pets welcome

SWEETCOMBE COTTAGE HOLIDAYS,
ROSEMARY COTTAGE, WESTON, NEAR SIDMOUTH, DEVON EX10 0PH
Tel: 01395 512130
e-mail: enquiries@sweetcombe-ch.co.uk • www.sweetcombe-ch.co.uk

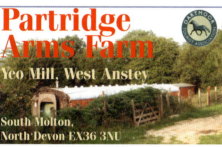

SB

SB

Westward Ho!, Woolacombe

WEST PUSEHILL FARM COTTAGES

SB

Resident proprietors, The Violet Family have been welcoming visitors to West Pusehill Farm for over twenty years, and many return time and time again.

Ideal for family summer holidays, restful spring/winter breaks, or a perfect base to explore Devon's outstanding coast and countryside and many outdoor activities.

West Pusehill Farm Cottages not only give you the freedom and independence of a self-catering holiday, but the local area offers a wide range of excellent restaurants and cafes, so your holiday can be enjoyed by every member of the family.

- ❖ Located in an Area of Outstanding Natural Beauty
- ❖ Eleven sympathetically converted cottages
- ❖ BBQ area
- ❖ Children's playground
- ❖ On-site heated outdoor pool
- ❖ Laundry room
- ❖ Golf, fishing, walking, exploring, shopping
- ❖ Family attractions

West Pusehill Farm
Westward Ho!
North Devon EX39 5AH
Tel: 01237 475638/474622
e-mail: info@wpfcottages.co.uk
www.wpfcottages.co.uk

Resthaven
Holiday Flats

On the sea front overlooking the beautiful Combesgate beach. Fantastic views of Morte Point and the coastline.
Contact Brian Watts for details and brochure.
Tel: 01271 870248

★ Two self contained flats, sleeping 5 & 9 ★ Family, double and bunk bedrooms all with washbasins ★ All-electric kitchens. Electricity on £1 meter ★ Bathrooms with bath & shower ★ Colour TVs with DVD players ★ Free parking, lighting, hot water and laundry ★ Terms £160 to £1000 per week

The Esplanade, Woolacombe, Devon EX34 7DJ
e-mail: rhflats@orange.net • www.resthavenflats.co.uk

Woolacombe

SB

CHICHESTER HOUSE HOLIDAY APARTMENTS

Chichester House is situated on the sea front overlooking Barricane Beach in an area listed as being of outstanding natural beauty, with wonderful views of Baggy Point to the left, Morte Point to the right, and Lundy Island on the horizon. It is only a short level walk to the village and Woolacombe's three miles of golden sands, whilst a walk in the other direction takes you to Combesgate beach, the coastal path and Mortehoe.

FLATLETS • **Lundy Lights and Bay Views** • both situated on the first floor, with balconies with magnificent views over the Bay. **SLEEP 2.**

SELF CONTAINED APARTMENTS • all with sea views.

The Retreat • on the first floor with bathroom, bedroom with double bed, sitting room and combined kitchen, split level apartment. **SLEEPS TWO**

Shell Bay • on the second floor with double bedroom, bathroom, living room/kitchen overlooking the sea. **SLEEPS TWO PLUS**

Hartland View • very large apartment on second floor with lounge overlooking the sea, two bedrooms, each with a double and single bed. Kitchen diner. Bathroom. **SLEEPS UP TO SIX**

Morte View • on the first floor, with bathroom, sitting room/kitchen opening onto a balcony, double bedroom. **SLEEPS TWO**

Sea Spray • on the ground floor, with bathroom, dining/bed-sitting room with foldaway double bed, large bedroom with double and single beds. Kitchen. **SLEEPS FOUR.**

Well behaved dogs are welcome by prior arrangement • Resident Proprietor: Joyce Bagnall

The Esplanade, Woolacombe EX34 7DJ• Tel: 01271 870761

Dorset

The "Old Coastguards" Holiday Cottages
Abbotsbury

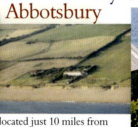

Luxury self-catering holiday cottages by the sea in Abbotsbury, West Dorset – ideally located just 10 miles from Weymouth and Dorchester, and on the edge of England's beautiful West Country. Built in 1823, these charming self-catering cottages are situated on stunning Chesil Beach, with fantastic sweeping views of the sea and the coast.

Ideal for a short break or a family summer holiday, our luxury self-catering holiday cottages have accommodation for up to 8 people. Each is comfortably furnished and well equipped, with fridge/freezer, microwave, hairdryer, iron and ironing board, colour TV, adjustable heating and an open fire. Bed linen and towels are provided in each cottage.

**laundry room • storage for bicycles, fishing rods etc • payphone for outgoing calls
free broadband internet connection • ample parking • dogs welcome by arrangement.**

Contact: Cheryl & John Varley
'The Old Coastguards', Abbotsbury, Dorset DT3 4LB • Telephone: 01305 871335 • Fax: 01305 871766
www.oldcoastguards.com

Contact **Mrs P.M. Wallbridge,
Watermeadow House,
Bridge Farm, Hooke,
Beaminster, Dorset DT8 3PD**
Tel: **01308 862619**

Orchard End & The Old Coach House
Hooke, Beaminster.

Hooke is a quiet village nine miles from the coast. Good walking country and near Hooke Working Woodland with lovely woodland walks. Coarse fishing nearby.

Orchard End is a stone-built bungalow, with electric central heating and double glazing. Four bedrooms, two bathrooms; sleeps 8. Well-equipped and comfortable. Enclosed garden and off-road parking.

The Old Coach House, a cottage sleeping 9, is also finished to a high standard. Four bedrooms, two bathrooms; central heating. Large garden; off-road parking.

Both properties (on working dairy farm) are equipped with washing machine, dryer, dishwasher, fridge/freezers, microwaves and payphones. Both properties ETC ★★★★
Terms from £300 to £760 inclusive of VAT, electricity, bed linen and towels.

enquiries@watermeadowhouse.co.uk • www.watermeadowhouse.co.uk

SB

SB

Six stunning cottages in a private hidden valley, surrounded by extensive gardens, grounds and ponds. Situated at Dorset's very centre, close to Milton Abbas, with a fine pub and restaurant (01258 880233), we make a great touring base not too far from anywhere.

Superior self-catering Holiday Cottages

Try our indoor pool, jacuzzi, swim jet and sauna, or gymnasium and games room on wet days. Play tennis, explore our farm on foot or bike, followed by a lakeside barbecue on dry ones. Go riding (01258 880057), shoot a clay, fish or just relax in a very peaceful setting.

There is something for everyone here at Luccombe

• Terms from £290 to £1275.

Please check our availability at www.luccombeholidays.co.uk or telephone 01258 880558

• Dogs welcomed by arrangement.

Luccombe, Milton Abbas, Blandford Forum, Dorset DT11 0BE

e-mail: luccombeh@gmail.com www.luccombeholidays.co.uk

BOURNEMOUTH HOLIDAY APARTMENTS

Proprietors Mike and Lyn Lambert have been catering for Bournemouth holidaymakers at Aaron and Lyttelton Lodge for over 35 years. These modern holiday apartments situated in a pleasant residential area of Boscombe offer accommodation for 1-10 persons in clean self-catering studios, one, two and four bedroom flats close to a superb sandy beach, shops and entertainments.

Holidaymakers are accommodated in either an elegant Victorian property or spacious new wing. Each flat is completely self-contained and provided with constant hot water from each flat's own gas boiler. **Free Wi-Fi access**.

Bournemouth town centre is a few minutes away by car or there is a frequent bus service. A car parking space is provided for each apartment in our own grounds.

Boscombe is an ideal base for touring many places of interest in the Dorset and Hampshire countryside, with to the east, the New Forest, Beaulieu and the Isle of Wight, and to the west, Poole with its magnificent harbour, Corfe Castle, the Jurassic coast and the picturesque Dorset villages.

16 Florence Road, Bournemouth BH5 1HF Tel: 01202 304925 or 01425 474007

www.selfcateringbournemouth.co.uk
e-mail: mikelyn_lambert@btinternet.com

Holiday Flats & Flatlets

Highly sought after location, a short walk to golden sandy beaches and pedestrianised shopping area. Buses, coaches and trains to all parts.

- A SHORT WALK TO GOLDEN SANDY BEACHES •
- MOST WITH PRIVATE BATHROOMS •
- CLEANLINESS AND COMFORT ASSURED •
- LAUNDRY ROOM • FREE PRIVATE PARKING •
- DOGS WELCOME • COLOUR TV IN ALL UNITS •
- NO VAT CHARGED •

**CONTACT: M. DE KMENT,
4 CECIL ROAD, BOURNEMOUTH,
DORSET BH5 1DU
TEL: 07788 952394**

Bridport

SB

Burton Bradstock, Sherborne

Mimosa

The Fossil & The Cross

Granary Lodge

1

Tamarisk Farm

Beach Road, West Bexington, Dorchester DT2 9DF
Tel: 01308 897784   Mrs Josephine Pearse

SELF CATERING

On slope overlooking Chesil beach between Abbotsbury and Burton Bradstock.
Three large (Mimosa is wheelchair disabled M3(i), Granary Lodge is disabled-friendly (M1) and The Moat) and two small cottages (VB 3/4 Stars). All have wide views of the sea and stand in own garden.
Glorious views from all front rooms along West Dorset and Devon coasts. Lovely walks by sea and inland. Part of mixed organic farm with arable, sheep, cattle, horses and market garden (organic vegetables, meat and wholemeal flour available). Sea fishing, riding in Portesham and Burton Bradstock, lots of tourist attractions and good markets. Good centre for touring Thomas Hardy's Wessex. Safe for children and excellent for dogs. Very quiet. Terms from £215 to £995.

e-mail: holidays@tamariskfarm.com •• www.tamariskfarm.com/holidays

SB

Self-Catering Cottages

White Horse Farm
ETC ★★★/★★★★

Set in beautiful Hardy countryside, we have six cottages furnished to high standards and surrounded by two acres of paddock and gardens with a duck pond. We lie between the historic towns of Sherborne, Dorchester and Cerne Abbas. Within easy reach of many tourist attractions. Next door to an Inn serving good food. Pets welcome. All cottages have central heating, colour digital TV and free film rental (500+). Heating, electricity, bed linen, towels inclusive. Ample parking. Good value.

The Willows sleeps 4/6; Otters Holt sleeps 6/8; Toad Hall sleeps 4; Badger's and Moley's sleep 2; Ratty's sleeps 2/4

SB

White Horse Farm, Middlemarsh, Sherborne, Dorset DT9 5QN
01963 210222

Pets welcome

Visit our website:
www.whitehorsefarm.co.uk
e-mail: enquiries@whitehorsefarm.co.uk

North Perrot - Wood Dairy. See P254 under Somerset

While every effort is made to ensure accuracy, we regret that FHG Guides cannot accept responsibility for errors, misrepresentations or omissions in our entries or any consequences thereof. Prices in particular should be checked. We will follow up complaints but cannot act as arbiters or agents for either party.

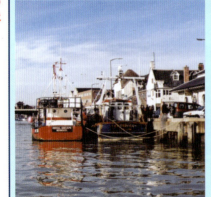

Dursley, Mitcheldean

Gloucestershire

South Cerney

SB

Luxury lakeside holidays in the Cotswolds

01285 861 839

www.orionholidays.com/fhg

Luxury Holidays

A collection of luxury 4/5* lakeside holiday homes situated across the Cotswold Water Park. We offer short breaks and pets are welcome.

Cotswold Water Park

The Cotswold Waterpark provides a variety of activities including walking, sailing, fishing, water sports, tennis, golf, swimming and a premier spa is on the doorstep.

Somerset

Somerset shares in the wild, heather-covered moorland of Exmoor, along with the Quantock Hills to the east, for walking, mountain biking, horse riding, fishing and wildlife holidays. Stretching inland from the Bristol Channel, historic villages and towns like medieval Dunster, the ancient harbour town of Watchet with its marina and pretty villages like Porlock all provide ideal bases for exploring the area. The forty miles of coastline with cliffs, sheltered bays and sandy beaches includes family resorts like Weston-super-Mare, with its famous donkey rides and all the other traditional seaside attractions. More family fun can be found at Minehead, the start of the South West Coast Path, Burnham-on-Sea and quieter Clevedon.

Toghill House Farm
SELF-CATERING COTTAGES

Situated just four miles north of Bath and within a few miles of Lacock, Castle Combe, Tetbury and the Cotswolds, the 17thC farm buildings have been converted into luxury self-catering cottages with well equipped kitchens.

Each cottage includes a lounge with kitchen/diner, bathroom and separate bedroom, with a choice of twin or double beds. All have colour TV, microwave, fridge-freezer, full cooker and hob. All bed linen, towels etc included. Pets welcome.

A laundry room complete with washing machine, tumble dryer and ironing facilities is available for all guests

B&B also available in warm and cosy 17thC farmhouse.

THE GARDEN COTTAGES (x 6) have one bedroom and sleep 2-3.

BARN COTTAGE has two bedrooms and sleeps 4.

THE COPSE has four bedrooms and sleeps 8.

LYNCH COTTAGE has two bedrooms and sleeps 4.
It is a five-minute drive from the farm.

**Toghill House Farm, Toghill, Wick, Near Bath BS30 5RT
Tel: 01225 891261 • Fax: 01225 892128 • www.toghillhousefarm.co.uk**

SB

Primrose Hill

Primrose Hill offers spacious, comfortable accommodation in a terrace of four bungalows with private enclosed gardens and panoramic views over Blue Anchor Bay. The games room and boule pitch are popular with both adults and children. In walking distance of picturesque Blue Anchor Bay with its sandy beach, pubs, beachside cafes and indoor swimming pool.
Within sight and sound of the West Somerset Railway.

Wheelchair-friendly • Dogs welcome • Internet connection

**Winner Accessible Somerset 2008 & 2009
and Exmoor Excellence Awards, 2006/2007**

**Primrose Hill Holidays, Wood Lane, Blue Anchor TA24 6LA
Tel: 01643 821200 • info@primrosehillholidays.co.uk
www.primrosehillholidays.co.uk**

Withy Grove Farm

Come and enjoy a relaxing and friendly holiday "Down on the Farm" set in beautiful Somerset countryside. Peaceful rural setting adjoining River Huntspill, famed for its coarse fishing. The farm is ideally situated for visiting the many local attractions including Cheddar Gorge, Glastonbury, Weston-super-Mare and the lovely sandy beach of Burnham-on-Sea. Self-catering cottages are tastefully converted, sleeping 4-5. Fully equipped with colour TV.

SB

★ *Heated Swimming Pool* ★ *Games Room*
★ *Licensed Bar and Entertainment (in high season)*
★ *Skittle Alley* ★ *Laundry*

For more information please contact: **Mrs Wendy Baker, Withy Grove Farm, East Huntspill, Near Burnham-on-Sea, Somerset TA9 3NP • Telephone: 01278 784471 • www.withygrovefarm.co.uk**

TAMARACK LODGE, CHARD

This luxurious, traditionally styled, ranch house-type log cabin enjoys extensive views of the delightful Yarty Valley. It was purpose-built to provide self-catering holiday accommodation for both able-bodied and disabled people, and sleeps up to eight. It is very wheelchair-friendly, and has two of the three double bedrooms on the ground floor, and a large ground floor wc/shower room. Tamarack Lodge is situated on a family-run beef and sheep farm in the beautiful Blackdown Hills, an Area of Outstanding Natural Beauty near the Somerset/Devon border.

SB

NATIONAL ACCESSIBLE SCHEME LEVEL 1.

Matthew Sparks, Fyfett Farm, Otterford, Chard TA20 3QP • 01823 601270
e-mail: matthew.sparks@tamaracklodge.co.uk • www.tamaracklodge.co.uk

---

CHEDDAR – SUNGATE HOLIDAY APARTMENTS
Church Street, Cheddar, Somerset BS27 3RA

SB

Delightful apartments in Cheddar village, each fully equipped. Sleep 2/4. Laundry facilities. Private parking. Family, disabled and pet friendly.

The apartments are within easy walking distance of shops, swimming pool, leisure centre, and the stunning **Cheddar Gorge and Caves**.
The bus stop is only a few paces away.
The Mendip Hills offer open countryside and great views for walkers and those wishing to walk along the Mendip Way to Wells or Weston-Super-Mare. Other facilities close to Cheddar include golf, fishing, sailing and an artificial ski slope with ski lift. There is so much to see and do in the area, as well as many local events, pubs and restaurants making this an ideal venue for a short break holiday.

Contact: Mrs. M.M. Fieldhouse for brochure.

Tel: 01934 842273/742264 • enquiries@sungateholidayapartments.co.uk
www.sungateholidayapartments.co.uk

Dunster

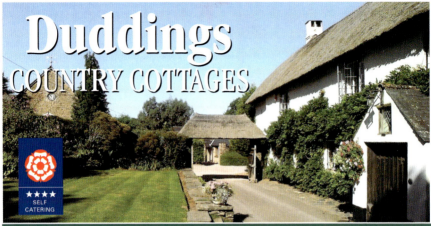

Duddings
COUNTRY COTTAGES

As resident owners, we personally guarantee immaculate presentation of cottages on arrival. Each cottage has tasteful decor with matching, highest quality fabrics and is fully central heated. Amenities include comfortable lounges with colour TV/video/DVD, fully fitted modern kitchens with fridge-freezer, cooker and microwave. Our facilities include heated indoor pool, hard tennis court, putting green, pool and table tennis, trampoline, football net and play centre. Trout stream in 8.5 acres for fishing or picnics. Families and pets welcome, walking, riding, beaches nearby. Short breaks available off season, open all year. Full details and plans of the cottages together with up to date prices and availablity can be found on our website, or please call for brochure.

Thatched longhouse and 12 cottages for 2-16 persons, beautifully converted from old stone barns and stables. Original beams and exposed stonework retain the character of the buildings. Two miles from the picturesque village of Dunster in the Exmoor National Park.

Luxury Cottages

Indoor Heated Pool

Tennis Court

Duddings Country Cottages
Timberscombe Dunster, Somerset TA24 7TB

Telephone: 01643 841123
www.duddings.co.uk
e-mail: richard@duddings.co.uk

Riscombe Farm Holiday Cottages – Exmoor National Park

Four charming self-catering stone cottages converted from barns surrounding an attractive courtyard with stables. Very comfortable, with log fires and equipped to a high standard, sleeping 2-6. Peaceful, relaxing location beside the River Exe in the centre of Exmoor National Park. Excellent walking and riding country in the valleys, across the moors or along the spectacular coast.

One and a half miles from Exford Village.
Dogs and horses welcome. Stabling provided.

Open all year   VisitBritain ★★★★

Leone & Brian Martin,
Riscombe Farm, Exford,
Somerset TA24 7NH
Tel: 01643 831480
www.riscombe.co.uk *(with vacancy info.)*

West Withy Farm

Situated in the beautiful Brendon Hill countryside on the edge of Exmoor National Park, West Somerset, West Withy Farm holiday cottages are a haven of peace and tranquillity. Set in a 23-acre small-holding, the two self-catering cottages have panoramic views across green pastures to the hills on the horizon.
Two local stone barns have been skillfully converted to create spacious, character holiday cottages offering centrally heated comfort, private, enclosed gardens and modern conveniences. Sleep 4/5.

Fully inclusive prices • From £200-£565 per week • Short breaks available

UPTON, NEAR DULVERTON, TAUNTON TA4 2JH • Tel: 01398 371 322
e-mail: westwithyfarm@exmoor-cottages.com • www.exmoor-cottages.com

Exmoor, Minehead

*W*intershead Self Catering Holiday Cottages
Character Cottages Amidst Breathtaking Scenery

Simonsbath, Exmoor, Somerset TA24 7LF

Wintershead is ideal for holiday makers looking for a relaxing break away from the crowded coastal resorts, occupying a unique location with breathtaking views. Five quality stone cottages converted from original farm buildings offer all the comforts of home, yet are not far from all the local attractions: the famous Doone valley and Oare church, Lynton, Lynmouth and Porlock, and the sleepy villages of Dunster, Dulverton and Exford. There is excellent fishing locally on the Barle, Exe, East and West Lyn rivers, or, if you want to be closer to nature, there are riding stables nearby; if you enjoy walking, the Two Moors Way is on the doorstep. The golden beaches of Croyde, Saunton Sands and Woolacombe are a short and pleasant drive away, passing quaint fishing villages, Ilfracombe, Combe Martin and the historic town of Barnstaple. If you would like an unforgettable day out, the Somerset Levels, Cheddar Caves and Wookey Hole are within easy driving distance, as are the Eden Project and the Lost Gardens of Heligan.

Wintershead is an ideal base from which to explore the beautiful West Country. Easy to find – yet so hard to leave. Colour brochure available.
Telephone Jane Styles on 01643 831222
or look at www.wintershead.co.uk

Four-star lodges and cottages sleeping from two in a cosy cottage up to 12 in our newly built Holly Lodge, all situated in two and a half acres of gardens overlooking the slopes of Exmoor.

Located between Minehead and Porlock and within five miles of Snowdrop Valley. Superb walking with National Park on two sides and with Minehead seafront, its shops, restaurants and pubs within 1½ miles, Woodcombe Lodges offer the best of both worlds. Full convector heating throughout. Dogs permitted in some lodges.

WOODCOMBE LODGES
Bratton, Near Minehead
Somerset TA24 8SQ
Tel & Fax: 01643 702789
nicola@woodcombelodge.co.uk www.woodcombelodge.co.uk

North Perrott, Taunton

WOOD DAIRY

**WOOD LANE, NORTH PERROTT
SOMERSET TA18 7TA**

Three well-appointed stone holiday cottages set around courtyard in two and a half acres of Somerset/Dorset countryside. Area of Outstanding Natural Beauty, close to Lyme Bay and Jurassic Coast. Excellent base for walking, trails and historic properties.

• Pets welcome by arrangement. • Wheelchair friendly.
• Direct access to Chedington Court Golf Club on the 8th and 9th greens.

**Tel & Fax: 01935 891532
liz@acountryretreat.co.uk
www.acountryretreat.co.uk**

Timbertop
Holiday Bungalows

01823 601378

www.timbertopbungalows.co.uk

Come and stay at one of our luxury bungalows and experience the best of both Devon and Somerset. You can visit the unspoilt Somerset hills of the Quantocks, Brendons, Exmoor and also Dartmoor in neighbouring Devon – not to mention the popular Devon coastal resorts. Lyme Regis, Sidmouth, Woolacombe and Minehead are within easy reach.
Three charming bungalows are available, one sleeping 4, the others 6.

**Mrs V D Manning, Timbertop Farm, Churchinford,
Taunton, Somerset TA3 7PR • Tel: 01823 601 378 / Mobile: 07811 362 740**

The city of Bath has all the features of a major 21st century centre, festivals, theatres, museums, galleries, gardens, sporting events and of course, shopping. Attracting visitors from all over the world, this designated World Heritage Site boasts wonderful examples of Georgian architecture and of course, the Roman Baths.

**Readers are requested to mention this FHG guide
when seeking accommodation**

Taunton, Watchet

Wells

Potting Shed Self-catering Holiday Cottages

offer perfect retreats near Glastonbury, Cheddar and historic Wells. Our cottages are made to relax in, and we invite you to enjoy our wonderful gardens, breathtaking Somerset landscapes, wildlife and luxury spa

Potting Shed Cottage • A perfect country hideway "a deux". Situated in the centre of Somerset.

Spider's End Cottage • A cottage surrounded by nearly two acres of garden.

In-B-Tween Cottage • A charming and unique little Mews place in central Wells. Very quiet and beautifully appointed.

Middle Earth • A charming and unique little Cottage. Very quiet and beautifully appointed and fully equipped.

Potting Shed Holiday Cottages
Harter's Hill Cottage, Pillmoor Lane, Coxley,
Near Wells, Somerset BA5 1RF
Tel: 01749 672857
www.pottingshedholidays.co.uk

Wiltshire

Trowbridge

John and Elizabeth Moody
Gaston Farm, Holt,
Trowbridge BA14 6QA
Tel: 01225 782203

The self-contained accommodation is part of a farmhouse, dating from the 16th century, on the edge of the village of Holt with views across open farmland. Within 10 miles of Bath, Bradford-on-Avon two miles, Lacock eight miles. Private fishing on River Avon available.

The apartment consists of a large lounge/dining room with open fire and sofa which converts into a double bed; two generously proportioned bedrooms upstairs, one twin-bedded, one with a double bed, both with washbasins; a separate toilet (downstairs); a large kitchen in the single storey wing, fitted with light oak finish units, electric cooker, microwave, refrigerator and automatic washing machine; shower room which opens off the kitchen. Electricity extra.

Off-road parking. Choice of pubs in village.
Terms £200 to £225. Brochure and further details available.

Olney

Buckinghamshire

The Old Stone Barn • Olney •

The Old Stone Barn is peacefully positioned on an arable farm $1\frac{1}{2}$ miles from the beautiful market town of Olney where there is a wide variety of shops, cafes, bars and restaurants.

The accommodation is a charming combination of old character and modern facilities, and consists of 7 spacious self-contained apartments (sleep 1-6), centrally heated and equipped with colour TV and payphone. Linen and towels are provided, and there is a laundry room with washing machines and a tumble dryer. Computer room and wifi available.

Guests can relax in the gardens, make use of the outdoor heated swimming pool, or take day trips to Oxford, Cambridge, London or the Cotswolds. Terms from £240 to £560 per week.

Mr & Mrs Garry Pibworth, Home Farm, Warrington, Olney MK46 4HN
Tel: 01234 711655 • Fax: 01234 711855
e-mail: info@oldstonebarn.co.uk
www.oldstonebarn.co.uk

SB

Only half an hour from London, the rolling hills and wooded valleys of the Buckinghamshire countryside provide a wonderful contrast to city life. Enjoy the bluebells in spring and the autumn colours of the woodland while following the innumerable footpaths, bridleways and National Trails that cross the county, looking at the local flora and fauna on the way.

There are fascinating historic towns and villages, including West Wycombe, owned by the National Trust, which also has many other interesting properties in the area. These include the stunning gardens at Cliveden, former home of the Astors and focus of the early twentieth century social scene. Shoppers will want to visit the complex at High Wycombe or for more specialised outlets, Amersham, the Georgian market town of Marlow, or Stony Stratford.

Lymington

Hampshire

Whether you prefer an active break or a quiet country holiday, Hampshire offers plenty of choices. There are gardens and country parks, historic houses and wildlife parks, museums and castles, and with its location on the Channel coast, all the activities associated with the seaside. Shopping and nightlife, the Historic Dockyard with HMS Victory and the spectacular views of the surrounding area from the Spinnaker Tower, taller even than the London Eye, make Portsmouth well worth a visit. There's plenty to do outdoors in Hampshire. Walking, cycling and horse riding on the heathland and ancient woodlands of the New Forest National Park, and for more thrills, paragliding and hang gliding at the Queen Elizabeth Country Park on the South Downs.

Isle of Wight

Island Cottage Holidays

Self Catering Holiday Cottage accommodation on the Isle of Wight

More than 75 charming individual cottages situated throughout the island, in lovely rural surroundings and close to the sea.

- Thatched cottages • Cottages with sea views or with short walk to the sea
- Larger cottages • Cottages accepting dogs and pets • Gold award cottages

Beautiful views, attractive gardens, delightful country walks.

All equipped to a high standard and graded for quality by the Tourist Board ★★★ to ★★★★★

For a brochure please **Tel: (01929) 480080 • Fax: (01929) 481070**
e-mail: enq@islandcottageholidays.com
www.islandcottageholidays.com

Open all year (Sleep 1 - 12) £185– £1595 per week. Short breaks available in low season (3 nights) £155 – £399

All kinds of watersports are available along the coast, but of course the Isle of Wight, only a short ferry ride away from the mainland, is the ultimate destination, with award-winning beaches, water sports centres, seakayaking, diving, sailing and windsurfing. For land-based activities there are over 500 miles of interconnected footpaths, historic castles, dinosaur museums, theme parks and activity centres, while the resorts like Sandown, Shanklin, Ryde and Ventnor offer all that is associated with a traditional seaside holiday. There is a thriving arts community, and of course two internationally renowned music festivals held every year. Something for everyone!

Kent

SB

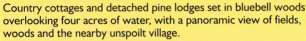

Ashby Farms - Holiday Cottages

Country cottages and detached pine lodges set in bluebell woods overlooking four acres of water, with a panoramic view of fields, woods and the nearby unspoilt village.

Eight detached PINE LODGES beautifully situated by the water's edge, with views across the water to the village of Woodchurch a mile or so away. Sleep up to 6.
attractive living/dining areas • lakeside terrace • sun decks • fully equipped pine kitchens • one double bedroom, two twin bedrooms • bathroom

ROUGHLANDS BUNGALOW, with its own large garden, set well back from the quiet country road between Appledore and Woodchurch. Sleeps up to 5.
attractive kitchen/dining area • fully equipped pine kitchen • one bedroom with double and single bed, one twin bedroom • large garden • off-road parking

Three terraced COTTAGES with views across the fields to the church. Sleep up to 5.
attractive kitchen/dining areas • fully equipped pine kitchens • one double bedroom, one twin bedroom, one single bedroom • off-road parking

**ASHBY FARMS LTD, PLACE FARM,
KENARDINGTON, ASHFORD TN26 2LZ
Tel: 01233 733332 • Fax: 01233 733326
e-mail: info@ashbyfarms.com
www.ashbyfarms.com**

SB

Sunset Lodge at Great Field Farm
Stelling Minnis, Canterbury, Kent CT4 6DE
Tel: 01227 709223

Ground floor Lodge in lovely private position with panoramic views over beautiful countryside and magnificent sunsets. Light, spacious and modern with open-plan living, dining and kitchen area, spiral staircase to snug/kid's room. Two en suite bedrooms, 1 double with wet room with shower, 1 twin-bedded room with bath. Free internet access. Open all year.
Also available in the main farmhouse on the SE corner is a cosy flat with a double bedroom, sitting room, kitchen and bathroom. Free internet access.
Both properties are also available for B & B, and we have 2 more en suite rooms for B & B, if required.
ETC ★★★★ and Breakfast Award
Lovely and quiet, yet easily accessible position, approximately 15 minute drive to Canterbury, Folkestone, Ashford and Eurotunnel.
Ample off-road parking, flexible start and finish days.
Please phone or Email for prices and availability.
Self-Catering • Bed & Breakfast
greatfieldfarm@aol.com • www.great-field-farm.co.uk

Maidstone

Apple Pye
Self-Catering Cottage

SB

Cottage on farm set in 45 acres, surrounded by beautiful rolling Kentish countryside. Well away from the road and next to the farmhouse B&B, it is only 10 minutes' drive from M20, J8. Central location for visiting Kent's many attractions, 6 miles from Leeds Castle, Canterbury half-hour drive, Dover one hour's drive, London 1¼ hours by train.

e-mail: diane@bramleyknowlefarm.co.uk • www.bramleyknowlefarm.co.uk

Sleeps four. One double room en suite, one twin with own shower room; living room/kitchen/dining room with washer/dryer, fridge/freezer, electric cooker, microwave, TV, DVD, wireless broadband. Full Central heating. Garden and patio. Suitable for disabled. Rent £295-£495 per week. B&B from £30 per person.

Mr & Mrs Leat, Apple Pye Cottage, Bramley Knowle Farm, Eastwood Road, Ulcombe, Maidstone, Kent ME17 1ET
Tel: 01622 858878

Oxfordshire

Pangbourne

Brambly Thatch

Merricroft, Goring Heath RG8 7TA
Tel: 01189 843121 • Fax: 01189 844662

An attractive 17thC thatched cottage within easy reach of Oxford and London. The acccommodation comprises living room, dining room, fully equipped kitchen, 3 bedrooms (one downstairs), and bathroom. TV and VCR. Parking available. Sleeps 5. A variety of local attractions include National Trust properties and the Childe-Beale Wildlife Trust and further afield, Windsor Castle and Legoland Windsor and more. Open all year.

Oxford

SB

Apartments in Oxford
58 St Thomas Street, Oxford OX1 1JP
Tel: 01865 254000 • Fax: 01865 254001

Apartments in Oxford offers 34 high quality serviced apartments in a quiet location in the centre of Oxford; each apartment is beautifully decorated, fully furnished and well equipped. The kitchens have all the modern conveniences you would expect, and the sitting rooms have all the comforts of home, making it preferable to other hotels in Oxford.

ETC ★★★★ *Serviced Apartments.*

In addition, each apartment has wireless internet access (chargeable), two dedicated telephone lines, a radio/CD player and 24-hour reception. Housekeeping services are provided daily except on Sundays.

e-mail: based@oxstay.co.uk • www.oxstay.co.uk

East Sussex

Chiddingly

CHIDDINGLY, EAST SUSSEX

Adorable, small, well-equipped cottage in grounds of Tudor Manor. Two bedrooms, sleeps 4-6. Full kitchen and laundry facilities. Telephone. Use of indoor heated swimming pool, sauna/jacuzzi, tennis and badminton court. Large safe garden. Pets and children welcome. From £420-£798 per week incl. Short Breaks £258-£360.

Apply: Eva Morris, "Pekes", 124 Elm Park Mansions, Park Walk, London SW10 0AR • Tel: 020-7352 8088 • Fax: 020-7352 8125 ETC
★★★ **•e-mail: pekes.afa@virgin.net • www.pekesmanor.com**

Heathfield

Cannon Barn, a Sussex wheat barn built in 1824, has been sympathetically converted to provide modern comforts. Boring House is a small working farm with sheep. There are ponds and a stream on the farm, and plenty of footpaths in the area, including one which crosses the farm, giving plenty of choice for walkers.

Tel: 01435 812285

Locally, there is a good selection of pubs for meals, and also a great variety of things to do and places to visit for all the family.

Please visit our website for photographs and further information.
Short Breaks available out of season. Sleeps 8-10. Prices £200-£950.

Contact: Mrs A. Reed, Boring House Farm,
Nettlesworth Lane, Vines Cross, Heathfield TN21 9AS
e-mail: info@boringhousefarm.co.uk
www.boringhousefarm.co.uk

West Sussex

Storrington

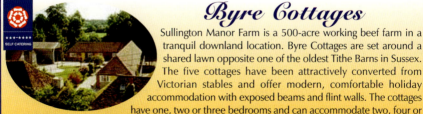

Byre Cottages

Sullington Manor Farm is a 500-acre working beef farm in a tranquil downland location. Byre Cottages are set around a shared lawn opposite one of the oldest Tithe Barns in Sussex. The five cottages have been attractively converted from Victorian stables and offer modern, comfortable holiday accommodation with exposed beams and flint walls. The cottages have one, two or three bedrooms and can accommodate two, four or six people. Outdoor swimming pool, tennis court, private patios, BBQs.

Mr G. Kittle, Sullington Manor Farm, Storrington, West Sussex RH20 4AE
Tel/Fax: 01903 745754 • e-mail: kittles@waitrose.com

Ely

Cambridgeshire

Cathedral House

17 St Mary's Street, Ely
Cambridgeshire CB7 4ER

Tel: 01353 662124

The Coach House has been imaginatively converted into a delightful abode full of character and charm, situated close to Ely Cathedral.

Arranged on two floors, the accommodation downstairs comprises a sitting room and country-style kitchen. Upstairs there are two charming double rooms (one has a view of the Cathedral), and a cosy single room. All have an en suite bathroom, with a toilet, wash hand basin and a half-size bath with shower taps.

Gas central heating. Linen, towels, toilet soap, cleaning materials and some basic provisions are provided.

Prices range from £300 to £750 depending on season and length of stay. Special rates for two people.

www.cathedralhouse.co.uk
farndale@cathedralhouse.co.uk

symbols

	Totally non-smoking		*Pets Welcome*
	Children Welcome		*Short Breaks available*
	Suitable for Disabled Guests		*Licensed*

Billericay, Colchester

Essex

The Pump House Apartment

The Apartment is self-contained on two floors, with two living rooms, a dining room, a fully fitted kitchen and the choice of one, two or three bedrooms with one, two or three bath/shower rooms (two are en suite). First floor rooms are air conditioned. Wi-Fi internet access is available throughout the apartment.

Facilities: TV, video, hi-fi (CD), DVD, fridge, freezer, electric oven/hob, microwave, dishwasher, washing machine, tumble dryer, telephone, trouser press.

In the grounds there is an open-air swimming pool (heated May to September), a spa/hot tub with fully glazed gazebo, summer house, barbecue facilities, garden games and garden furniture. Parking for 2 cars.

For the benefit of other guests no smoking is permitted in the Apartment and no pets are allowed. All linen and towels are provided. No charge for heating and lighting.

Contact:
Edwina & John Bayliss
Pump House
Church Street
Great Burstead
Essex CM11 2TR
Tel: 01277 656579

e-mail: **enquiries@thepumphouseapartment.co.uk**
www.thepumphouseapartment.co.uk

Rye Farm   www.ryefarm.org.uk

Rye Lane, Layer de la Haye, Colchester CO2 0JL
Tel: 01206 734350/07976 524276
e-mail: peterbunting@btconnect.com

Three attractive holiday apartments converted from a 17thC cart lodge on a working farm adjacent to Abberton Reservoir, an internationally important wetland and wildfown haven.

Furnished and equipped to a high standard, the apartments sleep 2-4, with central heating, colour TV/DVD. Two apartments are on the ground floor, and one is designed and equipped for disabled guests. Laundry facilities. Patio with table and chairs.

Norfolk

Bacton-on-Sea

Bacton-on-Sea

For one of the best value holidays on the glorious North Norfolk Coast, welcome to Castaways Holiday Park

A small, family-run business situated in the quiet, peaceful village of Bacton, with direct access to fine sandy beach, and ideal for beach fishing and discovering Norfolk and The Broads.

Stunning sea views from most of our accommodation:
Fully equipped modern Caravans, comfortable three bedroom pine lodges and a choice of 2 ground floor and 2 first floor flats with all amenities. Licensed Club. Entertainment. Amusement Arcade. Children's Play Area.

PETS WELCOME

Enquiries and Bookings to:
Castaways Holiday Park,
Paston Road, Bacton-on-Sea,
Norfolk NR12 0JB
BH & HPA approved

on-line booking facility available

Booking Hotline: 01692 650 436
www.castawaysholidaypark.net

Kings Chalet Park
Cromer, Norfolk
Sleep 2-4
Open March to October

Comfortable, well-equipped chalets situated on beautiful, landscaped, quiet site. Ideally placed for walks to adjacent woods, cliffs and sandy beaches. 10 minutes' walk to town. Golf course and local shops nearby. Plenty of local places of interest to visit. One twin, one double room, bathroom, colour TV, microwave, well-equipped kitchenette. Children welcome. Pet welcome free of charge.

Short Breaks in Spring/Autumn 2 nights or more from £80
Spring/Autumn £150-£230 per week
June-September £250-£320 per week

DETAILS FROM: MRS I. SCOLTOCK, SHANGRI-LA, LITTLE CAMBRIDGE, DUTON HILL, DUNMOW, ESSEX CM6 3QU TEL: 01371 870482 / Mobile: 07710 904048

Holiday Properties (Mundesley) Ltd
6a Paston Road, Mundesley, Norwich NR11 8BN

We are a small family business that has been established over 50 years.

We have a choice of landscaped chalet sites that are close to the beach and village amenities.

Our chalets are heated and well equipped with all the essentials and include a comfortable lounge area, a fitted kitchen, 2 bedrooms and a bathroom. They are graded from 1 to 3 stars with the East of England Tourist board.

Also available are our Manor Court Bungalows. These are newly built. Spacious accommodation with en suite facilities, a large fully equipped kitchen and luxuries such as 32" Flat Panel TV, dishwasher and washing machine. They have good access and parking and each one has their own private courtyard.

Phone: 01263 720719
www.holidayprops.co.uk
info@holidayprops.co.uk

Clippesby Hall

Superbly appointed
Lodges, Cottages
& Apartments

Surrounded by the
Natural Beauty of
The Norfolk Broads

www.clippesby.com   01493 367800

Along the Norfolk coast from King's Lynn to Great Yarmouth the broad, sandy beaches, grassy dunes, nature reserves, windmills, and pretty little fishing villages are inviting at all times of year. An important trade and fishing port from medieval times, the historic centre of King's Lynn is well worth a visit, and take a break at Great Yarmouth for family entertainment, 15 miles of sandy beaches, traditional piers, a sea life centre and nightlife with clubs and a casino. On the low-lying Fens, the Norfolk Broads or through the ancient pine forests and heathland of The Breck there are walking, cycling and horse riding trails, and market towns and villages to explore. In contrast to the quiet and calm of coast and country, in the medieval city of Norwich with its historic streets and half-timbered houses, cathedral, Norman castle and museums you'll find not only history, but opera, ballet, theatre, music and restaurants .

The Holiday Estate with a difference

Winterton Valley Holidays

SB

A selection of modern superior fully appointed holiday chalets in a choice of locations near Great Yarmouth.

No straight lines of identical chalets on this delightfully landscaped 35 acre estate of holiday homes. It has private access to Winterton's fine sandy beaches, with no main roads for children to cross. A wonderful place for a real away from it all holiday, very quiet and yet only 8 miles from Gt Yarmouth. Both the beach and valley are ideal for dog walking, and pets are very welcome.

There are no shops, amusements or clubs on the site. The village of Winterton is a short distance away, with its well stocked stores and 300 year old pub which serves excellent food and drink at the bar or in the family room and garden.

Chalets are privately owned, sleep up to 6 people and each is of individual style. All have open plan lounge and dining areas adjoining the kitchens. Electric heating and TV. Kitchens are all equipped with an electric cooker, microwave and fridge. Bathrooms have a full size bath, wash basin and WC. Most chalets have a shower over the bath.

All chalets have two bedrooms which have a double bed in one room and either twin beds or bunk beds in the second bedroom. You are asked to supply your own bed linen: duvet covers, bottom sheets, pillow cases, towels and tea towels, but these can be supplied for hire if required. Pets are very welcome in most chalets at a small additional fee.

For those wanting a livelier holiday we also have chalets at nearby **California Sands.**

**For colour brochure please ring
01493 377175 or write to
15 Kingston Avenue,
Caister-on-Sea, Norfolk NR30 5ET**
www.wintertonvalleyholidays.co.uk

Suffolk

SB

Suffolk's 40 miles of unspoilt World Heritage coastline is perfect for a seaside holiday. Wander through the coastal forests or along the shingle and sandy beaches admiring the scenery, or hire bicycles for a family bike ride. Eat oysters at Orford or follow the Suffolk Coastal Churches Trail. Fishing is particularly popular on the Waveney as well as many on other rivers and golfers have a choice of short local courses and some of championship standard. Horse racing enthusiasts can't miss Newmarket, whether for a fun day out, to visit the National Horseracing Museum or to take a guided tour round the National Stud. However you choose to spend the day, the wonderful choice of locally produced food served in one of the many pubs, restaurants and cafes will provide the perfect end to your stay.

Badwell Ash

SB

Badwell Ash Holiday Lodges

A stunning resort of just four holiday lodges positioned around three fishing lakes. Set in five acres in the heart of Mid Suffolk.

As listed in The Sunday Telegraph article "The World's Best Over-Water Resorts

Badwell Ash offers the ultimate year round retreat:
a perfect place for a honeymoon, anniversary or simply
somewhere to spend time with friends and family.
Each of the 2 bedroom lodges is graded ★★★★.
VisitBritain Gold Award for 2009/10.

- Exclusively for adults.
- Personal outdoor hot tub for each lodge.
- Each lodge with a veranda over the lake.
- All furnished to a high standard with 4-poster beds,
  fully fitted kitchen and steam showers.
- Complimentary welcome hamper with Champagne,
  chocolates and many extras.
- All bedding, towels etc included.

An ideal base for exploring the historic market towns and cities,
quaint fishing villages, the beautiful coast and many other local
attractions that Suffolk has to offer.

BADWELL ASH HOLIDAY LODGES
Badwell Ash, Suffolk IP31 3DJ
Tel: 01359 258444
info@badwellashlodges.co.uk
www.badwellashlodges.co.uk

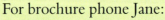

Southwold • Walberswick

Furnished Holiday Cottages, Houses and Flats, available in this charming unspoilt Suffolk seaside town. Convenient for beaches, sailing, fishing, golf and tennis. Near to 300 acres of open Common. Attractive country walks and historic churches are to be found in this area, also the fine City of Norwich, the Festival Town of Aldeburgh and the Bird Sanctuary at Minsmere, all within easy driving distance. Brochure available on request.

Durrants incorporating H.A. Adnams,
98 High Street, Southwold IP18 6DP
01502 723292 • Fax: 01502 724794
www.durrants.com

HolidayGuides.com

Looking for Holiday Accommodation? then visit our website

FHG

www.holidayguides.com

for details of hundreds of properties throughout the UK

Ashbourne

Derbyshire

SB

Paddock House Farm Holiday Cottages

★★★★ *Luxury Holiday Cottage Accommodation*

Surrounded by 5 acres of delightful grounds and reached along its own long drive, Paddock House nestles peacefully in a secluded spot between the famous villages of Alstonefield and Hartington.
Arranged around a courtyard, these charming cottages enjoy uninterrupted views.

The area is a walker's paradise, and there are excellent cycle trails along Dovedale, Tissington and the Manifold Valley.

An ideal base for families, the surrounding area boasts a wealth of attractions to suit all tastes. Nearby the attractive market town of Ashbourne offers shops, restaurants and other town amenities. Slightly further afield, the magnificent Chatsworth House is an impressive sight to behold. The spa towns of Matlock and Buxton are as popular as their 'magical' waters have ever been. Alton Towers 20 minutes.

Peak District National Park, Alstonefield, Ashbourne, Derbyshire DE6 2FT
Tel: 01335 310282 • Mobile: 07977 569618
e-mail: info@paddockhousefarm.co.uk • www.paddockhousefarm.co.uk

For walking, climbing, mountain biking and caving visit Derbyshire. There are activities available at every level and courses to suit everyone. From the gently rolling farmland and National Forest in the south to the rugged demanding landscape of the Dark Peak in the north there are trails for cyclists and walkers to follow, many along old railway lines. Everyone can visit Poole's Cavern to see the best stalagmites and stalactites in Derbyshire (and discover the difference!), and the Blue John Cave at Castleton where this rare mineral is mined, and perhaps buy a sample of jewellery in one of the local shops. Buxton was a spa from Roman times, but the main attractions now are concerts, theatre and the annual literary and music festival. Concerts are held at Calke Abbey and at Chatsworth, the best known of the stately homes, with impressive interiors and magnificent gardens and grounds, and period dramas at Haddon Hall at Bakewell.

Bakewell, Bamford, Buxton

BURTON MANOR
FARM HOLIDAY COTTAGES

Over Haddon, Bakewell, Derbyshire DE45 1JX

Situated in the heart of the Peak District, in an elevated position overlooking the delightful market town of Bakewell, our family-run dairy/sheep farm is an ideal base for visitors. Chatsworth House and Haddon Hall are just a short distance away. Excellent walking in all directions, with Lathkill Dale and Limestone Way close by. This barn conversion is in a courtyard and consists of six cosy cottages sleeping from 2-8, providing quality 4-star accommodation. Bed linen, towels and power are included, cots and high chairs are available. There is ample safe parking. Rates from £210 to £730.

Contact: Ruth Shirt, Holmelacy Farm, Tideswell, Buxton, Derbyshire SK17 8LW
Tel: 01298 871429 • Mobile: 07790 966707
e-mail: cshirt@burtonmanor.freeserve.co.uk • www.burtonmanor.freeserve.co.uk

SB

Shatton Hall Farm Cottages

On this quiet and beautiful upland farm, woodland and streamside walks, a hard tennis court and trout lake are there to enjoy, as are the gardens surrounding our three comfortable stone cottages. Furnished in old pine, with well equipped kitchens, tiled bathrooms with showers, double and twin bedrooms in each. Open all year. We can have a Derbyshire breakfast in your refrigerator if ordered in advance, to give you a superb start to a day's walking.
£300-£500 per week. Sleep 4-5. Low season short breaks available.
Bamford, Hope Valley S33 0BG
Tel/Fax: 01433 620635
e-mail: ahk@peakfarmholidays.co.uk
www.peakfarmholidays.co.uk

SB

STABLE COTTAGE
Upper Elkstones, Near Buxton SK17 0LU

Set in a peaceful rural location, this restored cottage retains many original features. The cosy accommodation for 2/3 comprises lounge, dining area, fully equipped kitchen, bathroom with power shower. On first floor: double bedroom, galleried landing with double put-u-up bed/settee. Pets by arrangement. Off-road parking. The cottage is central for the Peak District National Park, market towns including Buxton, Ashbourne and Leek, the China Trail, NT gardens and Alton Towers.

Contact: Mrs V. Lawrenson
Tel: 01538 300487
elkstones.t21@btinternet.com

Hartington

Wolfscote Grange
Farm Cottages

Hartington, Near Buxton,
Derbyshire SK17 0AX
Tel & Fax: 01298 84342

*Charming cottages nestling beside
the beautiful Dove Valley in stunning scenery.*

Cruck Cottage is peaceful 'with no neighbours, only sheep' and a cosy 'country living' feel.

Swallows Cottage offers comfort for the traveller and time to relax in beautiful surroundings. It sparkles with olde worlde features, yet has all modern amenities including en suite facilities and spa bathroom.

The farm trail provides walks from your doorstep to the Dales. Open all year. Dogs by arrangement only.

Weekly terms from £180 to £490 (sleeps 4) & £180 to £600 (sleeps 6).

e-mail: wolfscote@btinternet.com
www.wolfscotegrangecottages.co.uk

Herefordshire

Wye Valley Cottages are situated in the heart of rural Herefordshire close to the meandering River Wye. Our family home is Ruxton Farm at Hoarwithy where we offer bed and breakfast accommodation. The farm is also home to Ruxton Horses, an internationally renowned breeding and training centre. We have two cottages close to the farm, Ruxton Byre and Ruxton Mill, both of which have been refurbished to a very high standard.

•**Ruxton Mill ★★★★** sleeps 6
Ruxton Mill, dating from the seventeenth century, has been converted from a Cider Mill and Granary, to give very comfortable and attractive accommodation.

•**Ruxton Byre ★★★★** sleeps 5 - 6
Ruxton Byre, dating from the seventeenth century, has been converted recently from stables and granary, to give very comfortable and attractive accommodation.

Ruxton Farm, Kings Caple, Hereford HR1 4TX
Tel & Fax: (01432) 840 493 • e-mail: milly@wyevalleycottages.com
www.wyevalleycottages.com

Herefordshire, on the on the border with Wales, will appeal equally to outdoor lovers and enthusiasts for the arts, crafts and literature, as well as to all food lovers! There are endless opportunities for all kinds of outdoor activities, including white water canoeing through the steep-sided gorge at Symonds Yat, or longer, more gentle trips on the meandering sections of the River Wye. The Black and White Village Trail takes visitors through beautiful countryside to pretty little villages, each with its own individual characteristics and shops. Leominster specialises in antiques and fine art auctions, Ross-on-Wye in antiques and Ledbury, in the east, runs an annual poetry festival. The climate and fertile soil has resulted in wonderful local produce, particularly fruit and vegetables, beef and dairy products. All these are available to sample in restaurants, cafes and tearooms or to take home from farm shops as a reminder of the holiday.

Leominster

SB

Docklow Manor

Quietly secluded in five acres of garden and woodland, two delightful stone cottages have been simply but stylishly refurbished by the new owners. Guests are welcome to explore the extensive grounds, which enjoy superb westerly views towards the Black Mountains.

Table tennis, croquet and trampolining are all available, with excellent fishing, golf and walking nearby.

Excellent home cooked dinners available, served in your own cottage.

Docklow is ideally positioned for visiting the beautiful town of Ludlow, the Welsh Border castles, market towns and the Malvern Hills.

Leominster, Herefordshire HR6 0RX
Tel: 01568 760668
www.docklow-manor.co.uk

Visit the FHG website
www.holidayguides.com
for all kinds of holiday
acccommodation in Britain

symbols

Totally non-smoking	*Pets Welcome*
Children Welcome	**SB** *Short Breaks available*
Suitable for Disabled Guests	*Licensed*

Leicester

Leicestershire & Rutland

Set in the centre of the Midlands, the rolling countryside, canals, forests, beautiful villages, interesting market towns and history make Leicestershire and Rutland well worth a visit. Spend a peaceful hour or two cruising along the Ashby Canal in a narrowboat past Bosworth Battlefield where the Wars of the Roses ended in 1485. With over 1000 different species there's plenty to see at Twycross Zoo at Hinckley, or take a walk through Burbage Wood to see the native fauna. Wander along the banks of the River Soar at the conservation village of Blaby, or in summer try to find the way round the Maize Maze at Wistow. Rutland is England's smallest county with the largest man-made lake in Europe. Cycle round the shoreline, cruise on the water, walk round the lake, while the really energetic can take the walkers' route, Round Rutland, all of 65 miles long.

Barnoldby-Le-Beck

Lincolnshire

Three well appointed cottages and riding school situated in the heart of the Lincolnshire Wolds.
The tasteful conversion of a spacious, beamed Victorian barn provides stylish and roomy cottages, one sleeping 6, and two sleeping 4 in one double and one twin bedroom, comfy sittingroom and diningroom. Fully equipped kitchen. Bathroom with bath and shower.

You don't need to ride with us, but if you do....

The Equestrian Centre offers professional tuition, an all-weather riding surface, stabling for guests' own horses, and an extensive network of bridle paths.

GRANGE FARM COTTAGES & RIDING SCHOOL
Waltham Road, Barnoldby-le-Beck, N.E. Lincs DN37 0AR
For Cottage Reservations Tel: 01472 822216 • mobile: 07947 627663
www.grangefarmcottages.com

Coast or country, the choice is yours for a holiday in Lincolnshire. With award-winning beaches, miles of clean sand, theme parks, kite surfing, wake boarding and water skiing, there's action and excitement for everyone along the Fun Coast and at Cleethorpes on the Humber estuary. At Skegness, as well as all the fun on the beach, children will love watching the seals being fed at the seal sanctuary, and the exotic birds and butterflies flying overhead in the tropical house. Further north, at Cleethorpes with its wonderful beaches, take a ride on the Cleethorpes Coast Light Railway. Keen fishermen can always find a peaceful spot along the extensive network of rivers and canals and for golfers there's a wide variety and standard of courses, with the home of amateur golf in England at the National Golf Centre at Woodhall Spa. In Lincoln walk round the battlements at the Castle, explore the cobbled streets lined with medieval buildings and visit the imposing Gothic cathedral, one of the finest in Europe. Cruise on the Roman canal that flows through the city, shop at the boutiques, eat at the restaurants and cafes, and in the evening enjoy a concert or a visit to the theatre.

Brackenborough Hall Coach House Holidays

Three luxury self-catering apartments in a Listed 18th century Coach House in the beautiful county of Lincolnshire. Stables and Saddle Room sleep up to 4, Granary Apartment sleeps up to 8. Together can accommodate up to 24. Short Breaks all year round.

Winner 'Best Self-Catering Holiday in England 2009/10' Silver Award

Paul & Flora Bennett,
Brackenborough Hall, Louth, Lincolnshire LN11 0NS
Tel: 01507 603193
e-mail: PaulandFlora@BrackenboroughHall.com
www.BrackenboroughHall.com

Grange Cottages

MALTBY-LE-MARSH, ALFORD LN13 0JP
Tel: 01507 450267
e-mail: anngraves@btinternet.com

Farmhouse B&B and SELF-CATERING COUNTRY COTTAGES set in 15 idyllic acres of Lincolnshire countryside. Peaceful base for leisure and sightseeing.

• Two private fishing lakes • Many farm animals
• Brochure available. Contact Mrs Graves.
••**Pets welcome**••

www.grange-farmhouse.co.uk

Ludlow

Shropshire

SB

Sutton Court Farm

Little Sutton, Stanton Lacy, Ludlow SY8 2AJ
Tel: 01584 861305

Jane & Alan Cronin

Sympathetically converted from stone barns, these six cottages offer the ideal centre for exploring South Shropshire and the Marches (Ludlow 5 miles).

They are all furnished with care and attention to detail; well equipped kitchens, central heating (two have wood burning stoves), and stable doors allowing in sunshine and fresh air in fine weather.

Children's play room • Pets in some cottages by arrangement.
Breakfast packs, cream teas and home-cooked meals can be delivered to your cottage by arrangement.

www.suttoncourtfarm.co.uk • enquiries@suttoncourtfarm.co.uk

'A special place to return to'

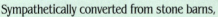

If you're looking for a break from the pace of life today, but with plenty to do and see, and with a choice of superb food to round off your day, Shropshire is the place to visit. Visit the Shropshire Hills Discovery Centre at Craven Arms, where you can take a simulated balloon ride and meet the Shropshire mammoth. Stokesay Castle, the finest 13th century fortified manor house in England, is just one of over 30 castles in the county, as well as stately homes and all kinds of gardens, including Hawkstone Historic Park and Follies, a fairytale kingdom near Shrewsbury. At the Ironbridge Gorge museums, as well as learning all about the early inventions leading to the start of the Industrial Revolution, discover how all kinds of present-day objects work – and make it happen yourself.

Sambrook Manor
Holiday Cottages
Sambrook, Newport TF10 8AL

SB

Set on the Shropshire/Staffordshire border, Sambrook Manor is the ideal place to stay to explore both counties. We have two beautifully converted barns: the **Old Shippon** is our biggest (sleeping 8/10), and **Churn Cottage** which sleeps 4 is also suitable for disabled guests. Both cottages have original exposed beams, well equipped kitchens, the luxury of underfloor heating, and their own gardens with fantastic views over the farm's grassy fields.

- *Short breaks.* • *Wi-Fi access.*
- *Children welcome.* • *Suitable for disabled.*
- *Non-smoking.*
- *Linen, towels, heat & electricity included.*

www.sambrookmanor.co.uk • Tel: 07811 632445

Oswestry

SB

Canal Central

Canal Central, Coed Y Rae Lane, Maesbury Marsh, Oswestry, Shropshire, SY10 8JG
Telephone: 01691 652168
e-mail: enquiries@canalcentral.co.uk
www.canalcentral.co.uk

The
Camping and
Caravanning
Club
The Friendly Club

Self contained first floor accommodation with open views, in an idyllic setting beside the Montgomery Canal. Canal Central is located in the hamlet of Maesbury Marsh, deep in the beautiful border countryside straddling England and Wales, and just a couple of miles from Oswestry. Available for stopovers or holidays, it is within easy distance of major ports and cities, and ideal for the many local attractions and outdoor activities in the area.

There is a spacious shower and toilet plus an additional separate toilet; kitchen and open plan living room; double bed/ twin bed, 2 single beds with truckle beds, ideal for children; or additional double beds and a sofa bed in the living room. No single supplement.

Canal Central's shop and tearoom provides convenience for both visitors and locals.
All essentials are available, and the emphasis is on supplying local produce as much as possible, including ice-cream from a neighbouring farm and specialty meats, dairy produce and bacon. There is a good selection of organic and fair trade goods, as well as unusual vegetarian options and foods for those with special dietary requirements. Quality wines, bottled beers and spirits are also available.

The tearoom provides a relaxed, airy environment with far reaching views over the Welsh hills. Simple, wholesome food and drinks are served daily. Wi-Fi internet access is available.

Camping with hook-ups and washroom.

Staffordshire

Situated in Staffordshire Moorlands, cosy 3 bedroomed cottage (sleeps 6), overlooking picturesque countryside. Fully equipped, comfortably furnished and carpeted throughout. Cottage, all on ground floor and with three bedrooms (one with four-poster). An ideal base for visits to Alton Towers, the Potteries and Peak District. Patio, play area. Cot and high chair available. Laundry room with auto washer and dryer. Electricity and fresh linen inclusive. Terms from £230 to £375.

SB

EDITH & ALWYN MYCOCK

'ROSEWOOD COTTAGE'

LOWER BERKHAMSYTCH

FARM, BOTTOM HOUSE,

NEAR LEEK ST13 7QP

Tel & Fax: 01538 308213

www.rosewoodcottage.co.uk

Situated right in the middle of England, Staffordshire is a county of open spaces and ancient woodlands, exciting theme parks, stately homes and castles, miles of canals and the largest street-style skate park in Europe at Stoke-on-Trent. There are thrills and fun for every age group at the theme parks. As well as the heart-stopping rides, walk through the Ocean Tank Tunnel at Alton Towers to watch the sea creatures from all the world's oceans and make a big splash in the Waterpark. Take a look at life in the past at the complete working historic estate at Shugborough near Stafford, with working kitchens, dairy water mill and brewhouse. Out in the open heathland of Cannock Chase in the south there are well maintained paths and trails for all levels of mountain biking, bikes to hire and fishing pools at Rugely and walking and cycling trails at Hednesford, or follow the Chase Heritage Trail.

Stoke-on-Trent

SB

Field Head Farmhouse Holidays

Field Head Farmhouse Holidays

Calton, Near Waterhouses
Stoke-on-Trent ST10 3LB
Tel & Fax: 01538 308352

Sleeps 13-15 plus two cots

Situated midway between Leek and Ashbourne within the Southern Peak District and the Staffordshire Moorlands, this Grade II Listed farmhouse with stables is set within its own grounds with open views. Well equipped, with spa bath, Sky TV, pets' corner and play area. Ample parking and space for the family caravan.

Set in beautiful secluded surroundings close to Dovedale and the Manifold Valley. Ideal country for the walker, horse rider or cyclist. Alton Towers 15 minute drive.

All pets and horses welcome. Open all year.

★★★★ SELF CATERING

Short breaks, bargain midweek breaks
Late booking discount • Contact Janet Hudson

e-mail: janet@field-head.co.uk • www.field-head.co.uk

Stratford-Upon-Avon

Warwickshire

Crimscote Downs Farm Self-catering Accommodation

SB

PARADISE COTTAGE is a romantic hideaway for two people in a newly converted former shepherd's retreat, with views over the downs.
It is full of character, and furnished and equipped to the highest standard.

THE DAIRY is ideal for a family visit, with fully equipped kitchen, sitting room and three en suite bedrooms. It has stunning views and is full of character with beams and wooden floors.

This is an excellent walking area, with several good routes around the village.
Stratford-upon-Avon 5 miles.

Terms from £210 to £445 • Electricity, heating, linen and towels incl.
Full central heating • No smoking • Ample parking

Mrs J. James, The Old Coach House, Whitchurch Farm,
Wimpstone, Stratford-upon-Avon CV37 8PD
Tel: 01789 450275 • e-mail: joan.james@tesco.net
www.stratford-upon-avon.co.uk/crimscote.htm

Weston Farm
Weston upon Avon, CV37 8JY

Five luxury holiday cottages converted from former barns and farm buildings on a working farm, four miles from Stratford upon Avon. All fully equipped including colour TV with basic Sky. Ample off-street parking. Electricity and linen included. Private fishing, golf and local cycle paths. We regret no pets. No smoking.
An ideal base from which to tour Warwickshire and Cotswold countryside or just to unwind.

SB

Tel: 01789 750688
info@westonfarm.co.uk • www.westonfarm.co.uk

Bishops Frome, Clifton-Upon-Teme

Worcestershire

SB

Five Bridges Cottages

Nestled in the heart of the Herefordshire cider apple and hop growing regions, the cottages are set within the owner's 4-acre garden and smallholding.

Formed from part of our Grade II Listed building, the cottages have been sympathetically converted into spacious self contained cottages which sleep 2 to 3 persons. They are all on the ground floor and each has an open plan lounge and fully equipped kitchen with beamed ceilings and ceramic tiled floors, double or twin bedroom, with a bed-settee in the lounge. All fuel, power and bed linen (duvet) and towels are included. Ample parking and shared garden. The market towns of Ledbury and Bromyard are within easy reach and you can stretch your legs on the Downs at Bromyard, a National Trust woodland, and Lower Brockhampton all offering good walking with unrestricted access.

Five Bridges Cottages, Near Bishops Frome, Worcester WR6 5BX
www.fivebridgescottages.co.uk • Tel: 01531 640340

SB

Set in a picturesque 25-acre location in the Teme Valley are our three lodges - Kingfisher, Woodpecker and Heron (each sleeps 6). Equipped and furnished to a high standard, with one double, one twin bedroom and bathroom upstairs, and en suite twin bedroom downstairs. Two suitable for wheelchair access.

Attached to the farmhouse is a timber-framed cottage - Chaff House (sleeps 2).

In its own grounds, and surrounded by orchards, is Pitlands Bungalow (sleeps 6). Two double bedrooms and one twin.

New for 2010, 3 two bedroom bungalows converted from redundant farm building. Eco-friendly with ground sourced heat pump and solar panels. Views over lower fishing pool.

The 3 lodges (ETC ★★★★) have stunning views over the coarse fishing pools (available for guests' use), and the valley beyond. Holistic Therapy by appointment. Outdoor spa. Games/function room - an ideal place to gather when booking multiple properties.

B&B also available in 15thC farmhouse - one twin, one triple en suite and one twin room with bathroom. All with TV and hospitality trays. ETC ★★★★

Mrs Diane Mann, Pitlands Farm, Clifton-upon-Teme,
Worcester WR6 6DX • Tel: 01886 812220
e-mail: info@pitlandsfarm.co.uk • www.pitlandsfarm.co.uk

Tenbury Wells

Rochford Park Cottages

SB

Tenbury Wells WR15 8SP
Tel & Fax: 01584 781392
e-mail: cottages@rochfordpark.co.uk

Located on one of the Teme Valley's working farms, this former dairy (sleeps 3), stable (sleeps 6) and barn (sleeps 8) are now stylish, comfortable retreats for any holidaymaker.

Explore the farm's footpaths and bridleways, fish in one of its lakes, play golf on the neighbouring 9-hole links. Further afield, walk the Malvern Hills, or valleys of the Welsh Marches. Hereford, Worcester and Ludlow are within 30 miles as are numerous National Trust and English Heritage houses and gardens. Youngsters will enjoy the Severn Valley Railway and Bewdley Safari Park.

enjoyEngland.com

★★★★
SELF CATERING

Open all year round.
For further details see our website.

www.rochfordpark.co.uk

Driffield

East Yorkshire

SB

Raven Hill Holiday Farmhouse

With delightful views overlooking the Yorkshire Wolds, ideally situated for touring the East Coast, Bridlington, Scarborough, Moors and York, this secluded and private four-bedroom **FARMHOUSE** is set in its own acre of woodland lawns and orchard, with garden furniture, summerhouse and children's play area. Sleeps 2-8 + 2 + cot.

Clean and comfortable and very well equipped including dishwasher, microwave, automatic washing machine and dryer; TV, video and games room. Fully centrally heated. Beds are made up for your arrival; cot and high chair available.

Three miles to the nearest village of Kilham with Post Office, general stores, garage and public houses. Available all year.

Terms per week from £290-£640. Brochure on request.

Mrs P. M. Savile, Raven Hill Farm, Kilham, Driffield YO25 4EG • Tel: 01377 267217

East Yorkshire is all about fun and action outdoors. From building sandcastles on the award-winning beaches along the North Sea coast in the east to walking in the Wolds inland, all the family will find an activity to enjoy. The Blue Flag beaches at Bridlington and Hornsea are ideal for children and if they tire of the sun and sand there's plenty of traditional entertainment too. Water sports aren't confined to the seaside, with windsurfing at Dacre Lakeside Park and jet skiing at Fossehill near Driffield, an ideal centre from which to explore both coast and country, and for golfers there's a choice of clifftop links and parkland courses inland and on the coast. For a taste of city life visit Hull, with its lovely waterfront, explore the Old Town while following the sculptures of the Seven Seas Fish Trail, enjoy modern drama at the Truck Theatre, and jazz, sea shanty and literature festivals, or watch football and rugby at the KC Stadium.

Old Cobbler's Cottage
North Dalton, East Yorkshire

A delightful mid-19th century terraced beamed cottage situated in the quiet, picturesque village of North Dalton nestling in the heart of the Yorkshire Wolds.

The cottage possesses a unique view overlooking the village pond and the 11th century village church.

Ideal for walkers as The Minster Way passes through the village, with the Wolds Way close by.

The village is a short drive from Driffield and Pocklington and the historic market town of Beverley. It is only twenty miles from York and the East Coast resort of Bridlington. Also accessible for Scarborough and Whitby.

The accommodation includes a fully equipped kitchen and living room with open fire, TV with DVD/Video/CD player and radio cassette player.

One double and one single bedroom, Z bed to sleep a 4th person, both with attractive views. The small conservatory leads onto a patio. Off-street parking for one car. Electric central heating is fitted throughout. Wi-Fi access available. Adjacent is an excellent, welcoming country pub serving good quality, pub grub, using locally grown produce.

**Details from: Chris Wade,
2 Star Row, North Dalton,
Driffield, E Yorkshire YO25 9UX
Tel: 01377 219901/ (day) • 01377 217523
(eve) 07801 124264 (any time)
e-mail:chris.wade@adastra-music.co.uk
www.waterfrontcottages.co.uk**

enjoyEngland.com
★★★
SELF CATERING

Coverdale

North Yorkshire

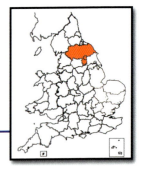

Panoramic views, waterfalls, wild birds and tranquillity

Stone farmhouse with panoramic views, high in the Yorkshire Dales National Park (Herriot family's house in 'All Creatures Great and Small' on TV). Three bedrooms (sleeps 6-8), sitting and dining rooms with wood-burning stoves, kitchen, bathroom, WCs.
House has electric storage heating, cooker, microwave, fridge, dishwasher, washing machine, colour TV, telephone. Garden, large barn, stables. Access from lane, private parking, no through traffic. Excellent walking from front door, near Wensleydale.
Pets welcome. Self-catering from £400 per week.

Allaker in Coverdale,
**West Scrafton, Leyburn,
North Yorks DL8 4RM**
For bookings telephone 020 8567 4862

**e-mail: ac@adriancave.com
www.adriancave.com/allaker**

The city of York in North Yorkshire is full of attractions for the visitor. View it gently floating through the air on a balloon trip, or if you prefer to keep your feet on the ground take a walk round the ancient walls, to get a first glimpse of the compact urban centre dominated by the magnificent York Minster, the largest medieval Gothic cathedral in northern Europe. Have fun finding your way through the the Snickelways, the maze of hidden alleyways, and enjoy a morning – or longer – in the interesting independent little shops and boutiques as well as all the top high street stores. Outside the city the vast open stretches of the North York Moors and the Yorkshire Dales National Parks and the golden sandy beaches of the coast are perfect for an active holiday. Walking, riding, cycling, horse riding, or just enjoying the great outdoors, North Yorkshire provides an ideal destination.

Mallard Cottage

25 Esk Valley, Grosmont, Whitby

SB

A steam enthusiasts' dream! Beside the North Yorkshire Moors Railway, this tastefully refurbished cottage retains much of its original character with beams, inglenook fireplaces and views over open countryside. A haven for walkers; Whitby and York within easy reach. Shop, cafe, post office and pub nearby.

◆ Two bedrooms ◆ double sofa bed
◆ bathroom with shower ◆ All fuel included
◆ electric cooking ◆ fridge/freezer
◆ microwave ◆ washing machine ◆ TV ◆ DVD
◆ storage heaters ◆ electric fire ◆ duvets and blankets
◆ garden & furniture ◆ private parking ◆ no pets ◆ no smoking
◆ all linen provided ◆ sleeps 4/6 ◆ "Heartbeat Country"

www.mallardcottageeskvalley.co.uk
e-mail: mallardcottage@gmail.com

For details contact: Mrs P. Robinson, 11 Scampton Close, Thornaby, Stockton-on-Tees TS17 0LH (01642 761317)

Cissy's Cottage

Hardraw • Hawes North Yorkshire

SB

A delightful 18th century cottage of outstanding character. Situated in the village of Hardraw with its spectacular waterfall and Pennine Way. Market town of Hawes one mile.

This unique, traditional stone-built cottage with its beamed ceilings and open fire, retains many original and unusual features. Sleeping four in comfort, in two bedrooms, it has been furnished and equipped to a high standard using antique pine and Laura Ashley prints.

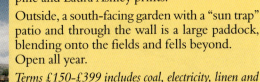

Sleeps 4

Outside, a south-facing garden with a "sun trap" patio and through the wall is a large paddock, blending onto the fields and fells beyond. Open all year.

Terms £150-£399 includes coal, electricity, linen and fishing rights. For more information and a brochure, contact:

**Mrs Belinda Metcalfe,
Southolme Farm, Little Smeaton,
Northallerton DL6 2HJ
Tel: 01609 881302/881052
e-mail: bm@adventuretoys.co.uk**

REGENT COTTAGE
Harrogate

Early 19thC Town House set in a private courtyard (shared by 6 residences). The property retains many of its original features and has been carefully restored and furnished to a high standard throughout (mainly with period pieces). The house comfortably sleeps 6, having one double and one twin-bedded bedroom with bathroom on the first floor, and bedroom with en suite bathroom in the semi-basement.

The well equipped kitchen/dining and sitting room are on the ground floor, with a further study/sitting room in the basement. Parking for two cars.

Contact: Robert Blake, 1a Moorfield Road, Woodbridge, Suffolk IP12 4JN
Tel: 01394 382565 • robert@blake4110.fsbusiness.co.uk
www.robertblakeholidays.co.uk

SB

Two well equipped holiday cottages in the award-winning Britain in Bloom village of Darley, between Harrogate and Pateley Bridge. Ideal for touring the Dales, with York within easy driving distance; riverside walks, local pub one mile. Bus stop for Harrogate and Pateley Bridge 200 yards from cottage. Rose Cottage *has two bedrooms, one double, one single, open plan lounge with kitchen and dining area.* Daffodil Cottage *is newly extended and refurbished with a new kitchen with dining area and large lounge. Three bedrooms, one en suite with bath, double and single bed. Further double bedroom and single room, shower room with basin and toilet. Large lawn area. Ample parking. Well behaved pets welcome.*

www.southfieldcottages.co.uk

Southfield Farm Holiday Cottages
Darley, Harrogate HG3 2PR • 01423 780258
e-mail: info@southfieldcottages.co.uk

Low Season £250/£320
High Season £350/£420

SB

12 Panorama Close, Pateley Bridge,
Harrogate HG3 5NY
01423 712062
info@abbeyholidaycottages.com

ABBEY HOLIDAY COTTAGES
Middlesmoor, Near Pateley Bridge HG3 5ST

Commanding unrivalled panoramic views of Nidderdale, and offering peace and tranquillity in an Area of Outstanding Natural Beauty. The cottages are an excellent base for walking, birdwatching and exploring the Dales, Brimham Rocks, Fountains Abbey, Stump Cross Caverns, Masham, Leyburn, Ripon, Harrogate, York and the North York Moors. Our traditional stone-built cottages have been modernised, refurbished and maintained to a high standard. The cottages sleep up to 6 people, and all have oil-fired central heating. All fuel, power, bed linen and towels provided; cot and high chair available. Off-road parking.

www.fhgahcottages.com

Leyburn, Low Bentham, Northallerton

Northallerton, Scarborough

Otterington Park

Situated in the Vale of York on a family-run farm, Otterington Park is a quality, purpose built 5-acre site designed to cater for up to 40 touring units. Electricity and luxury heated amenity block complete with individual bath/shower rooms, disabled facilities and laundry facilities available. Coarse fishing on site. Children and dogs welcome!

There is also a brand new development, adjoining the Touring Caravan site, ready for 40 Luxury Holiday Lodges and Static Caravans. Full details on request.

This is an ideal base for visiting the moors and dales of Yorkshire including locations from TV favourites such as *Heartbeat, Brideshead Revisited* and *Emmerdale*, market towns, leisure centres, golf courses, theme parks and other tourist attractions.

Otterington Park, Station Farm,
South Otterington, Northallerton DL7 9JB
Tel: 01609 780656
www.otteringtonpark.com • info@otteringtonpark.com

SB

BEDWYN'S SELF-CATERING ACCOMMODATION AGENCY
Easily find the ideal house, apartment or bungalow for your holiday

- 40 VisitBritain inspected properties.
- Coast or Village location.
- Ranging from apartments for couples to family houses.
- All of good quality and reasonably priced.
- Weekly prices per property from £145 to £895.

- Short Breaks from £35 per person.
- Pets go free. Absolutely no extra charges for bed linen, cots, high chairs, heating etc.
- Small independent local agency with the personal touch.

CALL 01723 516 700 - 7 DAYS - FOR BROCHURE
CHECK PRICES / AVAILABILITY / PHOTOS on **www.bedwyns.co.uk**

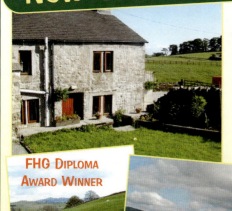

Staithes

Pennysteel Cottage

An old 19th century fisherman's cottage located in the beautiful fishing village of Staithes in North Yorkshire. The oak beamed and wood panelled cottage is set in the heart of the village and retains much of its original character, and has breathtaking views over the harbour from every room and from its sun terrace.

The cottage is situated only 20 yards from a local public house, serving excellent bar meals. The village also boasts two other pubs, a range of cafés and shops, as well as the Captain Cook Museum.

Fully fitted kitchen – including electric hob and cooker, microwave, fridge freezer and dishwasher. Lounge /dining room with TV/DVD/video/CD player, books and games.

One double and one single bedroom on the first floor, with twin (attic) bedroom and bathroom on the second floor. Cot and high chair available.

All rooms and the sun terrace overlook the sea

Details from: Chris Wade, 2 Star Row, North Dalton, Driffield, E Yorkshire YO25 9UX
Tel: 01377 219901/ (day) • 01377 217523 (eve) 07801 124264 (any time)
e-mail: chris.wade@adastra-music.co.uk
www.waterfrontcottages.co.uk

Whitby, York

SB

Self-catering two-bedroom cottages, all fully equipped. Central heating Whitby 2k • Close to sea and moors • Dogs welcome • Parking • Camping Site For further information phone

Mob: 07545641943
www.swallowcottages.co.uk
karl@swallowcottages.co.uk
KARL HEYES, 15 BEECHFIELD, HIGH HAWSKER WHITBY YO22 4LQ

SB

Pavilion Cottage is a converted cricket pavilion situated on the boundary of an active cricket club, beautifully renovated and retaining all its original charm and character and situated in lush parkland just a mile from York city centre. The cottage provides accommodation over four/five bedrooms sleeping up to 10 people comfortably and is decorated and equipped to a high standard. The cottage offers flexibility for large groups whilst maintaining a cosy welcome for smaller parties. Children of all ages are welcome as are well behaved dogs on payment of a returnable deposit.
Contact: **Mrs H. Whitaker, Pavilion Cottage, Shipton Road, York YO30 5RE**
Tel: 01904 639258 or 07974 853876
e-mail: pavcottage@yahoo.co.uk

www.pavilioncottage-holidayinyork.co.uk

---

symbols

     Totally non-smoking

     Children Welcome

     Suitable for Disabled Guests

 Pets Welcome

SB Short Breaks available

 Licensed

York Lakeside Lodges
Moor Lane, York YO24 2QU

A taste of the countryside, but with all the advantages of the City of York, just two miles away. Stroll in the parkland, relax by the lake (possibly doing a spot of fishing), catch a glimpse of the kingfisher, or go further afield to the North Yorkshire Moors, Yorkshire Dales or the coast.

York Lakeside Lodges is owned and run by the Manasir family who live in the grounds and are at hand for friendly help and advice.

The lodges are situated along one side of the 10-acre lake. Facing south, with beautiful views over the water, they are reached by a private road leading to a parking space beside each lodge.

The two adjoining brick cottages with balconies overlooking the lake have their own cottage garden. All properties are well insulated, double glazed and heated.

Throughout the grounds and in the lodges and cottages wireless internet access is available.

Tel: 01904 702346
e-mail: neil@yorklakesidelodges.co.uk
www.yorklakesidelodges.co.uk

Holmfirth, Todmorden

West Yorkshire

SB

Welcome to Heselwood Cottage

Set right in the heart of Summer Wine Country, Heselwood Holiday Cottage nestles on the edge of the Pennines, and a mile from the centre of Holmfirth. The accommodation comprises luxurious living space, kitchen, bathroom and two bedrooms. The cottage is ideal for couples wanting to explore the magnificent surrounding countryside, with wonderful walks, pubs and restaurants nearby. Heselwood Cottage is the ideal base for anyone wanting a peaceful and relaxing holiday. Children are most welcome. For details contact:

Jen & Chris Brook, Heselwood House,199 Woodhead Road, Holmbridge HD9 2NW
Tel: 01484 685175 • Fax: 01484 683955
e-mail: jenandchris@heselwoodcottage.co.uk • www.heselwoodcottage.co.uk

SB

Shoebroad Barn **Todmorden**

Shoebroad Barn is a substantial semi-detached barn conversion enjoying a superb semi-rural setting and commanding wonderful views. The property is within one mile of the town centre and railway station and is convenient for hilltop pubs and local amenities.
The spacious accommodation boasts a grand reception hall with feature staircase and four double bedrooms.
Children are most welcome. Open all year. Short breaks available.
Plus adjacent twin bedded Studio Cottage.
Contact Mrs Horsfall • Tel: 01706 817015 • Mobile: 07966 158295
www.shoebroadbarn.co.uk • e-mail: lynne100@live.com

West Yorkshire is a mix of wild moorland and towns and cities with a long industrial heritage. Spend time in one of the many fascinating museums of past working life, then stride out over the moors, taking in the dramatic scenery, before a shopping spree or a wonderful afternoon tea. Leeds is the destination for a lively city break. Theatres, ballet, opera, festivals, restaurants, clubs, and of course, one of the best shopping experiences in the country, all are here to provide entertainment and a memorable stay. Visit the exclusive shops in the Victoria Quarter and find sought after brands in the new developments at The Light and Clarence Dock on the waterside. If all this is too much for some family members, Harewood House with its wonderful interior, gardens, and adventure playground is nearby, as well as the Yorkshire Planetarium.

Durham

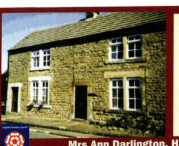

Laneside

Self Catering Holiday Cottage
Forest-in-Teesdale

Laneside, a luxury cottage for up to 6 persons, situated in the Area of Outstanding Natural Beauty in Upper Teesdale, is a haven of tranquillity, combining the best features of traditional Dales life with modern facilities.

This former farmhouse occupies an elevated position and enjoys breathtaking south-facing panoramic views of the Upper Raby Estate. It is situated on a carpet of ancient meadows with botanical species and supporting an array of wildlife.

Prices from £300.00 per week.
For further details please contact:

Raby Estates Office, Staindrop,
Co Durham DL2 3NF
Tel: 01833 660207
e- mail: lynda.currie@rabycastle.com
www.rabycastle.com

Northumberland

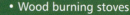
Alnwick

Alnwick

BILTON BARNS

Come and relax in one of our well appointed self-catering cottages either on our working farm or in the seaside village of Alnmouth, which has an InterCity station, or in Seahouses with its shops, pubs and other amenities.

SB

The three cottages on the farm sleep six comfortably and are very well equipped, have parking for two cars and shared garden and lawn area.

Jacksons Cottage in Alnmouth sleeps four/five and has "upside down" accommodation which takes advantage of the delightful views towards the sea. Very well furnished and comfortable.

Fishermans Cottage in a quiet location in the old part of the fishing village of Seahouses, sleeps six and is modernised to a very high standard.

B&B also available in the farmhouse. Full details and prices on request.

Brian & Dorothy Jackson, Bilton Barns, Alnmouth, Alnwick, Northumberland NE66 2TB
Tel : (01665) 830427 Fax: (01665) 833909 • e-mail : stay@biltonbarns.com • www.biltonbarns.com

BUSTON FARM

HOLIDAY COTTAGES • WARKWORTH

Come and enjoy the enchanting coast of Northumberland from one of our luxury four-star self-catering cottages, sleeping 2 to 6. Three cottages on a working farm just outside the historic village of Warkworth, whilst another is nestled within the pretty coastal village of Newton-by-the-Sea, just north of Alnwick. All are truly a home from home, charmingly decorated and extensively equipped, providing you the best possible base for a relaxing break. The Alnwick Garden, Cheviot Hills, Holy Island, Hadrian's Wall and a bounty of castles are but a few local treasures for you to explore. Pets and children welcome.

FARM COTTAGES

Tyelaw, Coquet and Cheviot Cottages.

Each sleeps 4. Master bedroom with four-poster and en suite /jacuzzi bathroom, twin bedroom en suite, lounge/dining area, superbly equipped kitchen.

LOW NEWTON-BY-THE-SEA

Seawinds sleeps 6. Four bedrooms, sitting room, games room, dining room. 200 yards from sandy beach, 5 miles from Seahouses.

Contact:
Mrs Jo Leiper
Buston Farm
Holiday Cottages

Bygate,
Black Heddon,
Newcastle Upon
Tyne NE20 0JJ

Tel: 01661 881506

e-mail: stay@buston.co.uk
www.buston.co.uk

Alwinton, Beadnell

Fellside Cottage
within Northumberland National Park

Nestling at the foot of the Cheviot Hills in the beautiful Upper Coquet Valley, lies our cosy self-catering Northumbrian cottage.

Described as a 'gem', our wonderful cottage and beautiful garden is situated in the hamlet of Alwinton, gateway to the Cheviot Hills, within the glorious Northumberland National Park.
Furnished and equipped to a high standard, this cottage sleeps three. Very comfortable and tasteful interior, with an open log fire. Having stunning views of the Upper Coquet Valley and Cheviot Hills, this is a very special place to relax and unwind. A memorable stay. A walkers' paradise.

**Contact: Mrs D. Straughan,
Bedlington Lane Farm, Bedlington NE22 6AA
Tel: 01670 823042
e-mail: stay@fellsidecottcheviots.co.uk
www.fellsidecottcheviots.co.uk**

Shore Cottage • Beadnell

Detached property just a few metres from the beach, furnished and equipped to high standard.
3 bedrooms (sleeps 5/6) • All power and bed linen incl. • Spacious living/dining room with wood-burning stove, TV with DVD/Freeview.
Kitchen with electric cooker, gas hob, dishwasher, microwave etc. Washer/dryer • Travel cot and high chair on request.
No smoking • Regret no pets

**Contact: Mrs L. Barnett,
North East Coast Holidays,
7 Alnside Court, Alnwick NE66 3PD
Tel: 0191 286 9351
e-mail: d_barnettuk@yahoo.co.uk
www.northeastcoastholidays.co.uk**

Rambling over the heather-clad Cheviot moorlands, exploring the castles and pele towers built to ward off invading Scots, watching the feast of wildlife on the coast and in the countryside, breathing in the wonderful sea air on a golden sandy beach, you'll find it all in Northumberland. At the lively market town of Alnwick visit the castle, Hogwarts in the Harry Potter films, with the newly redeveloped gardens, magnificent water features and even a poison garden! Rare and endangered wildlife is found all along the coast and the ultimate destination for enthusiasts is the Farne Islands, with boat trips from the family resort of Seahouses to watch the grey seals and seabirds, including puffins, in the breeding seasons. Hexham and Haltwhistle are good bases for a visit, and these and other market towns and villages make a stay here a very pleasant one.

WAREN LEA HALL

Waren Mill, Bamburgh

*Luxurious Self-Catering
Holiday Accommodation
for families, parties and friends.*

HOLIDAYS AND SHORT BREAKS on the beautiful Northumberland coast.

Standing on the shore of beautiful Budle Bay, an Area of Outstanding Natural Beauty and a Site of Special Scientific Interest for its birdlife, lies spectacular WAREN LEA HALL. This lovely, gracious old Hall, set in 2 ½ acres of shoreline parkland and walled gardens, enjoys breathtaking views across the bay and sea to Lindisfarne. In addition to THE HALL there are two entirely self-contained apartments, GHILLIE'S VIEW and GARDEN COTTAGE.

THE HALL *(for up to 14 guests, with 6 bedrooms)*

Beautifully furnished to complement its Edwardian grandeur, with high ceilings, chandeliers, sash windows, fireplaces and polished wooden floors.

Breathtaking views from every room. Large drawing and dining rooms opening on to floodlit terrace; large, fully equipped kitchen/breakfast room. Ground floor twin bedroom and cloakroom/shower room; upstairs five further twin/double/en suite family bedrooms including en suite master with four-poster; family bathroom. Own private garden and use of walled garden and parkland bordering the shore. ETB Gold Award 2010/11.

GHILLIE'S VIEW *(for up to 10 guests, with 4 bedrooms)*

Accommodation is all on one level, with luxurious furnishings throughout. Fully equipped kitchen/dining room, semi-circular drawing room with balcony, and master bedroom with four-poster and en suite shower; all with fine views across the river and bay to Holy Island. Family, double and twin bedrooms, one en suite, and family bathroom. Guests have use of secluded walled garden and parkland bordering the shore. ETB Gold Award 2010/11.

GARDEN COTTAGE *(for up to 4 guests, with 2 bedrooms)*

The terrace wing of Waren Lea Hall, reached through its own entrance from the garden. All the light and sunny rooms are prettily furnished with high quality fabrics, pine furniture and polished wooden floors throughout, and face the lovely gardens which guests can use. The well equipped kitchen/dining room, lounge, double and twin bedrooms, one en suite, and family shower room are all on one level. Guests have use of the secluded walled garden and parkland bordering the shore. ETB Gold Award 2010/11.

For further information please contact the owners:

Carolynn and David Croisdale-Appleby
Abbotsholme, Hervines Road
Amersham, Buckinghamshire HP6 5HS
Tel: 01494 725194 • Mobile: 07901 716136
e-mail: croisdaleappleby@aol.com
www.selfcateringluxury.co.uk

**Warenford,
Near Belford
Northumberland
NE70 7HZ**

Originally the stable and blacksmith's forge for the Cottage Inn, Etive is a beautiful appointed old stone cottage, tastefully converted to offer comfortable accommodation for your holiday. Lying to the west of the A1 on the outskirts of the hamlet of Warenford, the cottage has sweeping views over open countryside towards the coast.

Accommodation is on one level, well equipped and comfortable, with central heating and double glazing throughout.

There are two bedrooms, one twin and one double, both with washbasins, shaver points, radio alarm clocks, extra bedding and hot water bottles. All bedding is supplied for your stay.

Etive Cottage is a convenient base for exploring Northumberland along the Heritage Coast, with its many castles including Lindisfarne, Bamburgh, Walkworth, and Dunstanburgh all a short drive away; the Farne Islands with seals and bird life are also worth a visit. The historic county town of Alnwick is 12 miles away.

Give your dogs the holiday they deserve.

A welcome grocery pack is provided for you and your dogs.

**For brochure contact Jan Thompson
Tel: 01668 213233
www.etivecottage.co.uk
janet.thompson1@homecall.co.uk**

Milecastle Inn Cottages

These two newly built cottages have excellent views to Hadrian's Wall and are ideally situated next to a traditional pub/restaurant, renowned for its good food and well kept ales. The cottages provide an excellent base for walkers, cyclists and golfers, or indeed anyone visiting the many attractions in the area.

There are a number of quality golf courses within a 20 mile radius, the new Hadrian's Wall Cycle Route follows the wall for 174 miles and passes the cottages and Carlisle, Hexham or Newcastle are all easily accessible for those interested in horse racing.

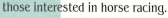

- *Each sleeps 2* • *No children under 12 years*
- *Non-smokers only* • *Minimum stay 3 nights*

**Contact: Mrs C. Hind,
Milecastle Inn, North Road,
Haltwhistle NE49 9NN • Tel: 01434 321372
e-mail: clarehind@aol.com
www.milecastle-inn.co.uk**

SB

Self Catering Holiday Cottage in Hadrian's Wall Country
Sleeps 5

CHAPEL • • HOUSE

Welcome to Chapel House

5 star self-catering cottage located in an Area of Outstanding Natural Beauty and situated in the hamlet of Whitley Chapel, 5 miles south of the medieval market town of Hexham near Hadrian's Wall, Northumberland.

Lovely detached Northumbrian sandstone cottage tucked away down a tree-lined drive. There are wonderful panoramic views of Slaley Forest and the heather-covered North Pennine hills. The cottage sits in four acres of pasture rich in wild flowers and biodiversity

Contact Joan Liddle, Peth Head Cottage, Bed and Breakfast, Juniper, Hexham, Northumberland NE47 0LA
Tel 01434 673 286 • E-mail info@chapel-house.co.uk
www.chapel-house.info

Hexham

High Dalton Cottage

Cosy and comfortable cottage on a family-run working farm set in 270 acres of beautiful scenery and wildlife.

SB

The cottage has been converted from stables and has two double rooms and one twin, each with en suite bath/shower room. The cottage is in an area of Northumberland's most picturesque and interesting countryside and has private parking and an enclosed garden with patio. The quaint Roman towns of Hexham and Corbridge are nearby.

The award-winning championship golf courses of Slaley Hall and Matfen Hall are a short distance away; other attractions include Newcastle, Kielder Water and Gateshead Metro Centre.

For details contact **Mrs J. Stobbs, High Dalton Farm, Hexham NE46 2LB • tel: 01434 673320 e-mail: stobbsjudy@aol.com**

Moorgair Cottage

SB

Slaley, Hexham NE47 0AN
Tel: 01434 673473
Contact: Vicki Ridley
e-mail: g_ridley@lineone.net
www.moorgair.co.uk

This charming cottage for 4/5 people is attached to the owner's home on a small working farm in rural Northumberland, home of Moorgair Alpacas. The cottage is furnished to a high standard and has every convenience to make your holiday stress free and enjoyable. Cot and high-chair available. Private garden and parking.

From the doorstep there are miles of forest tracks and country lanes for walkers and cyclists, and the cottage is ideally situated to explore Northumberland, Durham and the Scottish Borders. A small shop, post office and two pubs serving food (one with an excellent adventure playground) are within 1½ miles of the cottage.

Isaacs Cottage
Sparty Lea, Allendale, Northumbria.

A semi-detached cottage set in the beautiful rolling countryside of Allendale, perfectly placed for exploring Northumberland, Cumbria and the Northern Dales by car. Very comfortably furnished, accommodation comprises sitting room, dining kitchen; one double, one twin and one family bedroom; bathroom and shower room. Full oil-fired central heating and log fires. **Sleeps 7**. Fishing, walking and cycling on the doorstep.

Hannah's & Rose Cottage Allenheads, Northumbria.

Two semi-detached cottages in peaceful rural surroundings within the North Pennines Area of Outstanding Natural Beauty, both traditionally furnished with panoramic views. Centrally heated with open fires; TV/DVD/video; well equipped kitchens; large shared garden. Linen provided. Off-road parking. No smoking. Abundant opportunities for walking, cycling and exploring the region. Allendale is 5 miles away with friendly pubs, tea rooms and craft shops. **Sleeps 6**

Contact:
Mrs H. Robson • Allenheads Farm
Hexham, Northumberland NE47 9HT
Tel: 01434 685312

Two spacious stone-built cottages sleeping 4-6.
Recently converted and modernised to give you every facility you require.
Located in the heart of Northumberland on a very tidy working farm with private gardens.
Bolam Lake two miles, Belsay Castle four miles, coast 20 minutes, Hadrian's Wall 30 minutes,
to name only a few attractions.
All linen, heating, electricity included in price.
Sorry, no pets. All children welcome. Brochure on request. Terms from £275 to £470.

SB

Mr & Mrs A.P. Coatsworth
Gallowhill Farm
Whalton, Morpeth NE61 3TX
Tel: 01661 881241
www.gallowhillcottages.co.uk

Bosley

Cheshire

The Old Byre
Pye Ash Farm, Leek Road, Bosley, Macclesfield

SB

The Old Byre at Pye Ash Farm is particularly well designed to suit two families wishing to spend their holidays together in the countryside.

Set amongst the fields but only half a mile from Bosley Village, with a choice of two pubs, many walks can be taken from the farm, into the fields and woods. Bosley Minns overlooks the reservoir and forms part of the Gritstone Trail. Alton Towers is 15 miles away. All accommodation is on the ground floor, suitable for the less able visitor. The Cow Shed and the Sheep Shed both sleep four, with well equipped kitchen and shower room; rear porch with washing and drying facilities. Ample parking. **ETC ★★**.

For further details please contact: Dorothy Gilman, Woodcroft, Tunstall Road, Bosley, Macclesfield SK11 0PB Tel & Fax: 01260 223293 e-mail: dotgilman@hotmail.co.uk • www.bosley-byre-stay.co.uk

In Cheshire, just south of Manchester, combine a city break in historic Chester with a day or two at one of relaxing spas either in the city itself or in one of the luxury resorts in the rolling countryside. Time your visit to the historic Georgian mansion at Tatton Park to coincide with one of the wide choice of events held there throughout the year, including the annual RHS Flower Show. All the family will be fascinated by a visit to the giant Lovell Telescope at Jodrell Bank Visitor Centre near the old silk weaving town of Macclesfield or meeting the native animals and birdlife at the Cotebrook Shire Horse Centre. The walkways in nearby Delamere Forest provide pleasant and not too challenging walks, or hire a mountain bike to ride round the forest trails. Chester, with its wonderful array of Roman, medieval and Georgian buildings is a fascinating place to visit. Walk round the most complete example of city walls in the whole country, past the beautiful cathedral, before browsing through the wonderful range of shops, art galleries and museums.

Cumbria

SB

• • Betty Fold • •
Hawkshead Hill,
Ambleside LA22 0PS

Situated near Hawkshead and Tarn Hows, this large country house in spacious grounds is in the heart of Lake District National Park.

Betty Fold offers self-catering accommodation in a comfortable ground floor apartment with private entrance, sleeps 4. One double en suite and one small twin with dressing room and bathroom. Open-plan kitchen/livingroom with electric cooker, fridge, freezer, microwave, colour TV with Freeview and DVD player. Well behaved pets are welcome.

Terms incl.heat, light, power, bed linen and towels.

015394 36611
e-mail: claire@bettyfold.co.uk
www.bettyfold.co.uk

RAMSTEADS COPPICE,
Outgate, Ambleside LA22 0NH
Mr Evans • 015394 36583

Six timber lodges of varied size and design set in 15 acres of mixed woodland with wild flowers, birds and native wild animals.

There are also 11 acres of rough hill pasture. Three miles south west of Ambleside, it is an ideal centre for walkers, artists, birdwatchers, and country lovers.

No pets • Children welcome • Open March to November

SB

Quality Holiday Homes in England's Beautiful Lake District

Hundreds of VisitBritain inspected and graded properties throughout the southern and central Lake District.
Lakelovers are sure to have a property to meet your needs.

Tel: 015394 88855 • Fax: 015394 88857
e-mail: bookings@lakelovers.co.uk • www.lakelovers.co.uk
Lakelovers, Belmont House, Lake Road,
Bowness-on-Windermere, Cumbria LA23 3BJ

symbols

 Totally non-smoking

 Children Welcome

 Suitable for Disabled Guests

 Pets Welcome

 SB *Short Breaks available*

 Licensed

SB

43A Quarry Rigg
Bowness-on-Windermere

Ideally situated in the centre of the village close to the Lake and all amenities, the flat is in a new development, fully self-contained, and furnished and equipped to a high standard for owner's own comfort and use. Lake views, ideal relaxation and touring centre. Close to Beatrix Potter Museum.

Accommodation is for two/three people. Bedroom with twin beds, lounge with TV, video and DVD; convertible settee; separate kitchen with electric cooker, microwave and fridge/freezer; bathroom with bath/shower and WC. Electric heating. Parking for residents.

Rates: Low season £190 to £275; High Season £240-£350

• Weekends/Short Breaks also available. • Sleeps 2/3 • Sorry, no pets.

SAE, please, for details to E. Jones, 45 West Oakhill Park, Liverpool, Merseyside L13 4BN

Tel: 0151-228 5799
e-mail: eajay@btinternet.com

Fisherground Lodges
Eskdale, Cumbria

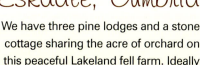

We have three pine lodges and a stone cottage sharing the acre of orchard on this peaceful Lakeland fell farm. Ideally suited for walkers, nature lovers, dogs and children, offering space, freedom and tranquillity. Children of all ages will love the raft pool and the games room, – and we even have our own station on the Eskdale miniature railway! Good pubs nearby serve excellent bar meals.

Ian & Jennifer Hall, Orchard House, Applethwaite, Keswick CA12 4PN
Tel: 017687 73175
e-mail: holidays@fisherground.co.uk
website: www.fisherground.co.uk

3 Randle How
Self Catering Cottage

SELF CATERING

★★★★

WALKERS WELCOME

Situated in the Esk Valley in the west of the Lake District, 3 Randle How is an 18th century cottage located in Eskdale Green, Cumbria.

The cottage is in a quiet part of the village and is an excellent base for walking, touring or a quiet relaxing rest throughout the year. It has modern facilities while maintaining its traditional style and comfortably accommodates four people.

Two bedrooms, a twin and one double, sitting room and dining room.
Log fires, full central heating. Well equipped kitchen. Parking. £285 - £485 weekly.
A visit to the Roman Fort, Hard Knot or a trip on the Ravenglass and Eskdale Railway, known as La'al Ratty is worthwhile as is a trip to Muncaster Castle to see the gardens and Owl Centre.

Details from Susan Wedley, Randle How,
c/o Long Yocking How, Eskdale Green,
Holmrook CA19 1UA • Tel: 01946 723126
e-mail: jswedley@btinternet.com
www.3randlehowselfcatering.com

Hawkshead

SB

Large enough to offer choice... small enough to care

- Choice of more than 60 cottages in and around Hawkshead
- Pets Welcome
- Traditional and contemporary cottages
- Short breaks available
- Award winning website, online booking

'Hawkshead – The prettiest village in the Lake District'

The Square, Hawkshead, Cumbria LA22 0NZ | Tel: 015394 42435 | Fax: 015394 36178
Email: bookings@lakeland-hideaways.co.uk | www.lakeland-hideaways.co.uk

Keswick, Kirkoswald

Kirkby Lonsdale, Lake District

Cragside

**Harrison Farm,
Whittington,
Kirkby Lonsdale,
Carnforth,
Lancashire LA6 2NX
Tel: 015242 71415**

SB

Near Hutton Roof, three miles from Kirkby Lonsdale and central for touring Lake District and Yorkshire Dales. Coast walks on Hutton Roof Crag, famous limestone pavings.

Property sleeps 8; one room with double and single bed, one with double and cot, third bedroom with three single beds. Bathroom. Sitting room, dining room and kitchen. Electric cooker, microwave, fridge, kettle, iron, immersion heater and TV. Everything supplied but linen. Electricity and coal extra. Parking space. Pets permitted.

*Terms from £250 per week.
SAE brings quick reply.*

Other cottages available, sleeping 2-8.

"Your own country house in the Lakes"

Two luxury holiday houses available to rent in the Lake District.

Routen House

Routen House is a beautiful old farmhouse set in 4 acres in an outstanding position with fabulous views over Ennerdale Lake. Fully modernised while retaining the character of the old farmhouse, it has been furnished to a very high standard. Sleeps 12 plus cot.

Little Parrock is an elegant Victorian Lakeland stone house a short walk from the centre of Grasmere with large rooms and a wealth of period features. Lovely private garden. Fully modernised to a very high standard; real log fires. Sleeps 10 plus cot.

Little Parrock

Both houses are non-smoking but pets are very welcome.

Please contact:

Mrs J. Green • **Tel & Fax: 01604 505115**
e-mail: joanne@routenhouse.co.uk
www.routenhouse.co.uk • www.littleparrock.co.uk

Lamplugh

Little Langdale, Mungrisdale, Penrith

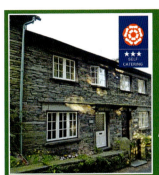

★ ★ ★ ★ ★

LUXURY HOLIDAY COTTAGES
on the fringe of the
LAKELAND FELLS

Carrock Cottages

★ ★ ★ ★ ★

Home-from-home accommodation for
single's to groups of 18

★ ★ ★ ★ ★

Easy access to the Lakes, Pennines and Borders

★ ★ ★ ★ ★

Games room with table tennis table and pool table

★ ★ ★ ★ ★

Top quality fittings, wide screen TV's,
DVD's & games consoles

★ ★ ★ ★ ★

Pets Welcome

★ ★ ★ ★ ★

Home-cooked meal service

For our full colour brochure contact
Malcolm & Gillian Iredale
Carrock Cottages, How Hill, Hutton Roof
Penrith, Cumbria CA11 0XY
Tel: 01768 484 111 Fax: 017684 888 50
E.Mail: info@carrockcottages.co.uk
www.carrockcottages.co.uk

SB

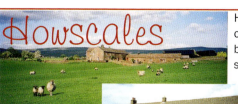

Howscales was originally a 17th century farm. The red sandstone buildings have been converted into five self-contained cottages, retaining many original features.

SB

NATIONAL ACCESSIBILITY SCHEME: CATEGORY 2

Set around a cobbled courtyard, the cosy, well-equipped cottages for 2-4, are surrounded by award-winning

  ♿

gardens and open countryside. Shared laundry facilities.

Cared for by resident owner. Ideal base from which to explore the Eden Valley, Lakes, Pennines and Hadrian's Wall.

Please contact us or see our website for details.

- **£250 to £580 weekly • Sleep 2/4**
- **Non-smoking • Open all year**
- **Short breaks available**
- **Well-behaved pets welcome by arrangement**

Liz Webster, Howscales, Kirkoswald, Penrith CA10 1JG
Tel: 01768 898666 • Fax: 01768 898710
e-mail: liz@howscales.co.uk • www.howscales.co.uk

Middle Brig How
Near Ambleside

SB

Middle Brig How is tucked away up a private drive surrounded by a well kept garden. The accommodation comprises a good sized living room with open fire and French doors opening out onto the garden. There is a large kitchen/dining area which has been extensively modernised and contains every convenience. Bathroom and separate wc; good sized double bedroom with king size bed. Sleeps 2.

Tel: 015394 31176 (Roberta) • 015394 37635 (Wheelwrights)
enquiries@wheelwrights.com • www.wheelwrights.com

Visit the FHG website
www.holidayguides.com
for all kinds of holiday
acccommodation in Britain

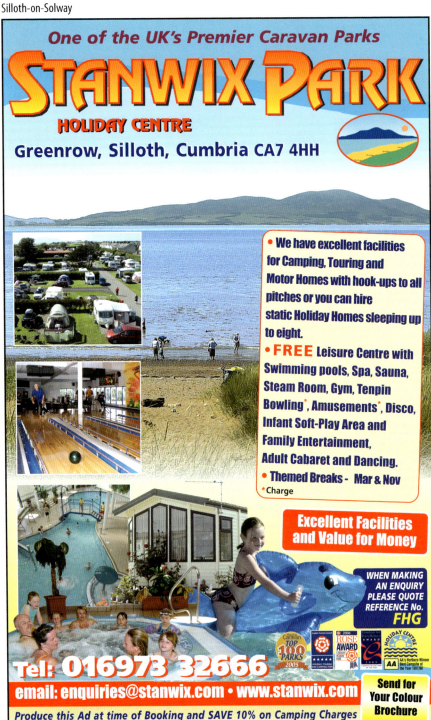

One of the UK's Premier Caravan Parks

STANWIX PARK

HOLIDAY CENTRE

Greenrow, Silloth, Cumbria CA7 4HH

- We have excellent facilities for Camping, Touring and Motor Homes with hook-ups to all pitches or you can hire static Holiday Homes sleeping up to eight.
- **FREE** Leisure Centre with Swimming pools, Spa, Sauna, Steam Room, Gym, Tenpin Bowling*, Amusements*, Disco, Infant Soft-Play Area and Family Entertainment, Adult Cabaret and Dancing.
- Themed Breaks - Mar & Nov

*Charge

Excellent Facilities and Value for Money

WHEN MAKING AN ENQUIRY PLEASE QUOTE REFERENCE No. **FHG**

Tel: **016973 32666**

email: **enquiries@stanwix.com** • **www.stanwix.com**

Send for Your Colour Brochure

Produce this Ad at time of Booking and SAVE 10% on Camping Charges

Lancashire

WHITE SYKE FARM Farmhouse Tranquillity overlooking Pendle Hill

THIS LARGE 18THC RURAL FARMHOUSE SLEEPS 8 PEOPLE AND IS
CENTRALLY HEATED AND FULLY EQUIPPED, WITH LARGE LAWNED
GARDENS AND PRIVATE PARKING. ALL FUEL, POWER, BED LINEN AND
TOWELS ARE INCLUDED IN THE RENTAL. WELL BEHAVED PETS ARE
WELCOME IN THE GROUND FLOOR ROOMS AND THE GARDEN. PANORAMIC
VIEWS. SITUATED IN PICTURESQUE PENDLE, BETWEEN THE YORKSHIRE
DALES AND BRONTË COUNTRY. WALKING, FISHING, GOLF, CANAL
CRUISES, SWIMMING AND GYMNASIUMS ARE AVAILABLE LOCALLY, AND
THERE ARE PLENTY OF SHOPS, PUBS AND RESTAURANTS IN THE AREA.

**White Syke Farm, Aynhams Farm, Brogden Lane, Barnoldswick BB18 5XE
• Tel: 01282 815731•**

Rakefoot Farm
Chaigley, Near Clitheroe BB7 3LY
Tel: (Chipping) 01995 61332 or 07889 279063 • Fax: 01995 61296
e-mail: info@rakefootfarm.co.uk • www.rakefootfarm.co.uk

VisitBritain ★★★★
VisitBritain ★★★/★★★★

SB

Family farm in the beautiful countryside of the Ribble Valley in the peaceful Forest of Bowland,
with panoramic views. Ideally placed for touring Coast, Dales and Lakes. 9 miles M6 Junction
31a. Superb walks, golf and horse riding nearby, or visit pretty villages and factory shops. Warm
welcome whether on holiday or business, refreshments on arrival.
BED AND BREAKFAST or SELF-CATERING in 17th century farmhouse and traditional
stone barn conversion. Wood-burning stoves, central heating, exposed beams and
stonework. Most bedrooms en suite, some ground floor. Excellent home cooked meals
service, pubs/restaurants nearby. Garden and patios. Dogs by arrangement. Laundry.
**B&B £25 - £35pppn sharing, £25 - £40pn single
S/C four properties (3 can be internally interlinked)
£111 - £695 per property per week. Short breaks available.**

Generations of excited holiday-makers have visited Lancashire's coastal resorts, and amongst
them Blackpool stands out as the star attraction. For seaside fun, amusements and
entertainment it's difficult to beat, but the quieter resorts along the coast with traditional
seaside attractions have their own appeal. For an outdoor break there are all kinds of activities
from hot air ballooning to fishing on offer inland, from the lowland plain, along the winding
valleys of the Ribble and the Lune, up into the Forest of Bowland and on to the moors of the
western Pennines. There's fun for all ages in Blackpool, Britain's most popular resort, from the
Big Wheel on Central Pier, the thrilling rides at the Pleasure Beach, and the Winter Gardens with
award-winning shows, jazz and rock concerts, to the tropical sharks and reef fish at Sealife, the
Sandcastle Waterpark, and a ride in a historic tram along the newly renovated Central
Promenade, not forgetting sand, sea and donkey rides.

At Morecambe take part in the Catch the Wind Kite Festival held on the sands in July, just one of a number of events in the town each year. With the winds blowing in every direction conditions on this Irish Sea coast are perfect for kite-surfing, and instruction is available at Fleetwood, a family-orientated Victorian resort where the Fylde Folk Festival is held every September. Experience being locked in the dungeons at Lancaster Castle, on a visit to this historic centre with its cobbled streets and lively bars and restaurants. Preston, with everything from high street names to farmers' shops and markets, is the destination for shopping, as well as the National Museum of Football. Follow the Ribble Valley Food Trail to sample the wonderful produce on offer, and wherever you are look out for the panopticons, the modern sculpture installations in town and countryside.

Preston, Southport

Channel Islands

Well equipped holiday homes, close to the beach, ideal as a base to explore and enjoy the island. Each flat is fully furnished, with bedroom(s), lounge, bathroom/toilet, kitchen/diner. Bed linen, towels, cots and high chairs (by request), TV, kettle, electric heaters, hot water, fridge/freezer, oven and microwave. £1 slot meter for electricity. The premises are under the supervision of the proprietor, who will help you to enjoy your stay here. A taxi or hire car can be arranged to meet you at the harbour or airport if required.

Les Clotures, L'Ancresse, Guernsey GY3 5AY
Tel/Fax 01481 249633
www.swallowapartments.com
swallowapt@aol.com

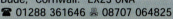

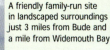

❖ Carnevas Farm Holiday Park ❖

Carnevas Farm, St Merryn, Padstow PL28 8PN
01841 520230

◆Situated only half a mile from golden sandy beach, fishing, golf, sailing etc.

◆Quaint harbour village of Padstow only four miles.

◆Bungalows/chalets sleep 4/5, have two bedrooms, bathroom, kitchen/diner, airing cupboard, colour TV.

◆Caravans four-berth or six-berth, all have showers, toilets, fridge, colour TV (also separate camping and caravan facilities).

◆Converted barn available, sleeps 4/6 persons, furnished to a high standard. Brochure on request.

www.carnevasholidaypark.co.uk

Bone Valley Holiday Park

Situated in a pretty valley, ideal for exploring the countryside and coast of West Cornwall, this small, family-run park is surrounded by mature hedges and trees. There is also a pretty stream running along the park. We are located approx. ¾ mile from the centre of Penzance, in the village of Heamoor which has shops, a pub and a regular bus service.

17 pitches (some hardstanding) • Pitches for tents • Electric hook-ups available • Static Caravans, fully equipped • Budget Caravans On-site facilities include: showers, kitchen/laundry room (microwave, electric kettle etc), shop, campers' lounge with digital TV, public telephone, free ice pack service, chemical disposal, gas and Camping Gaz, BBQ loan.

Bone Valley *Holiday Park*
Heamoor, Penzance TR20 8UJ
www.bonevalleyholidaypark.co.uk

Please contact Mrs Ward • Tel & Fax: 01736 360313

---

symbols

 Totally non-smoking
 Children Welcome
 Suitable for Disabled Guests

 Pets Welcome
SB *Short Breaks available*
 Licensed

Redruth

Globe Vale
Holiday Park
Radnor, Redruth, Cornwall TR16 4BH

Globe Vale is a quiet countryside park situated close to the town of Redruth and the main A30. There are panoramic views across green fields to the coast; 10 minutes' drive to the nearest beach. Campers/tourers; static caravans for hire, and also plots available if you wish to buy your own new static holiday home. Facilities on site include fully serviced pitches, electric hook-ups, modern shower/toilet block, launderette and chemical disposal. Licensed bar with games room. Evening meals served. There is also a children's play area, and open spaces for ball games. We are happy to accept pets on site at extra charge. Caravan storage available.

Contact
Paul and Louise Owen on
01209 891183
www.globevale.co.uk
e-mail: info@globevale.co.uk

Ambleside

Greenhowe
Caravan Park
Great Langdale, English Lakeland.

Greenhowe is a permanent Caravan Park with Self Contained Holiday Accommodation. Subject to availability Holiday Homes may be rented for short or long periods from 1st March until mid-November. The Park is situated in the heart of the Lake District some half a mile from Dungeon Ghyll at the foot of the Langdale Pikes. It is an ideal centre for Climbing, Fell Walking, Riding, Swimming or just a lazy holiday.

Greenhowe Caravan Park
Great Langdale,
Ambleside
Cumbria LA22 9JU
For free colour brochure
Tel: (015394) 37231
Fax: (015394) 37464
www.greenhowe.com

LODGES also available • Please ask about Short Breaks

Three six-berth, modern, well-equipped caravans situated on a quiet family-run farm site with beautiful views over Coniston Water.

Pets are welcome, and pony trekking can be arranged from the farm. A good base for walking and touring the area. We have a good pub 200 yards down the road.

Weekly terms on request.

Showers, toilets, gas cookers, fires and water heaters; electric lighting, fridge, TV, kettle, toaster and microwave.

Mrs E. Johnson, Spoon Hall, Coniston LA21 8AW
Telephone: 015394 41391

Waters Edge
CARAVAN PARK

Modern purpose-built park with top class amenities just ¾ of a mile from M6 Exit 36. Within easy reach of the Lakes, Yorkshire Dales, West Coast and Morecambe Bay.

With licensed lounge bar, off-licence, TV lounge, pool table, facilities for the disabled, shop, Calor gas, barbecues, picnic tables, fully tiled private showers, toilets and wash cubicles, laundry and washing up facilities all with free hot water. All hardstanding pitches with electric hook-ups. Many suitable for awnings.

Please telephone or write for our free colour brochure. Call for bar opening times.

Crooklands, Near Kendal LA7 7NN Tel: 015395 67708
www.watersedgecaravanpark.co.uk

SB

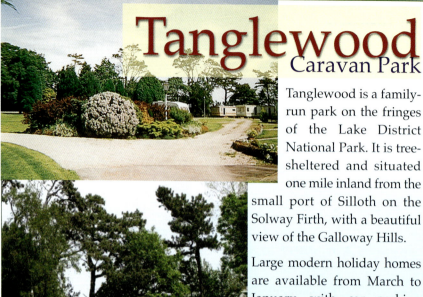

Tanglewood
Caravan Park

Tanglewood is a family-run park on the fringes of the Lake District National Park. It is tree-sheltered and situated one mile inland from the small port of Silloth on the Solway Firth, with a beautiful view of the Galloway Hills.

Large modern holiday homes are available from March to January, with car parking beside each home.

Fully equipped except for bed linen, with central heating, electric lighting, hot and cold water, toilet, shower, gas fire, fridge and colour TV, all of which are included in the tariff. Touring pitches also available with electric hook-ups and water/drainage facilities, etc. Play area. Licensed lounge with adjoining children's play room. Pets welcome free but must be kept under control at all times. Full colour brochure available.

AA ►►►
⛺🚐🏠

English Tourism Council
★★★
HOLIDAY, TOURING
AND CAMPING PARK

Mike Bowman
Tanglewood Caravan Park
Causewayhead
Silloth-on-Solway
Cumbria CA7 4PE
Tel: 016973 31253

e-mail: tanglewoodcaravanpark@hotmail.com
www.tanglewoodcaravanpark.co.uk

Penrith

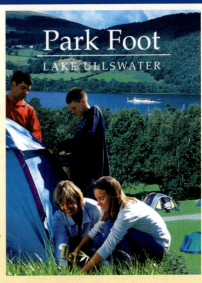
Buxton

STATIC CARAVANS
TOURING SITE

Friendly, family-run touring site and static
caravans situated in unspoilt countryside.
Spectacular views to Dartmoor.
Two modern shower blocks; electric hook-ups.
Bar and restaurant with area for dogs. Large
dog-walking fields. Shop, launderette and
indoor/outdoor play areas. 12 miles to coast.
Short Breaks available.

**HIGHER MEAD FARM,
ASHBURTON, DEVON TQ13 7LJ**
Tel: 01364 654869 • Fax: 01364 654004
e-mail: parkersfarm@btconnect.com
www.parkersfarmholidays.co.uk

North Morte Farm Caravan & Camping
Dept. FHG, Mortehoe, Woolacombe EX34 7EG
(01271 870381)

*The nearest camping and caravan park to the sea,
in perfectly secluded beautiful coastal country.*

Our family-run park, adjoining
National Trust land, is only 500
yards from Rockham Beach, yet
only five minutes' walk from the
village of Mortehoe with a Post
Office, shops, cafes and pubs.

Four to six berth holiday
caravans for hire and pitches for
tents, dormobiles and touring
caravans, electric hook-ups available. We have hot showers and flush toilets, laundry
room, shop and off-licence; Calor gas and Camping Gaz available; children's play area.
Dogs accepted but must be kept on lead. Open April to end October.
Brochure available.

e-mail: info@northmortefarm.co.uk • www.northmortefarm.co.uk

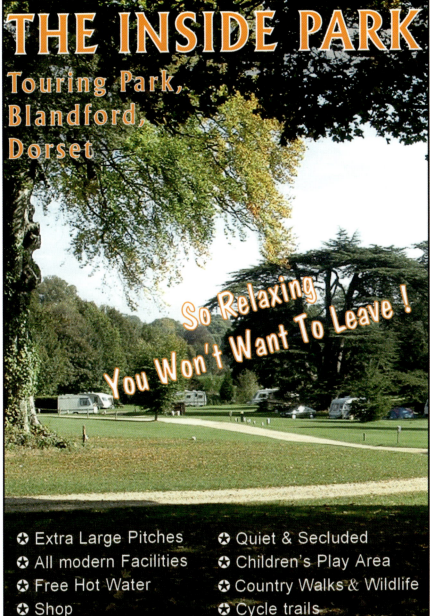

THE INSIDE PARK

Touring Park, Blandford, Dorset

So Relaxing You Won't Want To Leave !

- ✿ Extra Large Pitches
- ✿ All modern Facilities
- ✿ Free Hot Water
- ✿ Shop
- ✿ Ideal Family Site

- ✪ Quiet & Secluded
- ✪ Children's Play Area
- ✪ Country Walks & Wildlife
- ✪ Cycle trails
- ✪ Caravan Storage

01258 453719
www.theinsidepark.co.uk

SB

Hayling Island

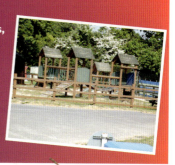
Leominster

Mundesley

Sandy Gulls
Caravan Park Ltd
Cromer Road, Mundesley, Norfolk NR11 8DF

Found on the Mundesley cliff tops, this quiet private park, managed by the owning family for over 30 years, offers a warm welcome to all visitors. The touring park has grass and non-turf pitches, all have uninterrupted sea views, electric/TV hook-ups and beautifully refurbished shower rooms. Holiday caravans for sale or hire, which are always the latest models.

Our charges include gas and electricity.
Superbly situated for exploring the beauty of North Norfolk including The Broads National Park.

ADULTS ONLY TOURING PARK

Samantha
01263 720513

Hexham

SB

GREENCARTS FARM
www.greencarts.co.uk

Greencarts is a working farm situated in Roman Wall country, ideally placed for exploring by car, bike or walking. It has magnificent views of the Tyne Valley. Campsite for 30 tents with facilities, and bunk barn with 12 beds, showers and toilet are now open from Easter until the end of October. Prices for campsite are £5 to £10 per tent, plus £1pp. Bunk barn beds from £10. Linen available. Bed and Breakfast also available from £25 to £40 .

Mr & Mrs D Maughan, Greencarts Farm, Humshaugh, Hexham NE46 4BW
Tel/Fax: 01434 681320
e-mail: sandra@greencarts.co.uk.

Tuxford

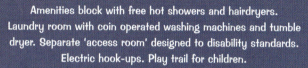

Bridgwater

Bridgwater

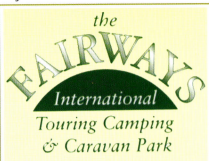

HIGHER TOWN

Dulverton, Somerset TA22 9RX

Tel: 01398 341272

Our farm is situated half-a-mile from open moorland, one mile from the Devon/Somerset border and four miles from Dulverton. 80 acres of the farm is in the Exmoor National Park. We let two caravans which are quarter-of-a-mile apart and do not overlook each other. Both have lovely views, situated in lawns with parking space. Both are 8-berth, with a double end bedroom, bunk bedroom, shower, flush toilet, hot/cold water and colour TV.

The caravans are modern and fully equipped except linen. Cot and high chair available. One caravan with three bedrooms. Visitors are welcome to watch the milking or walk over our beef and sheep farm. Riding and fishing nearby. Open May to October.

Price from £120, includes gas and electricity.

Quantock Orchard Caravan Park

Award-winning, family-run campsite set amidst the stunning Somerset countryside.

Quantock Orchard is situated in an idyllic setting surrounded by picturesque views of the Quantocks, in an Area of Outstanding Natural Beauty. This peaceful park is close to Exmoor, the coast and the West Somerset Railway. Relax and unwind among these beautiful surroundings whilst enjoying our Five Star facilities.

• fully heated toilet and shower block • launderette • games room • adventure playground • shop • outdoor heated pool • gym with jacuzzi, steam room and sauna • cycle hire • caravan storage

Tents, tourers and motorhomes welcome
Luxury static holiday homes for sale or hire
Open all year

Michael & Sara Barrett, Quantock Orchard Caravan Park, Flaxpool, Crowcombe, Near Taunton TA4 4AW
01984 618618
e-mail: qocp@flaxpool.freeserve.co.uk
www.quantock-orchard.co.uk

DE LUXE PARK

Lowestoft

Marston

BLACK BULL CARAVAN PARK

Family Caravan and Camping Park one mile south of Pickering on the A169, behind a public house. The gateway to the North York Moors! Good base for walking, cycling, visiting the coast and numerous other local attractions.

On-site facilities: playground • games room • sports field
refurbished amenities with free hot showers • dishwashing and laundry

Touring pitches in open level field with some shelter. Fully serviced and fully equipped holiday caravans also for hire. Double-glazed and heated.

**Terms from £115 to £410.
Four caravans for hire,
sleeping six.
Touring pitches available,
from £12 per night**

**Why not view our website
for more photographs?
Malton Road,
Pickering,
North Yorkshire
YO18 8EA**

**www.blackbullpark.co.uk
Tel: 01751 472528**

Middlewood Farm Holiday Park

SB

Small, peaceful, family park. A walkers', artists' and wildlife paradise, set amidst the beautiful North Yorkshire Moors National Park, Heritage Coast and 'Heartbeat Country'. Relax and enjoy the magnificent panoramic views of our spectacular countryside. Five minutes' walk to the village PUB and shops. Ten minutes' walk to the BEACH and picturesque Robin Hood's Bay. SUPERIOR LUXURY HOLIDAY HOMES FOR HIRE, equipped to the highest standards (Open all year). TOURERS and TENTS: level, sheltered park with electric hook-ups. Superb heated facilities, free showers and dishwashing. Laundry. Gas. Children's adventure playground. Adjacent dog walk and cycle route. Credit cards accepted. Signposted. A warm welcome awaits you.

**Robin Hood's Bay, Near Whitby, Yorkshire YO22 4UF
Tel: 01947 880414
e-mail: info@middlewoodfarm.com
www.middlewoodfarm.com**

Scotland

see Wilderness Cottages, page 428.

Aberdeen, Banff & Moray

Aberdeen

Furain Guest House, on the A93 8 miles west of Aberdeen centre, is a late Victorian house built from red granite. We have some of the most beautiful countryside in the UK right on our doorstep, offering plenty of scope for walkers. Drum and Crathes Castles are only a few minutes' drive. Golf can be arranged at Peterculter Golf Club, our local course.

• 3 Double rooms • 2 Family rooms
• 1 Single room • 2 Twin rooms

Contact: Mr Reid, Furain Guest House, 92 North Deeside Road, Peterculter, Aberdeen AB14 0QN

**Tel: 01224 732189 • Fax: 01224 739070
e-mail: furain@btinternet.com
www.furain.co.uk**

Woodside of Glasslaw

Modern bungalow with six centrally heated en suite bedrooms with
colour TV and hospitality trays. Accessible for disabled guests.
Wifi available. Stonehaven two miles.

MRS AILEEN PATON, 'WOODSIDE OF GLASSLAW',
STONEHAVEN AB39 3XQ

Tel: 01569 763799
aileen@woodsideofglasslaw.co.uk
www.woodsideofglasslaw.co.uk

Brechin

Angus & Dundee

Brathinch Farm
By Brechin DD9 7QZ
01356 648292 • Fax: 01356 648003
brathinch@tesco.net

Brathinch is an 18th century farmhouse on a family-run working arable farm, with a large garden, situated off the B966 between Brechin and Edzell.

Rooms are en suite, TV and tea/coffee making facilities. Shooting, fishing, golf, castles, stately homes, wildlife, swimming and other attractions are all located nearby.

Easy access to Angus Glens and other country walks. Open all year.

Double £26pppn, twin £27pppn, single £30-£35pn.

We look forward to welcoming you.

The Firth of Tay and westwards from the North Sea coast towards the highlands of the Cairngorm National Park, lies the former Pictish stronghold of Angus, its historic burghs and villages and the university city of Dundee. The marine and industrial heritage of this lively city, the quiet glens and hills inland, the rivers and coast, all with a wide range of outdoor pursuits on hand, make this an ideal destination. The area is renowned for golf, and with 50 golf courses within 30 miles of Dundee, from classic links like Carnoustie to the heathland at Edzell in the north, it's a golfers' dream. In Dundee at Discovery Point is the home of the RRS Discovery, the ship that took Captain Scott on his ill-fated journey to the Antarctic. The story of the jute industry, on which the wealth of the city was built, is retold at the Verdant Works. But this city formerly associated with jute, jam and journalism now looks to the future too at the Sensation Science Centre, where everyone can experiment with interactive exhibits involving robotics, cybernetics and even keyhole surgery.

SB

Muirhouses is a livestock and arable farm set amidst beautiful Angus countryside, close to the Cairngorm National Park.

The accommodation is very comfortable with en suite rooms and central heating.

Every comfort is assured, from the homely welcome on arrival to the delicious breakfast. An excellent base for golf, walking and cycling.

**Cortachy, Kirriemuir,
Angus DD8 4QG**
Tel: 01575 573128 • *Mrs S. McLaren*
e-mail: susan@muirhouses.plus.com
www.muirhousesfarm.co.uk

Other British holiday guides from FHG Guides

**PUBS & INNS • 300 GREAT HOTELS
SHORT BREAK HOLIDAYS
The bestselling and original PETS WELCOME!
THE GOLF GUIDE - Where to Play, Where to Stay
SELF-CATERING HOLIDAYS • BED & BREAKFAST STOPS
CARAVAN & CAMPING HOLIDAYS • FAMILY BREAKS**

Published annually: available in all good bookshops or direct from the publisher:
**FHG Guides, Abbey Mill Business Centre, Seedhill, Paisley PA1 1TJ
Tel: 0141 887 0428 • Fax: 0141 889 7204**
e-mail: admin@fhguides.co.uk • www.holidayguides.com

Ballachullish

Argyll & Bute

Mr & Mrs J.A. MacLeod
Lyn-Leven Guest House
Ballachulish PH49 4JP
Tel: 01855 811392 • Fax: 01855 811600
www.lynleven.co.uk
Bed and Breakfast from £25
DB&B from £235 to £255 per person per week
Credit and debit cards accepted

Lyn-Leven
a superior, award-winning licensed guest house overlooking Loch Leven, with every comfort, in the beautiful Highlands of Scotland, is situated one mile from historic Glencoe village. Four double, two twin and two family bedrooms, all rooms en suite; sittingroom and diningroom. Central heating. Excellent and varied home cooking served daily. Children welcome at reduced rates. An ideal location for touring. Fishing, walking and climbing in the vicinity. The house is open all year except Christmas. Car not essential but private car park provided.

Argyll & Bute is a wonderfully unspoilt area, historically the heartland of Scotland and home to a wealth of fascinating wildlife. Here you may be lucky enough to catch a glimpse of an eagle, a wildcat or an osprey, or even a fine antlered stag. On the upper reaches of Loch Caolisport can be found St Columba's Cave, and more recent times are illustrated at the Auchindrain Highland Township south of Inveraray, a friendly little town with plenty to see, including the Jail, Wildlife Park and Maritime Museum. Bute is the most accessible of the west coast islands, and Rothesay is its main town. Explore the dungeons and grand hall of Rothesay Castle, or visit the fascinating Bute Museum. The town offers a full range of leisure facilities, including a fine swimming pool and superb golf course.

Killean Farmhouse

Killean Farmhouse is located just a few miles outside Inveraray. Ideally situated for walking, climbing, pony trekking or just touring. There is fishing for trout, pike or salmon, and opportunities to enjoy boating, water skiing or windsurfing. The whole area is steeped in history and the town of Inveraray itself is a classic example of 18th century Scottish town planning. With all this in mind, the cottages provide high quality accommodation for family holidays.

Mrs Semple, Killean Farmhouse, Inveraray PA32 8XT • Tel: 01499 302474

Gigha Hotel

SB

The community-owned Isle of Gigha (Gaelic: God's Island) is known as The Jewel of the Inner Hebrides. The Atlantic's crystal clear waters surround this six-mile long magical isle, and lap gently on to its white sandy beaches - creating an aura of peace and tranquillity.

The Gigha Hotel caters admirably for the discerning holidaymaker with comfortable accommodation and first class cuisine, including fresh local seafood. There are also holiday cottages available.

A must for any visitor is a wander around the famous sub-tropical Achamore Gardens, where palm trees and many other exotic plants flourish in Gigha's mild climatic conditions.

The Isle of Gigha Heritage Trust retails quality island-related craft products, some of which have utilised the Trust's own tartan.

Other activities on offer include organised walks, bird watching, sea fishing, a nine-hole golf course and alternative therapies.

Call us on 01583 505254 • Fax: 01583 505244
www.gigha.org.uk

Small, family-run guest house where we aim to make your stay as comfortable as possible. All rooms have central heating, colour TV and hospitality trays; some en suite. A full Scottish breakfast is served, although Continental is available if preferred. We have ample private parking at the rear of the house. Situated 10 minutes' walk from the town centre, train, boat and bus terminals. Oban boasts regular sailings to the Islands, and an excellent golf course, as well as walking, cycling, fishing, or just letting the world go by.

A warm welcome awaits you all year round.

MRS STEWART, GLENVIEW, SOROBA ROAD, OBAN PA34 4JF • Tel: 01631 562267
e-mail: morven.stewart@hotmail.com

A warm welcome awaits you in this delightful bungalow set in 20 acres of farmland where we breed our own Highland cattle which graze at the front. It is a peaceful location as we are set back from the road, and an ideal spot for touring, with the main ferry terminal at Oban just 10 minutes away. Our luxurious rooms have their own special sitting room attached where you can enjoy your coffee or a glass of wine in peace, and we also have our own restaurant where you can dine.

Mrs J. Currie, Hawthorn, 5 Keil Crofts, Benderloch, Oban PA37 1QS • 01631 720452
e-mail: june@hawthorncottages.com
www.hawthorncottages.com

SB

Oban

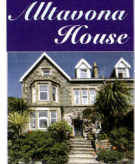

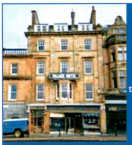

SB

Superb Bed & breakfast
Spectacular views
Spacious Suites
Relax and enjoy this
Victorian Lodge

The Moorings is a charming Victorian Lodge situated in its own grounds on a quiet conservation shoreline with spectacular views and close to all amenities.

- Spacious suites comfortable beds and seating
- Premier, double, twin, single and family suites available • En suite facilities in all rooms
- Hospitality trays • Colour TV and VCR in all rooms
- Hairdryer, shaving point and radio alarm
- Complimentary fruit bowl • Garden seating
- Free guest book and video library
- Private car parking • Wedding parties especially welcome • Full central heating • Secure storage area for walkers & cyclists • Choice of breakfast menu

The Moorings seafront location gives great views across the bay

The Moorings, 7 Mountstuart Road, Rothesay PA20 9DY
Tel: 01700 502277 • Mobile: 07810 515003
e-mail: fjhbute@aol.com
www.themoorings-bute.co.uk

SB

West Loch Hotel

By Tarbert
Loch Fyne
Argyll
PA29 6YF

Tel: 01880 820283
Fax: 01880 820930

An attractive, family-run, 18th century coaching inn of character, the West Loch Hotel is well situated for a relaxing holiday. It is renowned for outstanding food. After dining, guests can relax in front of an open fire, perhaps sampling some of the local malt whiskies. With glorious scenery, the area is excellent for hillwalking and enjoying the wide variety of wildlife. Visits to Islay, Jura, Arran and Gigha can be pleasant day trips, and attractions in the area include castles, distilleries, gardens and sandy beaches. Fishing, golf and boat hire are all available locally.

www.westlochhotel.co.uk • e-mail: westlochhotel@btinternet.com

Ayr

Ayrshire & Arran

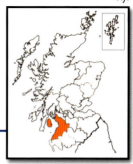

SB

Brodick, Kilmarnock, Largs

Borders

SB

The
Old School House
— TILLMOUTH —

Bed & Breakfast in a superb rural setting

Old school and headmaster's house, set in mature
gardens, sympathetically converted into a private
family home offering a friendly, warm welcome,
relaxing atmosphere and home cooking.
Situated perfectly for excursions in Northumberland
and the Scottish Borders. Tastefully furnished
double suite with its own private stairs and bathroom,
and a ground floor single suite with
the same level of comfort.

Judith Hodgson, The Old School House, Tillmouth,
Cornhill-on-Tweed, Northumberland TD12 4UT
Telephone : 01890 882463
e-mail : noelhodgson@btinternet.com
www.tillmouthschoolhouse.co.uk

Covering about eighteen hundred miles, The Scottish Borders stretch from the rolling hills and moorland in the west, through gentler valleys to the rich agricultural plains of the east, and the rocky Berwickshire coastline with its secluded coves and picturesque fishing villages. Through the centre, tracing a silvery course from the hills to the sea, runs the River Tweed which provides some of the best fishing in Scotland. As well as fishing there is golf – 18 courses in all, riding or cycling and some of the best modern sports centres and swimming pools in the country. Friendly towns and charming villages are there to be discovered, while castles, abbeys, stately homes and museums illustrate the exciting and often bloody history of the area. It's this history which is commemorated in the Common Ridings and other local festivals, creating a colourful pageant much enjoyed by visitors and native Borderers alike.

SB

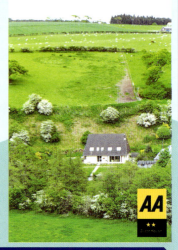

Castle Douglas

Dumfries & Galloway

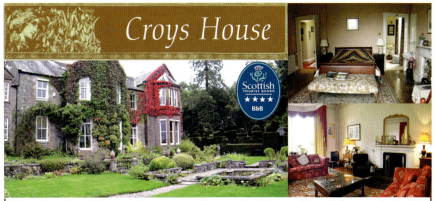

Croys House

Croys is an elegant Georgian House lying in 35 acres of parkland and beautiful gardens in the Urr Valley, three miles from Castle Douglas and close to the famous Threave Gardens. Watersports and fishing are available at nearby Loch Ken, and golf at Southerness, only 30 minutes away. Accommodation consists of two double rooms, one en suite, one four-poster with private bathroom, and one twin room. There is a large comfortable lounge with open fireplace (and log fires in cold weather), and a formal dining room. Breakfasts, and evening meals if required, include fresh produce from the garden. Vegetarian meals available on request.

Croys House, Bridge of Urr, Castle Douglas DG7 3EX
Tel: +44 (0)1556 650237 • Fax: +44 (0)1556 650561
e-mail: alanwithall@aol.com • www.croys-house.co.uk

Dumfries & Galloway is a mixture of high moorland and sheltered glens, and presents abundant opportunities for hill walking, rambling, fishing for salmon and sea trout, cycling, bird watching and field sports. There are at least 32 golf courses, ranging from the challenging Stranraer course at Creachmore to the scenic, clifftop course at Portpatrick. The Stranraer course has the distinction of being the last course designed by James Braid. The warming influence of the Gulf Stream ensures a mild climate which makes touring a pleasure, and many visitors come here to visit the dozens of interesting castles, gardens, museums and historic sites. In addition, pony trekking and riding plus a never-ending succession of ceilidhs, village fairs, country dances, classical music concerts and children's entertainment guarantee plenty of scope for enjoyment.

"Four Oaks" Bed & Breakfast

Canonbie
Dumfriesshire
DG14 0TF
Tel: **01387 371329**
camon@onebillinternet.co.uk
www.4-oaks.co.uk

Enjoy Bed and Breakfast accommodation in a comfortable, peaceful family-run home with open views of lovely rolling countryside and farm land. Near the village of Canonbie off the A7 just north of Carlisle, this is an excellent base for touring the beautiful Borderlands, with good fishing in the area.

The accommodation is in en suite twin and double rooms with tea and coffee facilities and TV. There is also private lounge with TV.

We have half an acre of enclosed garden surrounded by fields, and ample car parking space. £27-£29pppn.

Aston Hotel

The Crichton, Bankend Road, Dumfries DG1 4ZZ
Tel: **01387 272410** • Fax: **01387 267303**
golf@astonhoteldumfries.co.uk • **www.astonhotels.co.uk**

Ideal venue for Short Breaks

The Aston Hotel is located on the Crichton Estate, which extends to over 100 acres. With 71 de luxe bedrooms, we offer Scottish hospitality in an atmosphere of luxurious simplicity.
The Crichton Golf Course is directly opposite the hotel and transport to and from courses can be arranged.

Stranraer

Bathgate

Edinburgh & Lothians

This 17th century farmhouse is situated two miles from M8 Junction 4, which is midway between Glasgow and Edinburgh. This peaceful location overlooks panoramic views of the countryside. All rooms are on the ground floor, ideal for disabled visitors, and have central heating, colour TV and tea/coffee making facilities. We are within easy reach of golf, fishing, cycling (15 mile cycle track runs along back of property).

Scottish
TOURIST BOARD
★★★
B&B

SB

Ample security parking.
Open January to December.
Children and pets by arrangement

Twin Room from £44-£55,
Family Room £60-£80

**Mrs F. Gibb, Tarrareoch Farm,
Station Road, Armadale,
Near Bathgate EH48 3BJ
Tel: 01501 730404
nicola@gibb0209.fsnet.co.uk**

In the area known as Edinburgh & The Lothians, Scotland's capital is home to a wide range of attractions offering something for visitors of all ages. The Royal Mile holds many of the most historic sights, but within a short distance there are fine gardens to visit or the chance to sample the latest in interactive technology. A network of signposted paths allow walkers of all abilities to enjoy the contrasts of the area, whether for a leisurely stroll or at a more energetic pace. The annual Festival in August is part of the city's tradition and visitors flock to enjoy the performing arts, theatre, ballet, cinema and music, and of course "The Tattoo" itself. At the Festival Fringe there are free shows and impromptu acts, a jazz festival and book festivals. East Lothian has beautiful countryside and dramatic coastline, all only a short distance from Edinburgh. Once thriving fishing villages, North Berwick and Dunbar now cater for visitors who delight in their traditional seaside charm.

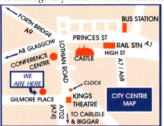

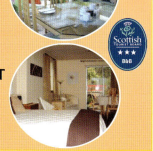

Fife

THE PEAT INN
RESTAURANT WITH ROOMS

Beautiful 5 Star restaurant with rooms situated just 6 miles from St Andrews in the village named after the Inn.

The restaurant has earned an international reputation over 30 years offering fresh Scottish produce, creativity and value, and is consistently voted one of the best restaurants in Scotland. A few steps away is 'The Residence', with 8 individual luxury suites, offering peace and comfort of the best of small country house hotels, but with a convivial and unpretentious atmosphere.

Peat Inn, by St Andrews, Fife KY15 5LH
Tel: 01334 840206 • Fax: 01334 840530
e-mail: stay@thepeatinn.co.uk
www.thepeatinn.co.uk

Fife - whether as 'County', 'Region' or more traditionally 'Kingdom', this has always been a prosperous part of Scotland. The coast, with small ports such as Crail, Anstruther, Pittenweem, St Monance, Elie and the more commercial Methil, Burntisland and Kirkcaldy, has always been interesting and important. St Andrews with its university, castle, cathedral and golf, is the best known and most visited town. Dunfermline has a historic past with many royal associations and was the birthplace of the philanthropist, Andrew Carnegie.Cupar, Falkland, Kinross (for Loch Leven), Auchtermuchty and Leuchars are amongst the many other historic sites in Fife, and at North Queensferry is one of Fife's most popular attractions, Deep Sea World.

SB

Meldrums Hotel
Ceres, By Cupar, Fife KY15 5NA

Nestled by the Ceres Burn in the charming village of Ceres, only 6 miles from St Andrews, the Home of Golf. Meldrums is surrounded by a vast selection of world class courses. Visitors can enjoy all levels of rounds, from a relaxing 9 holes to the toughest of the links courses.

- 7 en suite rooms • Private parking • B&B from £48
- Family restaurant serving breakfast, lunch, dinner, and Sunday high tea.

Tel: 01334 828286 • Fax: 01334 828795

www.meldrums-hotel.co.uk • meldrumshotel@btconnect.com

Fernie Castle Hotel

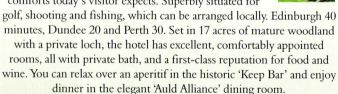

Fernie Castle is in a superb location for anyone visiting Scotland. This 450 year old castle can offer all the character of the past with the comforts today's visitor expects. Superbly situated for golf, shooting and fishing, which can be arranged locally. Edinburgh 40 minutes, Dundee 20 and Perth 30. Set in 17 acres of mature woodland with a private loch, the hotel has excellent, comfortably appointed rooms, all with private bath, and a first-class reputation for food and wine. You can relax over an aperitif in the historic 'Keep Bar' and enjoy dinner in the elegant 'Auld Alliance' dining room.

Letham, Near Cupar, Fife KY15 7RU
Tel: 01337 810381 • Fax: 01337 810422

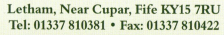

mail@ferniecastle.demon.co.uk
www.ferniecastle.demon.co.uk

Only two miles from St Andrews on the picturesque A917 road to Crail, Spinkstown is a uniquely designed farmhouse with views of the sea and surrounding countryside. Bright and spacious, it is furnished to a high standard.

Accommodation consists of double and twin rooms, all en suite, with tea/coffee making facilities and colour TV; diningroom and lounge. Substantial farmhouse breakfast to set you up for the day.

The famous Old Course, historic St Andrews and several National Trust properties are all within easy reach, as well as swimming, tennis, putting, bowls, horse riding, country parks, nature reserves, beaches and coastal walks.

Plenty of parking available. Bed and Breakfast from £33.

Mrs Anne Duncan,
Spinkstown Farmhouse,
St Andrews KY16 8PN
Tel & Fax: 01334 473475
e-mail:
admin@spinkstown.com
www.spinkstown.com

Glasgow & District

symbols

 Totally non-smoking

 Pets Welcome

 Children Welcome

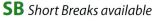 *Short Breaks available*

 Suitable for Disabled Guests

 Licensed

Highlands

•We are a family-run guest house situated in the Highland village of Ballachulish. Set on the shores of Loch Leven and only one mile from the majesty of Glencoe, Ballachulish makes an ideal centre for exploring much of Scotland's natural beauty. Attractions in and around Glencoe, Fort William, Oban, Skye, Mull, Loch Ness, Loch Lomond and many others are easily accessible.

Imposing craggy mountains, beautiful lochs, waterfalls and forestry can all be found locally and wildlife such as seals, dolphins, otters, deer, pine-martens and eagles thrive.There are a multitude of beautiful and interesting walks, from strolls to view historic Glencoe or around the Lochan trails to mainland Britain's most challenging mountain ridge - Glencoe's Aonach Eagach (The Notched Ridge).

•All of our rooms have en suite facilities, colour TV, DVD player, hospitality tray and individually controlled room heaters.

•We have a comfortable guest lounge, snack bar, separate dining room, drying room, bike store and large car park.

•We can also offer our guests wi-fi internet and access to leisure facilities including a swimming pool, jacuzzi, sauna and gym.

•Easy to find, next door to the Tourist Information Centre.

•B&B from £20.

Mike and Christine Richardson
Strathassynt Guest House, Loanfern,
Ballachulish, Near Glencoe PH49 4JB
Tel: 01855 811261
e-mail: info@strathassynt.com
www.strathassynt.com

Sunnyholm Guest House

is situated in a large mature, secluded garden in a pleasant residential area within six or seven minutes walking distance of the town centre, tourist information office and all essential holiday amenities.

 The front of the house overlooks the garden, with the rear allowing easy access to guests' private parking.

All rooms are ground floor level and bedrooms are all en suite with colour TV, tea/coffee making facilities, hairdryers, central heating and double glazing. The lounge is a spacious tastefully furnished room with bay window overlooking the garden, as is the diningroom which overlooks the conservatory and garden beyond.

Double/Twin from £30pppn,
Single from £40pppn.

**Mrs A. Gordon, Sunnyholm Guest House,
12 Mayfield Road, Inverness IV2 4AE
01463 231336 • e-mail: sunnyholm@aol.com
www.invernessguesthouse.com**

Kingussie, Kinlochbervie

A former hunting lodge situated within two acres of private grounds, Ardselma has magnificent views of the Cairngorm Mountains. Accommodation comprises two family and one double en suite rooms, one twin room with private facilities, and one single and one twin room with shared facilities. TV lounge available with tea/coffee making facilities; central heating. A three minute walk to the high street or to the golf course.

• Groups catered for, discounts available
• Children and pets welcome • Safe cycle storage
• Bed and Breakfast from £25pppn.

Valerie J. Johnston, Ardselma, The Crescent,
Kingussie PH21 1JZ • Mobile: 07786 696384
e-mail: valerieardselma@aol.com
www.kingussiebedandbreakfast.co.uk

Ardselma

The *Kinlochbervie Hotel*

Pet-friendly and friendly family-run hotel situated in one of the most stunning areas on the North West coast of Scotland, with views of open seas, surrounding majestic hills and unforgettable sunsets.

Supremely comfortable guest rooms, some with sea views, from £35 per person for bed & breakfast. Self-catering available.

Kinlochbervie, By Lairg, Sutherland IV27 4RP
Tel: 01971 521275 • Fax: 01971 521438
e-mail: info@kinlochberviehotel.com
www.kinlochberviehotel.com

Polcraig Guest House

SB

nestles on the hillside, centrally in Lochinver village. Family-run, with six very comfortable en suite bedrooms (three twin and three double). Each room is equipped with tea/coffee tray, colour TV, hairdryer and shaving point. Wireless Internet access available.

Enjoy hearty breakfasts in our dining room, with local produce used whenever possible. Generous helpings of fresh salmon, smoked haddock, sausage, bacon, eggs and black pudding will set you up nicely for the day ahead. The area is a paradise for anglers (permits available), climbers, walkers, birdwatchers and photographers. Drying area. Car park.

Mr C. MacLeod,
Polcraig Guest House, Lochinver IV27 4LD
Tel & Fax: 01571 844429
e-mail: cathelmac@aol.com
www.smoothhound.co.uk/hotels/polcraig.html

**Nethy Bridge
Inverness-shire
PH25 3DF**

Located in quiet woodland on the edge of Nethy Bridge, near Aviemore, in the heart of Scotland's beautiful Strathspey (Speyside) country and with the Cairngorm mountains on our doorstep, we can offer you ideal accommodation for enjoying the full range of outdoor recreation available in the Scottish Highlands. Both you and your pets are welcome.
If walking, cars can be parked free at Mondhuie while walking the Speyside Way.

We offer a very personal and friendly bed and breakfast facility in our home. An evening meal is also an option. You are invited to share our home, and our pets, with us and we will do everything we can to make your stay comfortable and enjoyable.

David & June Mondhuie
Tel: 01479 821 062

E-mail: david@mondhuie.com • www.mondhuie.com

Roy and Margaret King
Alvey House, Golf Course Road
Newtonmore
SB **Inverness-shire PH20 1AT**
01540 673260
e-mail: enquiries@alveyhouse.co.uk

Alvey House

Situated in the traditional Highland village of
Newtonmore, our hotel provides first class accommodation
and excellent meals, in a very relaxing environment.
The hotel is set in an acre of gardens with ample parking for
all guests, but only a few minutes walk from the village.
Newtonmore is just south of Aviemore and lies within the
border of the new Cairngorms National Park. No other area
of the UK offers such a wealth of things to do and see in such
fabulous mountain scenery and with activities on offer at all
levels of ability. What ever you like to do to offset the day-to-
day stresses and strains of life - touring and sightseeing,
walking, skiing, golf, cycling, water sports, pony trekking or
maybe just relaxing with a good book - you will return to an
excellent meal and a peaceful evening at Alvey House.

www.alveyhouse.co.uk

Tom-na-Creige
BED & BREAKFAST

Onich/North Ballachulish,
Near Fort William PH33 6RY
01855 821 547
e-mail: info@tom-na-creige.co.uk

Located in Onich, on the edge of Glencoe
and just south of Fort William, the house
overlooks Loch Linnhe and offers stunning
views of Glencoe to the east and the Isle of
Mull to the west.

Tom-na-Creige is open all year and is an ideal stop-over for Skye, Mull and the Road to the
Isles and a perfect base for enjoying the many activities the area has to offer, whether it be
walking, climbing, mountain biking, watersports, fishing or sightseeing. Ben Nevis is located
just to the north, offering skiing in the winter months, and the historic town of Fort William
is only a short drive away. Onich is also the location of the Corran Ferry, for trips to the Isle
of Mull, the Morvern Hills and the wilds of the Ardnamurchan peninsula. And with such a lot
to see and do, our hearty full Scottish or vegetarian breakfasts will be just what
you need to keep you going for the day!

• We operate a quiet policy at Tom-na-Creige so there are no TVs in the
bedrooms but a large screen Sky TV is available to view in the lounge.

• Broadband connection is available

• We can provide a laundry service if required.

Thurso

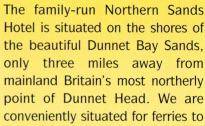

The family-run Northern Sands Hotel is situated on the shores of the beautiful Dunnet Bay Sands, only three miles away from mainland Britain's most northerly point of Dunnet Head. We are conveniently situated for ferries to the Orkney Isles at Gills Bay and Scrabster. The Castle of Mey and John O' Groats are also close by.

The Hotel has 12 comfortable en suite rooms, and public and lounge bars as well as our restaurant, which is known for being one of the finest in the north, featuring finest local produce cooked fresh for you.

The Northern Sands Hotel
Dunnet, Caithness KW14 8XD
Tel: 01847 851270 • Fax: 01847 851626
www.northernsands.co.uk
e-mail: northernsands@btinternet.com

Biggar

Lanarkshire

WALSTON MANSION FARMHOUSE

SB

Welcome to Walston Mansion Farmhouse, well known for its real home-from-home atmosphere, where guests return year after year. There is a hearty breakfast menu and delicious evening meals, using home produced meat, eggs, organic vegetables and freshly baked bread. All room have TV/video and tea/coffee making; there is a children's toy cupboard and lots of small animals to see. Pets by arrangement. In lovely walking area and an ideal touring base for the Scottish Borders and Clyde Valley; Edinburgh 24 miles, Glasgow 30 miles. Terms from £23 standard, £25 en suite.

**For details contact: Margaret Kirby, Walston, Carnwath, By Biggar ML11 8NF
Tel: 01899 810338 • Fax: 01899 810334
e-mail: margaret.kirby@walstonmansion.co.uk • www.walstonmansion.co.uk**

Lesmahagow

A modern farmhouse bungalow on Dykecroft Farm, set in lovely surroundings in a rural area on the B7086 (old A726) and within easy reach of the M74, making it the ideal stop between north and south; also convenient for Glasgow and Prestwick airports. Centrally situated for touring Glasgow, Edinburgh, Ayr, Stirling and New Lanark - all within one hour's drive. Nearby is Strathclyde Country Park with all watersports activities; other sporting facilities within two miles include sports centre, golf, fishing, quad bikes, rifle and clay pigeon shooting, and swimming. Guests will enjoy the open fires in our TV lounge and the good breakfasts; TV and tea making facilities in all rooms. A warm and friendly welcome awaits all guests.

Dykecroft Farm

Kirkmuirhill, Lesmahagow ML11 0JQ
e-mail: Dykecroft.bandb@tiscali.co.uk

Tel & Fax: 01555 892226
www.Dykecroftfarm.co.uk

Crianlarich

Perth & Kinross

Set just outside the village of Crianlarich, Inverardran House is sited in an elevated position with views across Strathfillan to Ben Challum.
This property offers excellent fishing, walking and touring prospects.
We can offer you Bed and Breakfast accommodation for up to nine people in two double rooms and one twin (all en suite) and one triple room with a private bathroom.
Tea/coffee making facilities in the rooms. Self-catering cottage also available.
Open all year • Prices from £23 to £26 per person per night based on two sharing, £8 surcharge for a single person. Discounts for longer stays
Evening meals and packed lunches on request.

John and Janice Christie, Inverardran House, Crianlarich FK20 8QS
Tel: 01838 300240 • e-mail: janice@inverardran.demon.co.uk
www.inverardran.demon.co.uk

Inverardran

Scottish
TOURIST BOARD
★★★
GUEST
HOUSE

Perth & Kinross embraces both Highland and Lowland. Close to where the two Scotlands meet, a cluster of little resort towns has grown up: Crieff, Comrie, Dunkeld, Aberfeldy, and Pitlochry, set, some say, right in the very centre of Scotland. Perthshire touring is a special delight, as north-south hill roads drop into long loch-filled glens - Loch Rannoch, Loch Tay or Loch Earn, for example. No matter where you base yourself, from Kinross by Loch Leven to the south to Blairgowrie by the berryfields on the edge of Strathmore, you can be sure to find a string of interesting places to visit. If your tastes run to nature wild, rather than tamed in gardens, then Perthshire offers not only the delights of Caledonian pinewoods by Rannoch and the alpine flowers of the Lawers range, but also wildlife spectacle such as nesting ospreys at Loch of the Lowes by Dunkeld. The main town of Perth has plenty of shops with High Street names as well as specialist outlets selling everything from Scottish crafts to local pearls. With attractions including an excellent repertory theatre and a great choice of eating places, this is an ideal base to explore the true heartland of Scotland.

Stanley

Newmill Farm

Stanley PH1 4QD
Mrs Ann Guthrie • 01738 828281
e-mail: guthrienewmill@sol.co.uk
www.newmillfarm.co.uk

This 330 acre farm is situated on the A9, six miles north of Perth. Accommodation comprises twin and double en suite rooms and a family room with private bathroom; lounge, sittingroom, diningroom; bathroom, shower room and toilet. Bed and Breakfast from £25.
The warm welcome and supper of excellent home baking are inclusive. Reductions and facilities for children. Pets accepted. Ample car parking area. Excellent local restaurants nearby.

The numerous castles and historic ruins around Perth are testimony to Scotland's turbulent past. Situated in the area known as "The Gateway to the Highlands" the farm is ideally placed for those seeking some of the best unspoilt scenery in Western Europe. Many famous golf courses and trout rivers in the Perth area. If walking or cycling are your interests, there are plenty of routes around the farm that are worth exploring to enjoy the views.

Stirling & The Trossachs

Callander

Riverview House

Leny Road, Callander FK17 8AL
Tel: 01877 330635

SB

Excellent accommodation in the Trossachs area which forms the most beautiful part of Scotland's first National Park. Ideal centre for walking and cycling holidays, with cycle storage available. In the guest house all rooms are en suite, with TV and tea-making. Private parking. Also available self-catering stone cottages, sleep 3 or 4. Sorry, no smoking and no pets. Call Drew or Kathleen Little for details.
e-mail: drew@visitcallander.co.uk
website: www.visitcallander.co.uk
B&B from £30.
Low season and long stay discounts available.
Self-catering cottages from £150 per week
(STB 3 & 4 Stars).

Strathyre

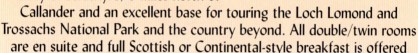

At the heart of Scotland, Stirling & The Trossachs has played a central role in most aspects of the nation's life. History and geography have converged here in road and rail routes, in decisive sieges and battles, in important industrial developments and heritage. The county enjoys the natural riches of the Forth valley and the economic wealth of Grangemouth and Falkirk. The town of Stirling itself is a natural tourist centre, both for its own attractions, such as the historic castle and the excellent shopping facilities, and as a base for other visitor attractions close at hand. Villages and small towns such as Drymen, Killearn, Fintry and Kippen offer hospitality and interesting outings. Loch Lomond and The Trossachs National Park is less than an hour from Glasgow, yet feels worlds apart from the bustle of city life. Explore wild glens and sparkling lochs, and for the more energetic, low-level walking, cycling, and hill walking can be enjoyed.

Loch Harray (Orkney)

Scottish Islands

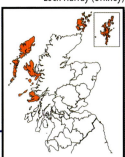

Merkister Hotel

Away from it all in the truest sense, this fine hotel provides a wonderful opportunity to commune with nature in peaceful surroundings and enjoy some of the best loch fishing in Britain and, what is more, the cuisine is really out of this world.

Guest rooms are delightfully furnished; all have en suite facilities, colour TV, direct-dial telephone, tea-makers and appointments that would shame many a 5-star establishment. Standing on the shores of Harray Loch, the emphasis here, naturally enough, is on fishing and many major events are held. Novices are welcomed and boats, outboards and ghillies may be arranged. The views from the hotel are breathtaking and other activities available include golf, squash and rock climbing.

**Loch Harray, Orkney KW17 2LF
Tel: 01856 771366 • Fax: 01856 771515
merkister-hotel@ecosse.net • www.merkister.com**

**Readers are requested to mention this FHG guide
when seeking accommodation**

Please note...

REDBURN HOUSE
Lochmaddy, North Uist

Redburn House is a Bed and Breakfast establishment in Lochmaddy, the main township of the wonderful Hebridean Isle of North Uist. Redburn House offers four en suite Bed and Breakfast rooms, a self-catering cottage (the Boat House), a self-catering annexe (the Studio) and a large self-catering Apartment.

Redburn House has recently undergone extensive renovation which has transformed it into the warm, cosy, clean and modern guesthouse it is now.

It is ideally located close to the post office, pub, Arts Centre, Sailing Club, Outdoor Centre, shop, Tourist Information Centre and Ferry Terminal.

Contact Donna at info@redburnhouse.com Tel/Fax: 01876 500301 or Redburn House, Lochmaddy, Isle of North Uist, Western Isles HS6 5AA www.redburnhouse.com

Glenlivet

Aberdeen, Banff & Moray

Reaching out into the North Sea from the Moray Firth in the north, extending south past Royal Deeside and dominated by the Grampian Highlands to the west, Aberdeenshire, Banff and Moray present a wonderful combination of countryside, coast and heritage for the holidaymaker to explore. Easily accessible from Aberdeen, where there are all the attractions of city life, this is an ideal corner of the country for an interesting and relaxing break. Why not follow one of the five tourist trails to see the spectacular scenery and learn more about the area at the same time? On the Victorian Heritage Trail follow in the footsteps of Queen Victoria to Royal Deeside to reach the best-known castle of all, Balmoral, visiting many of her favourite towns and viewpoints on the way. Golfers have 45 inland courses to choose from, some long-established, others more modern developments, like Inchmarlo, as well as the championship links. Aberdeen, a university city of sparkling granite buildings, has museums, art galleries, theatres, films and superb shopping, as well as beaches, golf and fishing.

Johnshaven

Angus & Dundee

Brawliemuir Holiday Cottages Kincardineshire

Two delightful stone-built cottages situated in a lovely country setting yet only three miles from the sea. Both cottages have central heating and are fully equipped to a high standard. Towels and bed linen included. This is a great base for exploring the Angus Glens, the Mearns countryside, the Castle Trail and the granite city of Aberdeen. Golf, fishing, horse riding, hill walking and a great beach are all nearby.

No smoking. Pets welcome. Available all year from £280 to £485 per week

Telephone Carole Duvall on **01561 362453** *or e-mail for further information.*

e-mail: carole@the-duvalls.com • www.brawliemuircottages.co.uk

SB

The Firth of Tay and westwards from the North Sea coast towards the highlands of the Cairngorm National Park, lies the former Pictish stronghold of Angus, its historic burghs and villages and the university city of Dundee. The marine and industrial heritage of this lively city, the quiet glens and hills inland, the rivers and coast, all with a wide range of outdoor pursuits on hand, make this an ideal destination. The area is renowned for golf, and with 50 golf courses within 30 miles of Dundee, from classic links like Carnoustie to the heathland at Edzell in the north, it's a golfers' dream. In Dundee at Discovery Point is the home of the RRS Discovery, the ship that took Captain Scott on his ill-fated journey to the Antarctic. The story of the jute industry, on which the wealth of the city was built, is retold at the Verdant Works. But this city formerly associated with jute, jam and journalism now looks to the future too at the Sensation Science Centre, where everyone can experiment with interactive exhibits involving robotics, cybernetics and even keyhole surgery.

Appin

Argyll & Bute

Campbeltown, Dalmally

Dalmally, Inveraray

Blarghour Farm

SB

**Loch Awe-side,
by Dalmally,
Argyll PA33 1BW
Tel: 01866 833246
Fax: 01866 833338**

At Blarghour Farm, by the shores of lovely Loch Awe, one may choose from four well equipped and comfortable holiday cottages sleeping from two to six people.

Kitchens are well appointed, lounges tastefully decorated and furnished with TV and gas fire, beds are made up and towels supplied, while the two larger houses have shower rooms in addition to bathrooms, all with shaver point.

The two larger houses are suitable for children and have cots and high chairs. Open all year with Short Breaks welcomed 29th October to end March. Non-smoking. No pets are allowed.

Centrally situated for touring. Illustrated brochure on request.

ASSC

**e-mail: blarghour@btconnect.com
www.self-catering-argyll.co.uk**

19th century Minard Castle beside Loch Fyne is a peaceful location for a quiet break. Stroll in the grounds, walk by the loch, explore the woods, or tour this scenic area with lochs, hills, gardens, castles and historic sites.

SB

THE LODGE • a comfortable bungalow with small garden and view through trees to the loch, sleeps 4-6.
THE MEWS APARTMENT • sleeps 4-5.
• Well equipped; central heating, hot water, electricity, linen and towels included.
• Terms £140 to £390 per week. Open all year.

Minard Castle
SELF-CATERING
**Minard, Inveraray PA32 8YB
Tel & Fax: 01546 886272
reinoldgayre@minardcastle.com
www.minardcastle.com**

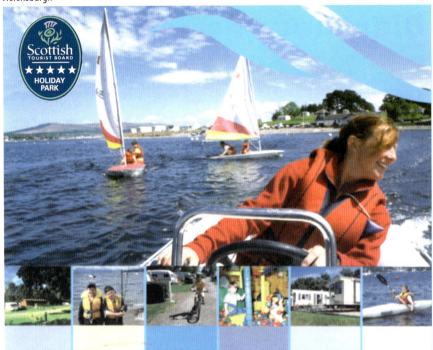

ROSNEATH CASTLE PARK
SO NEAR... YET SO FAR AWAY

Rosneath Castle Park has everything to offer if you are looking for a relaxing holiday. No more than an hour's drive from Glasgow, the 57 acres that the park occupies along the shore of Gareloch offer the perfect opportunity to relax and discover another world, and another you.

Thistle Awarded Luxury Self-Catering Holiday Homes with superb views. In a beautiful setting with first class facilities including an adventure playground, boat house, fun club, restaurant and bar, there's no end to the reasons why you would 'wish you were here'.

Rosneath Castle Park, Rosneath,
Near Helensburgh, Argyll G84 0QS
Tel: (01436) 831208
Fax: (01436) 831978
enquiries@rosneathcastle.demon.co.uk
www.rosneathcastle.co.uk

Halftown Cottages • St Catherine's •Argyll

In the heart of the West Highlands.
55 miles from Glasgow and across Loch Fyne from Inveraray.
Two radically modernised 18thC farm cottages.
Wholly secluded woodland site just above the loch.
A real 'chill out' place for humans and animals.
Extensive woodland, lochside and hillside walking.
Nearby top class restaurants. Extensive day touring. Beach BBQs.

Tel: 01369 860750 or book direct on
www.argyllcottages.com

Duntrune Castle Holiday Cottages

Five traditional self-catering cottages set in the spacious grounds of 12th century Duntrune Castle, which guards the entrance to Loch Crinan. All have been attractively modernised and accommodate two to five persons.

The estate comprises 5000 acres and five miles of coastline. Without leaving our land, you can enjoy easy or testing walks, sea or river fishing, and watching the abundant wildlife. Nearby are several riding establishments, a bicycle-hire firm, and a number of excellent restaurants.
Prices from £250 to £500 per week. Pets are welcome.

For further details please contact:
Robin Malcolm, Duntrune Castle,
Kilmartin, Argyll PA31 8QQ
01546 510283 • www.duntrune.com

Argyll & Bute is a wonderfully unspoilt area, historically the heartland of Scotland and home to a wealth of fascinating wildlife. Here you may be lucky enough to catch a glimpse of an eagle, a wildcat or an osprey, or even a fine antlered stag. On the upper reaches of Loch Caolisport can be found St Columba's Cave, and more recent times are illustrated at the Auchindrain Highland Township south of Inveraray, a friendly little town with plenty to see, including the Jail, Wildlife Park and Maritime Museum. Bute is the most accessible of the west coast islands, and Rothesay is its main town. Explore the dungeons and grand hall of Rothesay Castle, or visit the fascinating Bute Museum. The town offers a full range of leisure facilities, including a fine swimming pool and superb golf course.

SB

Inchmurrin Island
SELF-CATERING HOLIDAYS

Inchmurrin is the largest island on Loch Lomond and offers a unique experience. Three self-catering apartments, sleeping from four to six persons, and a detached cedar clad cottage sleeping eight, are available.

The well appointed apartments overlook the garden, jetties and the loch beyond. Inchmurrin is the ideal base for watersports and is situated on a working farm.

Terms from £407 to £850 per week, £281 TO £560 per half week.

A ferry service is provided for guests, and jetties are available for customers with their own boats. Come and stay and have the freedom to roam and explore anywhere on the island.

e-mail: scotts@inchmurrin-lochlomond.com
www.inchmurrin-lochlomond.com
Inchmurrin Island,
Loch Lomond G63 0JY
Tel: 01389 850245 • Fax: 01389 850513

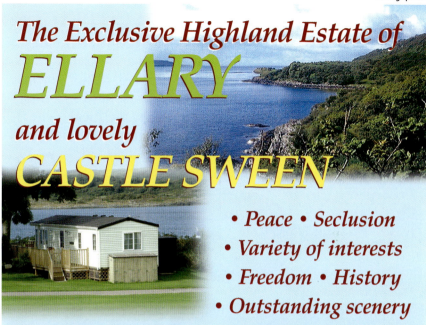

The Exclusive Highland Estate of
ELLARY
and lovely
CASTLE SWEEN

- *Peace • Seclusion*
- *Variety of interests*
- *Freedom • History*
- *Outstanding scenery*

This 15,000 acre Highland Estate lies in one of the most beautiful and unspoilt areas of Scotland and has a wealth of ancient historical associations within its bounds.

There is St Columba's Cave, one of the first places of Christian Worship in Britain, also Castle Sween, the oldest ruined castle in Scotland, and Kilmory Chapel where there is a fascinating collection of Celtic slabs. There is a wide range of accommodation, from small groups of cottages, many of the traditional stone-built estate type, to modern holiday chalets and super luxury caravans at Castle Sween.

Most of the cottages accommodate up to six, but one will take six/eight.

All units fully equipped except linen. Television reception is included.

Ellary is beautiful at all times of the year and is suitable for windsurfing, fishing, swimming, sailing and the observation of a wide variety of wildlife; there are paths and tracks throughout the estate for the visitor who prefers to explore on foot, and guests will find farmers and estate workers most helpful in their approach.

For further details, brochure and booking forms, please apply to:

ELLARY ESTATE OFFICE, by LOCHGILPHEAD, ARGYLL PA31 8PA

Tel: 01880 770232/770209
or 01546 850223
info@ellary.com
www.ellary.com

Oban

Taynuilt

SB

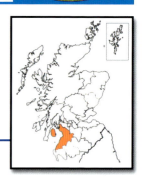
Ayrshire & Arran

Millport

SB

MILL HOUSE

Quality converted mill house sleeping 4 people on working farm, 3 miles from Jedburgh. Kitchen/dining room, 2 bedrooms, bathroom on ground floor. Large first floor living room with spectacular views across the Borders countryside. Excellent shops, restaurants and pubs in Jedburgh, with Edinburgh (50 miles) and Newcastle (60 miles) for further retail therapy. Millhouse is an ideal centre for exploring the Borders, sporting holidays or just chilling out in beautiful and peaceful surroundings.

Terms £290–£425 • Open all year • Bus three miles, airport 54 miles.

Mrs A. Fraser, Overwells, Jedburgh, Roxburghshire TD8 6LT
Telephone: 01835 863020 • Fax: 01835 864334
e-mail: abfraser@btinternet.com • www.overwells.co.uk

SB

£260-£430 per week.

Relax in your south-facing conservatory and enjoy the splendid view over the large secluded garden to the Cheviots. Nestle before a log fire in your clean, cosy, well equipped 4-Star cottage for two within the peace of Burnbrae. Within 40 minutes' drive of Edinburgh, fishing villages, superb coastal scenery, Borders towns, Cheviot and Ettrick Hills. Ideal for visiting a wealth of abbeys, gardens and stately homes. Fishing, walking, cycling, horse-riding and several golf courses nearby. Just 5km from Kelso with splendid square and abbey ruins.

• All on one level • Entirely non-smoking
• Free broadband wi-fi • Dogs welcome in one cottage only • Helpful proprietors live on site

SB

Burnbrae Holidays • Burnbrae Mill • Nenthorn • Kelso TD5 7RY • Tel: 01573 225570
e-mail: fhg@burnbraehol.co.uk • www.burnbraehol.co.uk

Plum Braes Barn Holidays

Self Catering Accommodation in the Scottish Borders and Edinburgh

Plum Tree Cottage • sleeps 2
A romantic cottage for two, beamed living room, Austrian Sleigh bed and beautiful views to the Cheviot hills.

Edmonston House • sleeps 6-10
chalet-style farmhouse, lounge with open fire. panoramic views over beautiful Border countryside.

Garden Bank • sleeps 4
all rooms on the ground floor, contemporary open plan living room.

Cockle Kitty • sleeps 4
The perfect place to stay, summer or winter. Sitting/dining room with Hemmel arch window.

Drummond St Apartment Edinburgh • sleeps 4+2
Situated in Old Town Edinburgh. A few minutes from The Royal Mile, Castle, etc.

All have barbecues, garden furniture, decking, Sky TV and internet connection. Beds are prepared for your arrival and towels are included. The cottages are off the beaten track yet only 3 miles from the bustling market town of Kelso.
The River Eden is a tributary of the River Tweed and meanders through Cliftonhill Farm.
Perfect for river walks, picnics and bird watching including kingfishers and the resident barn owls.
There is a new all-weather tennis court and coaching is available on request. In the area there is a great choice of golf courses, horse racing, Sunday Market, the Abbey walk way, coastal walks or quiet country roads for bike runs.
Explore Floors Castle and many other stately homes and their beautiful gardens.

Contact Maggie Stewart, Cliftonhill Farm, Kelso, Roxburghshire TD5 7QE
Tel: 01573 225028 • Mobile: 07789 220 468 • e-mail: maggie@kelsocottages.co.uk
www.kelsocottages.co.uk

Westwood House – Kelso

Overlooking Scotland's famous River Tweed
TOTAL "OFF LEAD" FREEDOM FOR DOGS
IN ENCLOSED AND SECLUDED GROUNDS

Renovated riverside cottage with
12 acres of paths, through walled
gardens and on own private island.
4 bedrooms sleeping 2-8 (+ child),
2 bathrooms, period features,
cosy log fire and centrally heated.
- Half mile Kelso town
- One hour Edinburgh/Newcastle
- Halfhour Berwick (station)
and Northumberland coast.

- 2 double bedrooms (one with en suite shower), 1 twin bedroom, 1 family bedroom with double and single bed.
- 1 bathroom and 1 downstairs cloakroom.
- 2 sitting rooms (both with TV).
- Dining room with table to seat 10.

Welcome Host

- Kitchen with dishwasher, fridge freezer and washer/dryer.
- An all inclusive holiday with linen and towels, electricity, central heating and trout fishing included.
- Dogs welcome free of charge.
- Cot and high chair also available.

2-person discounts available
Trout fishing also included

For brochure and tariff, from £385 per
week fully inclusive of all linen and
towels, electricity and heating, *contact:*

Debbie Crawford
Pippin Heath Farm,
Holt, Norfolk NR25 6SS
Tel: 07788 134 832

ACHIEVING GOLD IN
GREEN TOURISM AND
'HIGHLY COMMENDED'
IN SCOTTISH THISTLE AWARDS

Castle Douglas

Dumfries & Galloway

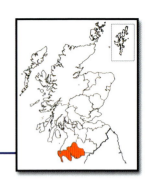

SB

An enchanting and peaceful "dark skies" holiday cabin ... with a difference.

A very well appointed and lavishly equipped log cabin with a touch of luxury • Nestling amongst trees in spectacular Galloway countryside in South West Scotland, visited daily by bird life and red squirrels • Sleeps 6 • Three bedrooms, two double (one en suite) and one twin • Bathroom • Log burner • Washer/dryer • Barbecue • All linen, fuel, use of bicycles included • Easy reach of market towns and Solway coast beaches • Pets by arrangement.

Contact John & Lesley Wykes, Cuckoo Stone St John's Town of Dalry, Castle Douglas DG7 3UA Tel: 01644 430375 e-mail: enquiries@cloudcuckoolodge.co.uk www.cloudcuckoolodge.co.uk

Dumfries & Galloway is a mixture of high moorland and sheltered glens, and presents abundant opportunities for hill walking, rambling, fishing for salmon and sea trout, cycling, bird watching and field sports. There are at least 32 golf courses, ranging from the challenging Stranraer course at Creachmore to the scenic, clifftop course at Portpatrick. The Stranraer course has the distinction of being the last course designed by James Braid. The warming influence of the Gulf Stream ensures a mild climate which makes touring a pleasure, and many visitors come here to visit the dozens of interesting castles, gardens, museums and historic sites. In addition, pony trekking and riding plus a never-ending succession of ceilidhs, village fairs, country dances, classical music concerts and children's entertainment guarantee plenty of scope for enjoyment.

barncrosh

farm

Self-catering
farm holiday
cottages in South West Scotland

SB

Whatever your interests, from family groups relaxing on holiday together, to outdoor enthusiasts relishing out-of-season activities, you will find so much to enjoy in the peaceful surroundings of Barncrosh, on our farm in the heart of Dumfries & Galloway.

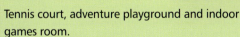

We offer a wide choice of self-catering holiday accommodation, sleeping from 2 people right up to 12. Many are ideal for holidays for disabled guests.

Tennis court, adventure playground and indoor games room.

Shops, pubs and restaurants in
Castle Douglas (4 miles) and Kirkcudbright (5 miles).

Barncrosh, Castle Douglas DG7 1TX
Tel: 01556 680 216 • Fax: 01556 680 442
e-mail: enquiries@barncrosh.co.uk
www.barncrosh.co.uk

Castle Douglas, Dalbeattie

AIRDS FARM

*Our two holiday homes, **Airdside** (3 Star) & **Airdsmill** (4 Star), catering for up to 5 and 8 persons respectively, are situated in the scenic and picturesque Galloway landscape overlooking Loch Ken.*

*Facilities in **Airdside** include washing machine, microwave, fridge, 28" TV and full central heating, while **Airdsmill** offers the additional luxury of dishwasher, range cooker, log fire, 32" TV and many other features in a spacious environment.*

All power, bed-linen and towels are supplied (Airdside heating is charged extra by oil meter).

Airds Farm, a short drive away from Castle Douglas and 30 minutes from Dumfries, is ideal for walkers, bird-watchers, fishermen and those wishing to escape from urban stresses.

Airds Farm also provides B&B.

Tricia & Alan Keith, Airds Farm, Crossmichael, Castle Douglas DG7 3BG
Tel: 01556 670418 • www.airds.com

BAREND HOLIDAY VILLAGE

SANDYHILLS, DALBEATTIE DG5 4NU

SB

Escape to the beautiful South West Colvend coast, the perfect base for walking, touring and cycling in Dumfries & Galloway, which is Scotland in miniature, and only one hour's drive from England.

Our chalets, situated only a short walk from Sandyhills beach, are well equipped and centrally heated for all year comfort. Pets welcome or pet-free. Their decks overlook our loch or Colvend 18-hole golf course, and the surrounding countryside teems with wildlife - red squirrels, badgers and deer are our neighbours.

On-site boules courts, bar, restaurant, sauna and indoor pool. Wifi internet access available.

3 days minimum: any day of entry, prices include linen and swimming. From £260 for four for 3 days.

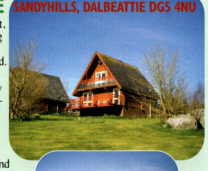

Tel: 01387 780663
www.barendholidayvillage.co.uk

Barend
HOLIDAY VILLAGE

Quote FHG50 for 5% discount

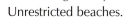

Portpatrick, Thornhill

SB

Dunskey Holiday Cottages are well equipped traditional comfortable country cottages, for those who love to experience the peace and tranquillity of glorious countryside by the sea. The picturesque harbour village of Portpatrick with its good pubs, restaurants, shops, etc is only 1½ miles away and Dunskey's own Glen Walks are located very close to the holiday cottages. Loch fishing, gardens and tearoom.
Blair Cottage sleeps 4 • Glen Cottage sleeps 5
Bed linen available to hire • Night store heaters throughout.
Log fires. • Short Breaks January to May
Mrs Orr Ewing, Dunskey House, Portpatrick DG9 8TJ
Tel: 01776 810211
info@dunskey.com • www.dunskey.com

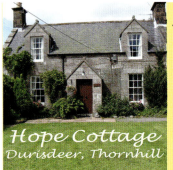

Hope Cottage
Durisdeer, Thornhill

Picturesque stone cottage in the peaceful conservation village of Durisdeer, the perfect place to relax and unwind. Plenty to do, see and explore in any weather for all the family. The nearby Solway coast with delightful towns like Kirkcudbright provides an alternative day out. If you fancy a day shopping or to get back to city life for a day, an hour in the car or train can get you to Edinburgh, Glasgow, Carlisle or Ayr. Comfortably furnished and equipped for 5/6 people with a large secluded garden. Towels, linen, heating and electricity included. Pets welcome.

For brochure telephone: Mrs S Stannett
01848 331510 • Fax: 01848 331810
e-mail: a.stann@btinternet.com • www.hopecottage.co.uk

Loch Lomond

Dunbartonshire

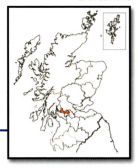

The Lorn Mill Cottages

Gartocharn, Loch Lomond
Dunbartonshire G83 8LX

Relax, unwind and recharge at The Lorn Mill - three peaceful
and pretty cottages within an 18th century water mill.
Tucked away in a secluded country estate overlooking
Loch Lomond, the cottages provide a unique four seasons
location in which to enjoy this gorgeous area of Scotland.
Tennis court with stunning views. Perfect for couples.
We look forward to welcoming you.

www.lornmill.com
e-mail: gavmac@globalnet.co.uk
Tel: 44 (0) 1389 753074

SB

The Gardeners Cottages
Arden, Loch Lomond

Secluded in the wooded grounds of Arden House by the shores of
Loch Lomond is the row of Gardeners Cottages, built as one side of
a magnificent Victorian walled garden.
Linnhe and **Lomond** are ideal for families or friends (sleeping 4 to 5
each), and **Luss** is a perfect hideaway for two. Only 6 miles from the picturesque village of
Luss and world famous Loch Lomond Golf Courses.
The cottages are warm, comfortable and full of character,
situated amidst breathtaking scenery.

The Gardeners Cottages, Loch Lomond G83 8RD
Tel/Fax 01389 850601
amacleod@gardeners-cottages.com
www.gardeners-cottages.com

SB

symbols

 Totally non-smoking

 Pets Welcome

 Children Welcome

SB *Short Breaks available*

 Suitable for Disabled Guests

 Licensed

Colinsburgh, Kirkcaldy, Pittenweem

Fife

East Neuk Cottage

Colinsburgh • Fife

Cottage to let in a conservation village in the attractive East Neuk of Fife, 3 miles from Elie and 11 from St Andrews.
Easy reach of sandy beaches, coastal walks and numerous golf courses.
Two bedrooms, lounge, kitchen/diner and a walled rear garden. Sleeps 4/5, pets welcome. Prices from £275 per week.

For further details, telephone
01788 890942 or see
www.eastneukcottage.co.uk

Kilrie Granary • Kilrie • Kirkcaldy • Fife KY2 5UW
Tel: 01592 269035 • Mobile 07801 465230
Newly renovated and refurbished Granary Cottage set in pretty gardens overlooking a loch set in farmland. Two-bedroom house with spacious kitchen/sitting area with TV, CD player, coffee-machine and dishwasher. Utility area with washing machine and microwave. One twin room, one family bedroom which could sleep 4-6, both en suite and decorated to a high standard. Cot available. There is a private driveway and plenty of room for parking.

e-mail: drumullion@gmail.com
www.kilriegranary.co.uk

Spindle Cottage
Pittenweem

The cottage comprises two doubles and a twin bedroom, bathroom and separate shower room, a beautiful living room with log-burning stove, and a lovely garden. Gas central heating, oven/hob, fridge/freezer and dishwasher, washing machine and tumble dryer, Freeview TV in the living room and all bedrooms, DVD player, broadband wireless internet access and telephone are all included. Maximum 4 guests only.

Ideally situated in the heart of the historic fishing village of Pittenweem on the Fife coast (East Neuk), only 10 miles from St Andrews and 45 miles from Edinburgh.

Sue Foan, 18 Cecil Avenue, Queens Park, Bournemouth BH8 9EH • Tel: 01202 257914
Mobile: 07977 467914 • www.spindlecottage.com • e-mail: sue@spindlecottage.com

Ardgay, Beauly

Highlands

Detached cottage, sleeps 5, standing in its own grounds with private parking.

Dornoch Cathedral (where Madonna and Guy Ritchie were married), Royal Dornoch Golf Course and beautiful safe sandy beaches only 14 miles away. Skibo Castle, Tain, Brora and Golspie golf courses all within easy reach.

Angling, mountain biking, hill walking, wildlife and forest walks available locally.

Tariff from £170 per week.

The cottage is clean, comfortable and well equipped. Immersion heater for hot water; open fires and electric fires in all rooms. No stairs.

Mrs M.C. MacLaren
The Poplars
Ardgay, Sutherland IV24 3BG • Telephone: 01863 766302

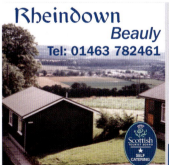

Rheindown
Beauly
Tel: 01463 782461

SB

Two self-catering chalets situated above and overlooking the village of Beauly with outstanding views of the river and surrounding hills. The chalets sleep two/six in two bedrooms, and a put-u-up in the living room. Fully equipped with full-sized cooker, fridge, microwave oven. Rheindown is a small working farm with breeding cows, sheep and poultry, and our friendly collie dog, Nell. Lots of country and hill walks. Beauly Pipe Band plays weekly in the square, with local children performing Highland dancing. Central for day trips to scenic areas in the north, south, east and west. Dolphins can often be seen from Fortrose in the Black Isle, eight miles away.

From £190-£275 per week.

Mrs M. M. Ritchie, Rheindown, Beauly IV4 7AB
e-mail: mm.ritchie@btopenworld.com

Tyndrum
Boat of Garten

Completely renovated, well furnished self-catering accommodation retaining the original pine panelling in the lounge.

Set in a rural village, Boat of Garten, in beautiful Strathspey, six miles from Aviemore, an ideal base for touring. Fishing is available locally on the River Spey, just two minutes away, with attractive riverside picnic spots. The famous Osprey nest is nearby, at Loch Garten RSPB Reserve.

Local steam train journeys, good golf and water sports; skiing at Cairngorm in season. Shop and pub half a mile.

Large lounge, attractive dining/sitting room, spacious fully fitted dining kitchen, shower room. First floor: bathroom, one double and one twin room, both with washbasin, and one single bedroom. Colour TV with Sky digital; dishwasher, microwave, washer/dryer and deep freeze. Electricity, bed linen and towels inclusive. Parking. Large garden.

Contact: Mrs N.C. Clark, Dochlaggie, Boat of Garten PH24 3BU
Tel: 01479 831242 • e-mail: dochlaggie99@aol.com

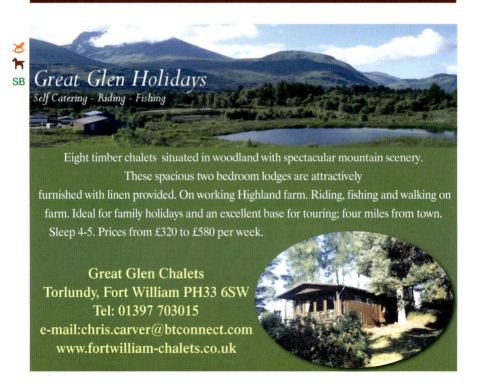

Great Glen Holidays
Self Catering - Riding - Fishing

Eight timber chalets situated in woodland with spectacular mountain scenery. These spacious two bedroom lodges are attractively furnished with linen provided. On working Highland farm. Riding, fishing and walking on farm. Ideal for family holidays and an excellent base for touring; four miles from town. Sleep 4-5. Prices from £320 to £580 per week.

Great Glen Chalets
Torlundy, Fort William PH33 6SW
Tel: 01397 703015
e-mail:chris.carver@btconnect.com
www.fortwilliam-chalets.co.uk

SB

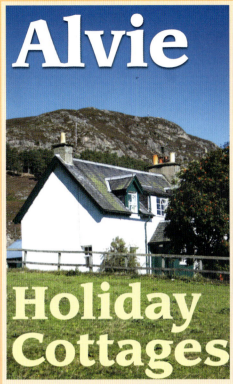

Alvie

Holiday Cottages

Situated amongst farm fields and woodland on a 13,000 acre Highland Estate. Located within the Cairngorm National Park, four miles south of Aviemore, Alvie can provide peace and quiet or an unsurpassed opportunity for recreation and activities. For details call **01540 651255** or see our website at ***www.alvie-estate.co.uk***
e-mail: info@alvie-estate.co.uk
Kincraig, Inverness-shire

Traditional cottages with superb views of the Cairngorms!

Alvie

BROOMVIEW and SUNSET

are situated in the quiet hamlet of Rhiroy on the south side of Loch Broom. These spacious properties with a homely atmosphere each have their own separate access. Broomview is on the ground floor, Sunset the upper.

Our accommodation offers comfort, peace and tranquillity in an area of unsurpassed beauty surrounded by open countryside overlooking picturesque Loch Broom, where panoramic views and spectacular sunsets can be seen. Idyllic location for bird watching, climbing, walking, fishing, photography, or just relaxing. A short drive away is the fishing village of Ullapool with its ferry terminal to the Western Isles.

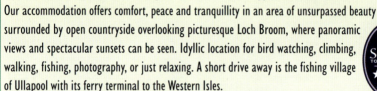

Prices from £210 to £410. For further information contact:

Mrs Linda Renwick, Spindrift, Keppoch Farm, Dundonnell, By Garve, Ross-shire IV23 2QR
Tel & Fax: 01854 633269 (Quote FHG)
e-mail: linda@lochbroomcottages.co.uk
www.lochbroomcottages.co.uk

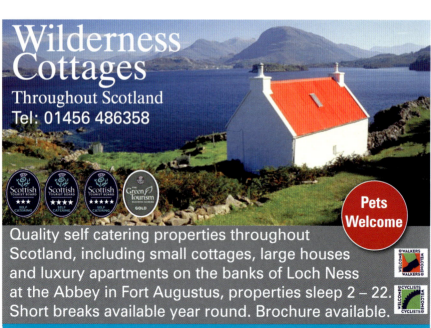

SB

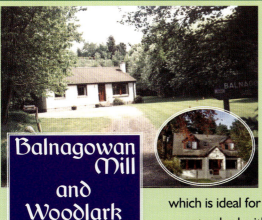

Spean Bridge

**Invergloy,
Spean Bridge
Inverness-shire
PH34 4DY**

Tel: 01397 712684

Riverside Lodges
...the ultimate Highland location

Set in 12 acres of grounds, just three uniquely designed lodges sleeping six comfortably. Private beach with free fishing, spectacular river gorge, specimen trees and plants. Ideal for all outdoor pursuits, or for just relaxing. Tariff from £460-£780 per week; discounts for small parties/long stay. Pets welcome. Linen included.
Open all year. Proprietors: Steve & Marilyn Dennis.

enquiries@riversidelodge.org.uk • www.riversidelodge.org.uk

Aberfeldy

Perth & Kinross

Perth & Kinross embraces both Highland and Lowland. Close to where the two Scotlands meet, a cluster of little resort towns has grown up: Crieff, Comrie, Dunkeld, Aberfeldy, and Pitlochry, set, some say, right in the very centre of Scotland. Perthshire touring is a special delight, as north-south hill roads drop into long loch-filled glens - Loch Rannoch, Loch Tay or Loch Earn, for example. No matter where you base yourself, from Kinross by Loch Leven to the south to Blairgowrie by the berryfields on the edge of Strathmore, you can be sure to find a string of interesting places to visit. If your tastes run to nature wild, rather than tamed in gardens, then Perthshire offers not only the delights of Caledonian pinewoods by Rannoch and the alpine flowers of the Lawers range, but also wildlife spectacle such as nesting ospreys at Loch of the Lowes by Dunkeld.

Aberfeldy, Blairgowrie

SB

LOCH TAY LODGES

Acharn, By Aberfeldy

This stone-built terrace houses six self catering lodges - three lodges sleep up to 4, two lodges sleep up to 6, one sleeps up to 8. They are fully equipped with colour television, washing machine, microwave, electric cooker & oven, and fridge. Bed linen, duvets and towels are all provided, electric blankets are also available. A separate drying area is available to hang up wet clothes or store bicycles. On the loch side 150 yards from the lodges there is access to a boat house to store sail boards, diving equipment and the like. A "starter pack' of groceries can be ordered from the village shop and will be delivered to your lodge prior to your arrival. Each lodge has own enclosed garden. Cots and highchairs available. Rates £230-£635.

Scottish TOURIST BOARD ★★★ SELF CATERING

Tel: 01887 830209
Fax: 01887 830802
e-mail: remony@btinternet.com
www.lochtaylodges.co.uk

ALTAMOUNT CHALETS

Set in mature grounds with majestic pines and abundant shrubs, bushes and flowers, the park achieves a blend of privacy and amenity 5 minutes' walk from Blairgowrie town centre. Set in the heart of beautiful Perthshire, Blairgowrie remains unspoilt and is an ideal touring centre for Perthshire and the Highlands in all seasons.

• **THE GLENISLA** 2 persons, One bedroom (double or 2 singles). •
• **THE GLENSHEE** 4 persons. Two bedrooms. (2 singles & 2 bunk beds). •
•**THE GLENESK** 6 persons. Three bedrooms. (1 double, 2 single & 2 bunk beds).

Coupar Angus Road, Blairgowrie, Perthshire PH10 6JN
Tel: 01250 872464 • www.crownparks.com
e-mail Tom & Sheila Smith on altamount@crownparks.com

AUCHAVAN STABLES, GLENISLA PH11 8QW

Contact: MRS GAMMELL, AUCHAVAN ESTATE
c/o LAGUNA HOUSE, MURTHLY, PERTH PH1 4HE

SB

Four Star stable conversion set in a quiet Highland glen, offering a very comfortable base to explore this peaceful area. Ideally placed to ski at Glenshee or for hillwalking or cycling from the doorstep in the Cairngorms National Park. Balmoral, Glamis and Blair Castles are a short drive as are no less than six fine golf courses. Shop and pub seven miles away. The house is non-smoking and comprises a spacious living room with open fire, large family room with open-plan dining and kitchen, utility room, 3 bedrooms (total of 8 beds), bathroom and shower room. Full oil CH, electricity and firewood along with bed linen and towels are included. Sat TV/ DVD/CD in both main rooms. Dog by arrangement. Prices £425-£800 weekly, Saturday to Saturday.

Tel: 01738 710440 • e-mail: sarah@thegammells.com

THE HAYLOFT AT AUCHAVAN, GLENISLA PH11 8QW

Contact: MRS GAMMELL, AUCHAVAN ESTATE
c/o LAGUNA HOUSE, MURTHLY, PERTH PH1 4HE

Five Star barn conversion set in a quiet Highland glen, offering a very **SB**
*comfortable hideaway in this peaceful area. Non-smoking adults-only
accommodation. Two double-bedded rooms, each en suite. Main
bathroom includes separate shower and leads to a sauna. Split-level
open-plan living room upstairs, gas cast-iron stove and kitchen/
dining downstairs with underfloor heating. Utility room and further
shower room. Electricity and gas along with bed linen and towels are
included. Satellite TV/DVD/CD in both rooms. Prices £360-£600.*

Tel: 01738 710440 • e-mail: sarah@thegammells.com

PRESNERB FARMHOUSE, GLENISLA PH11 8QW

Contact: MRS GAMMELL, AUCHAVAN ESTATE
c/o LAGUNA HOUSE, MURTHLY, PERTH PH1 4HE

Reputedly the oldest house in this quiet Highland glen, now fully **SB**
*modernised, offering a very cosy base to explore this peaceful area.
Ideally placed to ski at Glenshee or for hillwalking or cycling from the
doorstep in the Cairngorms National Park. Balmoral, Glamis and Blair
Castles are a short drive as are no less than six fine golf courses. Shop
and pub 7 miles away. The house is non-smoking and comprises a living room with wood burning stove, family
room with wood burning stove and open-plan dining and kitchen areas, utility room, 3 bedrooms, bathroom
and shower room. Full oil CH, electricity and firewood along with bed linen and towels are included. Sat
TV/DVD/CD in both main rooms. Dog by arrangement. Prices £382-£700 weekly, Saturday to Saturday.*

Tel: 01738 710440 • e-mail: sarah@thegammells.com

LAIGHWOOD HOLIDAYS
NEAR DUNKELD
For your comfort and enjoyment

We can provide properties from a large de luxe
house for eight to well-equipped cottages for two **SB**
to six, some open all year. All are accessible by
tarmac farm roads. Laighwood is centrally located
for sightseeing and for all country pursuits,
including golf, fishing and squash. Sorry, no pets.
Brochure on request from:

Laighwood Holidays, Laighwood, Dunkeld PH8 0HB.
Telephone: 01350 724241 • Fax: 01350 724212
e-mail: holidays@laighwood.co.uk • www.laighwood.co.uk

Visit the FHG website
www.holidayguides.com
for all kinds of holiday
acccommodation in Britain

Killin, Muthill

WESTER LIX

SB

At Wester Lix we offer two self contained properties both with their own unique character and style for that real "home from home" comfort. Wester Lix is set in a peaceful rural location surrounded by hills and overlooking our own private lochan.

We are three miles from Killin. Wester Lix is an excellent base for all outdoor activities including water sports, whilst also being ideally central for sightseeing.

Both Jonna's Cottage and The Farm House offer stylish accommodation for groups or families of 4 (5 by arrangement) with oil fired central heating and double glazing, wood burning stove/open fire and TV with Sky Digital. Jonna's has the addition of both bedrooms being en suite – plus it also offers a sauna as well as a private decking area with dining furniture. Well behaved pet, or pets are welcome by arrangement.

Gill and Dave Hunt, The Steading, Wester Lix, Killin, Perthshire FK21 8RD
Tel: 01567 820990 or 07747 862641
e-mail: gill@westerlix.co.uk • www.westerlix.co.uk

The Wee House   *A warm welcome awaits.....*

Self contained, 4 Star Holiday Cottage in Perthshire

The Wee House was originally the gardener's cottage and has been recently redesigned to provide the highest standard of comfort. Situated in the grounds of The Loaning, the Wee House lies a short walking distance from the historic village of Muthill in the picturesque Strathearn Valley. There are outstanding views across open fields to the market town of Crieff with a backdrop of the southern edge of the Grampian Mountains and Ben Chonzie – our local Munro!

An ideal centre for outdoor pursuits including golfing, fishing, sailing at Loch Earn, cycling, walking, rock climbing, pony trekking or the perfect hideaway for a romantic break in the Scottish Highlands.

SB

• Two twins or double bed with Egyptian cotton sheets • Shower and bath • Central heating • Patio with barbeque facilities
• Dishwasher, washing machine, microwave, full cooker • Flat-screen TV and DVD player • CD player • Welcome hamper
Alistair & Fiona Anderson, The Wee House at the Loaning, Peat Road, Muthill PH5 2PA
Tel: 01764 681 383 or 0798 0914 881 • e-mail: info@weehousescotland.co.uk • www.weehousescotland.co.uk

---

symbols

 Totally non-smoking

 Children Welcome

 Suitable for Disabled Guests

 Pets Welcome

 SB Short Breaks available

 Licensed

Alva

Stirling & The Trossachs

At the heart of Scotland, Stirling & The Trossachs has played a central role in most aspects of the
nation's life. History and geography have converged here in road and rail routes, in decisive sieges
and battles, in important industrial developments and heritage. The county enjoys the natural
riches of the Forth valley and the economic wealth of Grangemouth and Falkirk. The town of
Stirling itself is a natural tourist centre, both for its own attractions, such as the historic castle
and the excellent shopping facilities, and as a base for other visitor attractions close at hand.
Villages and small towns such as Drymen, Killearn, Fintry and Kippen offer hospitality and
interesting outings. Loch Lomond and The Trossachs National Park is less than an hour from
Glasgow, yet feels worlds apart from the bustle of city life. Explore wild glens and sparkling lochs,
and for the more energetic, low-level walking, cycling, and hill walking can be enjoyed.

Scottish Islands

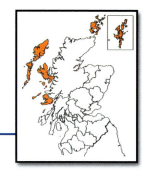

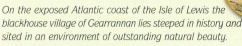

Irresistible Orkney

Hostel, Caravan and Camping Accommodation

Warbeth Beach overlooking the Hoy Hills

Point of Ness Caravan & Camping Site, Stromness

Stromness is a small picturesque town with impressive views of the hills of Hoy. The site is one mile from the harbour in a quiet, shoreline location. Many leisure activities are available close by, including fishing, sea angling, golf and a swimming & fitness centre.

Contact: stromnesscashoffice@orkney.gov.uk or recreation@orkney.gov.uk
www.orkney.gov.uk • Tel: 01856 850262

Birsay Outdoor Centre / Caravan & Camping Site
A new campsite located on the 3-Star hostel site in the picturesque north west of Orkney.

Hoy Centre
Four Star hostel accommodation with en suite facilities.
Ideal base for exploring Hoy's magnificent scenery and natural environment.

Rackwick Hostel
Rackwick is considered one of the most beautiful places in Orkney with towering cliffs and steep heathery hills. This cosy hostel has spectacular views over Rackwick's cliffs and beach.

For Birsay, Hoy and Rackwick contact recreation@orkney.gov.uk
Tel: 01856 873535 • www.hostelsorkney.co.uk

The Pickaquoy Centre and Camping Park, Kirkwall
Tel: 01856 879900

A 4-Star touring park with the latest in park amenities is situated at the Pickaquoy Centre complex, an impressive leisure facility offering a range of activities for all the family. Within walking distance of the St Magnus Cathedral and Kirkwall town centre.

e-mail: enquiries@pickaquoy.com • www.pickaquoy.co.uk

ORKNEY
ISLANDS COUNCIL

SB

Hannabreck
Dounby
Orkney Isles

Charming, recently refurbished old-style Orkney cottage. Two-bedroomed with old fashioned box beds. Bathroom with bath and level access shower. Living room has an open fire to burn peat, combined kitchen with dishwasher, washing machine/dryer. The flagstone and wooden floors are heated by ground source heat extracted from the surrounding land. Situated in quiet bird and wildlife conservation area. Many archaeological and historical sites nearby. Free local trout fishing. Internet access available.

Contact: Mrs P. Norquoy, Bigging, Dounby, Orkney Isles KW17 2HR • Tel: 01856 771340 e-mail: enquiries@lochlandchalets.co.uk www.hannabreck.co.uk

Scottish Tourist Board ★★★★ Self Catering

While every effort is made to ensure accuracy, we regret that FHG Guides cannot accept responsibility for errors, misrepresentations or omissions in our entries or any consequences thereof. Prices in particular should be checked. We will follow up complaints but cannot act as arbiters or agents for either party.

Kinlochleven

Dumfries

Newton Stewart

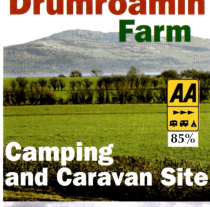
Laide

Almost a botanical garden, Linnhe is recognised as one of the best
and most beautiful Lochside parks in Britain. Magnificent gardens
contrast with the wild, dramatic scenery of Loch Eil and the

mountains beyond. Superb amenities, launderette,
shop & bakery, and free fishing on private shoreline
with its own jetty all help give Linnhe its Five
Star grading. Linnhe Lochside
Holidays is ideally situated for

day trips with Oban, Skye, Mull, Inverness and the
Cairngorms all within easy driving distance.

Holiday Caravans from £240 per week
Touring pitches from £16 per night
Tent pitches from £12 per night
 Pets welcome
Tourer playground, pet exercise area
Motorhome waste and water facilities
Recycling on park
Colour brochure sent with pleasure.

www.linnhe-lochside-holidays.co.uk/brochure
Tel: 01397 772 376 to check availability

Abingdon

Alyth

symbols

	Totally non-smoking		Pets Welcome
	Children Welcome	**SB**	Short Breaks available
	Suitable for Disabled Guests		Licensed

Dôl-Einion, see page 488.

Anglesey & Gwynedd

Conwy, Criccieth

Criccieth, Dulas Bay

SB

Cefn Uchaf Farm • Garndolbenmaen LL51 9PJ

A warm welcome awaits you at Cefn Uchaf, a family-run farm guest house set in beautiful open countryside overlooking Snowdonia's Cwm Pennant Valley. Our large modernised farmhouse offers comfort in a friendly, relaxed atmosphere.

There are eight well appointed bedrooms; all have colour TV, tea and coffee making facilities, hairdryers and radio alarm clocks. The comfortable residents' lounge has a log fire and a selection of games and books.

Start your day with a hearty breakfast, served at your own table. Choose from a selection of fruit juices, cereals, fresh fruits and yoghurts. Our full cooked breakfast includes Welsh bacon, sausage and free-range eggs.

Home-cooked evening meals are available. We are not licensed but please feel free to bring a bottle of wine to enjoy with your meal.

Wales Cymru ★★★

e-mail: enquiries@cefnuchaf.co.uk • www.cefnuchaf.com • Tel: 01766 530239

Beautiful Victorian Country House standing in 23 acres of woodland, gardens and fields.
High standard of accommodation in family, twin and double rooms, all en suite.

Guest lounge and dining room with panoramic view of Dulas Bay. Extensive garden with woodland walks.

Traditional Welsh breakfast with produce from own 'True Taste of Wales' Award-Winning Smokery.

Children welcome.

Pets welcome. Stabling/grazing available.
Mrs Gwen McCreadie

Deri Isaf

Dulas Bay, Isle of Anglesey LL70 9DX
Tel: 01248 410536 • Mobile: 07721 374471
e-mail: mccreadie@deriisaf.freeserve.co.uk
www.angleseyfarms.com/deri.htm

Wales Cymru ★★★★

SILVER ARIAN 2009 ANGLESEY TOURISM AWARDS GWOBRAU TWRISTIAETH MÔN

WINNER ENILLYDD 2010 ANGLESEY TOURISM AWARDS GWOBRAU TWRISTIAETH MÔN

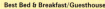
Best Bed & Breakfast/Guesthouse

Glanygors

This 3 Star guest house with two acres of land is situated 400 yards from a sandy beach, and has beautiful views of the mountains. It is 1½ miles from Harlech Castle, golf club and swimming pool, and within 500 yards of the train station. Ideal place for bird-watching. Presenting good home-cooking in a homely and relaxed atmosphere and run by a Welsh-speaking family.

One double, one twin and one family bedrooms (one en suite), all with washbasin, TV and tea-making facilities; bathroom, toilet; TV lounge, dining room. Central heating and electric blankets for winter months. Open all year.

B&B from £25pppn
Reduced rates for children.

Mrs G.M. Evans, Glanygors, Llandanwg, Harlech LL46 2SD • 01341 241410

Hotel Maes-y-Neuadd

Talsarnau, Near Harlech LL47 6YA
Tel: 01766 780200
Fax: 01766 780211
e-mail: maes@neuadd.com
www.neuadd.com

A warm welcome awaits you at this historic Welsh manor house, nestled on a hillside in the heart of Snowdonia, with fabulous views of the mountains and coast. Dating back to 14th century, this beautiful granite building is now a 4-Star Gold Award country house hotel, set amongst 80 acres of gardens, parkland, forest and vegetable/kitchen gardens. Happily, 21st century amenities together with excellent friendly service ensure a relaxing and comfortable stay! Ideally situated for exploring Snowdonia and its many attractions and with a range of rooms and prices to suit all tastes and budgets; an award-winning restaurant serving fresh local produce (much from our own gardens) and an excellent wine list – it's definitely a great place to stay and well worth paying us a visit!

We are open for morning coffee, lunch, afternoon tea, dinner or, if you fancy a treat, champagne and strawberries on the terrace!
Children welcome – children's menu, early teas, baby listening, family dining room.
Dogs also welcome in two of our Coach House rooms – dog sitting by arrangement.

Good Hotel Guide
Country House Hotel
of the Year 2003

Betws-y-Coed

North Wales

Conwy, Rhos-on-Sea

The Hand at Llanarmon

Standing in the glorious and hidden Ceiriog Valley, The Hand at Llanarmon radiates charm and character. With 13 comfortable en suite bedrooms, roaring log fires, and fabulous food served with flair and generosity, this is a wonderful base for most country pursuits, or just relaxing in good company.

Tel: 01691 600666
e-mail: reception@thehandhotel.co.uk
www.TheHandHotel.co.uk

Llanarmon DC
Ceiriog Valley
Near Llangollen
North Wales
LL20 7LD

Llanelli

Carmarthenshire

Best Western Diplomat Hotel
Felinfoel, Llanelli SA15 3PJ
Tel: 01554 756156 • Fax: 01554 751649
AA/WTB ★★★

The Diplomat Hotel offers a rare combination of charm and character, with excellent well appointed facilities to ensure your comfort. Explore the Gower Peninsula and the breathtaking West Wales coastline. Salmon & trout fishing, horse riding, golf, and motor racing at Pembrey are all within reach.

e-mail: reservations@diplomat-hotel-wales.com • www.bw-diplomathotel.co.uk

All our 50 bedrooms are stylish and modern, boasting much character and charm. Modern luxury and comfort is integrated with traditional furnishings, allowing relaxation with the familiar comforts of home. All of our rooms include the following: En-suite facilities • Direct-dial telephone Television • Tea & coffee-making facilities Hairdryer • High speed internet access Use of Chasens Health Club and Spa

Our chefs use the finest, freshest ingredients, sourced locally where ever possible, with imaginative presentation to excite the palate. Recently added to the front of the historic mansion, the Atrium is a wonderful fully glassed conservatory, which is comfortably air-conditioned. During the summer, drinks can be enjoyed on the terrace outside the conservatory. We are open to non-residents for morning coffee, lunch, afternoon teas and dinner.

Carmarthenshire is surely the best region for an activity or leisure break, with activities for everyone from cycling to bird watching, and from walking to sailing and fishing. The region also boasts many good golf courses , offering affordable golf to players of all abilities. The Millennium Coastal Park is one of the most popular tourist attractions in Britain, with breathtaking views of the Gower Peninsula, and a unique variety of attractions stretching from Pembrey Country Park with its acres of beautiful parkland, and one of the best beaches in the UK, as well as many excellent family attractions. Visitors will enjoy exploring the many interesting little villages, and there is an endless choice of places to eat and drink, including pubs, restaurants, inns and cafes.

Haverfordwest

Pembrokeshire

SB

There is a genuine welcome to our mixed working family farm. Quietly set in beautiful countryside surrounded by animals and wild life. Comfortable, well appointed accommodation. Bedrooms with tea/coffee tray, radio, TV and en suite facilities. Excellent quality food using home and local produce. Families welcome. Deductions for children and Senior Citizens.

Open January to December. Pretty flowers, lawns in relaxed surroundings. Personal attention. Unrestricted access.

Ideally situated in central Pembrokeshire for coastline walks. Sandy beaches. Bird islands, castles, city of St Davids, Tenby.

Bed and Breakfast • Bed, Breakfast and Evening Dinner. Terms on application.

**Mrs M. E. Davies, Cuckoo Mill Farm, Pelcomb Bridge, St David's Road, Haverfordwest SA62 6EA
Tel: 01437 762139
www.cuckoomillfarm.co.uk**

Pembrokeshire's entire coastline is a designated National Park, with its sheltered coves and wooded estuaries, fine sandy beaches and some of the most dramatic cliffs in Britain. The islands of Skomer, Stokholm and Grasholm are home to thousands of seabirds, and Ramsey Island, as well as being an RSPB Reserve boasts the second largest grey seal colony in Britain. Pembrokeshire's mild climate and the many delightful towns and villages, family attractions and outdoor facilities such as surfing, water skiing, diving, pony trekking and fishing make this a favourite holiday destination. .

Goodwick

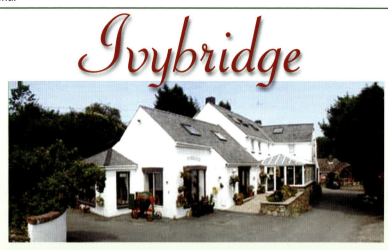

Welcome to Ivybridge

Situated in a quiet part of Goodwick, Ivybridge is a friendly, family-run guest house offering comfortable accommodation just outside of Fishguard, a picturesque area of Pembrokeshire, within easy reach of the Pembrokeshire coastal paths, the historic City of St David's and beautiful beaches.

Try our small heated indoor swimming pool, relax in our conservatory or put your feet up in front of a roaring fire in the bar/lounge area and enjoy the company and atmosphere at Ivybridge.

All rooms are en suite, with Freeview television, hairdryers and hot drink facilities. Wake up to a Full Welsh Breakfast or a Continental Breakfast. Vegetarian guests are welcome and all dietary needs can be catered for. At Ivybridge we offer home cooked evening meals by arrangement using fresh locally sourced ingredients wherever possible (please book before arrival). We serve evening meals between 6.30-7.30 pm. Our guests are more than welcome to bring friends and family to dine with them. We also cater for smaller functions and parties.

For further information
please contact us
Ivybridge, Drim Mill, Dyffryn,
Goodwick SA64 0JT
Tel: 01348 875366 • Fax: 01348 872338
e-mail: ivybridge5366@aol.com
www.ivybridgeleisure.co.uk

Wales
Cymru

★★★

SB

East Hook Farmhouse

SB

Jen welcomes you to this Georgian Farmhouse, which is surrounded by beautiful countryside, and is situated four miles from the coastline and three miles from Haverfordwest.

Spacious bedrooms offer comfort where you can relax and unwind. All are en suite or have private facilities, and are tastefully decorated.

Double, twin and family suites and ground floor rooms are available.

Relax in the breakfast room and enjoy a wide menu choice. Superb traditional home cooking is offered, including vegetarian, with home-made bread & preserves. Local produce is used whenever possible.

When you return to the farmhouse after a day out in the Pembrokeshire countryside you can relax in the comfortable lounge, which is furnished with antique pieces and large pictures for the guests to enjoy.

Bed and Breakfast from £32.50 to £45pp.

Mrs Jen Patrick, East Hook Farm, Portfield Gate, Haverfordwest, Pembroke SA62 3LN

★★★★

Tel: 01437 762211
www.easthookfarmhouse.co.uk

SB

LANGDON FARM GUEST HOUSE

Saundersfoot & Tenby

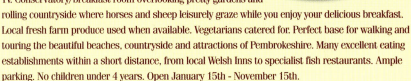

Beautifully appointed, idyllic farm guesthouse on working farm overlooking two small lakes in a perfect location close to Saundersfoot and Tenby. All bedrooms en suite with central heating, colour TV, radio alarm clock and tea/coffee/hot chocolate making facilities. Separate guest sitting room with colour TV. Conservatory/breakfast room overlooking pretty gardens and rolling countryside where horses and sheep leisurely graze while you enjoy your delicious breakfast. Local fresh farm produce used when available. Vegetarians catered for. Perfect base for walking and touring the beautiful beaches, countryside and attractions of Pembrokeshire. Many excellent eating establishments within a short distance, from local Welsh Inns to specialist fish restaurants. Ample parking. No children under 4 years. Open January 15th - November 15th.

Bed and Breakfast £32 - £35pppn (based on two sharing). Welcome Host Gold Award.

KILGETTY, NEAR SAUNDERSFOOT SA68 0NJ • TEL: 01834 814803
e-mail: mail@stayinpembrokeshire.co.uk   www.stayinpembrokeshire.co.uk

Powys

Llanbrynean is a fine, traditional, Victorian farmhouse peacefully situated on the edge of the picturesque village of Llanfrynach, 3 miles south-east of Brecon. We are in an ideal spot for exploring the area - the Brecon Beacons rise behind the farm and the Brecon/ Monmouth canal flows through the fields below.
We are a working family sheep farm with wonderful pastoral views and a large garden. The house is spacious and comfortable with a friendly, relaxed atmosphere. We have two double en suite bedrooms and one twin with private bathroom. All have tea/coffee facilities. There is a sitting room with TV. Excellent pub food within easy walking distance.

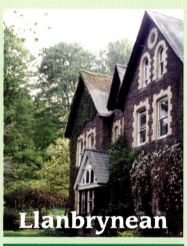

Llanbrynean

Bed and Breakfast from £28pp

Mrs A. Harpur, Llanbrynean Farm, Llanfrynach, Brecon LD3 7BQ

Tel: 01874 665222
e-mail: simon.harpur@tiscali.co.uk

Powys is situated right on England's doorstep and boasts some of most spectacular scenery in Europe. It is ideal for an action-packed holiday with fishing, golf, pony trekking, sailing and canal cruising readily available, and walkers have a choice of everything from riverside trails to mountain hikes. Offa's Dyke Path runs for 177 miles through Border country, often following the ancient earthworks, while Glyndwr's Way takes in some of the finest landscape features in Wales on its journey from Knighton to Machynlleth and back to the borders at Welshpool. There are border towns with Georgian architecture and half-timbered black and white houses to visit, or wander round the wonderful shops in the book town of Hay, famous for its Literary Festival each May. There are Victorian spa towns too, with even the smallest of places holding festivals and events throughout the year.

Brecon, Builth Wells

SB

SB

Llandrindod Wells, Montgomery

www.smoothHound.co.uk

Tastefully restored Tudor farmhouse on working farm in peaceful location. En suite bedrooms with breathtaking views over fields and woods, colour TV, beverage trays. Two lounges with log fires. Renowned for excellent food. Wonderful area for wildlife, walking, cycling, near Red Kite feeding station. Safe parking. Brochure on request.

Bed, Breakfast and Evening Meal weekly from £300 to £320. Bed and Breakfast from £28 to £38 per day.

Mrs Ruth Jones, Holly Farm, Howey, Llandrindod Wells LD1 5PP
Tel & Fax: 01597 822402 • Taste of Wales Tourism Award • Farm Stay UK Member

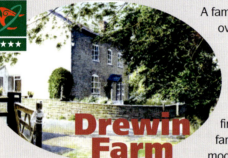

A family-run mixed farm set on hillside overlooking panoramic views of the most beautiful countryside.

The Drewin is a charming 17th century farmhouse retaining much of its original character with oak beams and large inglenook fireplace, separate lounge; twin and family rooms, both en suite and all modern amenities with colour TV.

Full central heating. Offa's Dyke footpath runs through the farm - a wonderful area for wildlife. Ideal base for touring the many beauty spots around. Good home cooking and a very warm welcome await our visitors.

Bed and Breakfast £28 for one night, £27 for more than one night
Evening-Meal by arrangement. Open March to October.

Featured in the BBC Travel Show. Holder of Essential Food Hygiene Certificate and Farmhouse Award from Wales Tourist Board, AA Best Breakfast in Wales Award.

Ceinwen Richards, The Drewin Farm, Churchstoke, Montgomery SY15 6TW • Tel: 01588 620325
drewinfarm@hotmail.com • www.offasdyke.co.uk/drewinfarm

Welshpool

Lane Farm

*A **warm welcome awaits*** on our working organic beef and sheep farm situated between Welshpool and Shrewsbury. Nestling beneath the tranquil Breidden Hills in the picturesque Severn Valley, ideally situated to explore The Marches, Shropshire Hills and Mid Wales. Accommodation consists of four spacious, modern, en suite bedrooms, two on the ground floor. All rooms have central heating, TV, beverage tray and radio alarm clock. Hearty farmhouse breakfasts. Local pubs offering excellent evening meals just a short drive or walk away.
Ample safe parking • Free fishing by arrangement • Non-smoking throughout.

Tel: 01743 884288 • Lane Farm, Criggion, Near Welshpool, Powys SY5 9BG
e-mail: lesley@lanefarmbedandbreakfast.co.uk
www.lanefarmbedandbreakfast.co.uk

South Wales

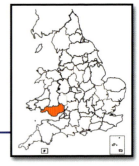

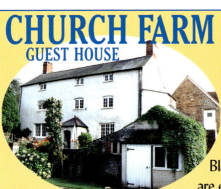

Wales' most complete resort

**Exhilarating cliff-top walks & stunning scenery
Special Short Break Packages available**

This magical location – once the 12th century estate of Lord St David – dominates the cliff-top overlooking Lydstep Bay and beautiful Caldey Island.

Set in the only coastal National Park in the UK, the original whitewashed stone buildings have been recreated as luxury cottages. Included in the price of your holiday are all our leisure facilities: a 9-hole golf course, indoor heated pool, hot-tub, gym, sauna and all-weather tennis courts.

Visit the only Elemis Premier Spa in West Wales with over 80 blissful treatments and holistic therapies designed to pamper and relax you.

Our stylish Italian influenced cliff-top restaurant Waves serves a variety of locally sourced à la carte dishes and our Welsh themed menu on a Thursday night is popular with locals and visitors alike.

Contact us to request our magazine to receive details of all our short break packages and how you can discover the Celtic Haven Experience.

**Lydstep, Near Tenby SA70 7SG
01834 870000 • www.celtichaven.co.uk
e-mail: welcome@celtichaven.com**

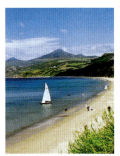

SB

Bala, Caernarfon

Anglesey & Gwynedd

Glanllyn Lodge

17th century gatehouse lodge lovingly restored with all new furnishings and fittings, comprising one en suite double bedroom, one twin and one single bedroom, luxury bathroom with spa bath, large oak kitchen/diner and a lounge with Sky TV and DVD player. All rooms are on ground floor level with level entry at front door suitable for wheelchairs. Occupants have access to 16 acres of parkland bordering on Wales' largest natural lake. This parkland is also a touring caravan and camping park from April to September. There is access to the lake and river for fishing, sailing and canoeing.

Megan W. Pugh, Glanllyn, Llanuwchllyn, Bala, LL23 7ST (01678 540227)
e-mail: info@glanllyn.com • www.glanllyn.com

THE CHALET is set in 200 acres of parkland, 1.5 miles east of Caernarfon, at the edge of the Snowdonia National Park. • fitted kitchen leading to lounge and dining area • bathroom • one double bedroom, the other with two single beds. It can accommodate a maximum of four people . Well behaved pets allowed (max. 2).

SB

Amenities on the park include: heated outdoor pool, club room, entertainment, bar meals, takeaway food, supermarket, launderette.

Enquiries/bookings: Mr H. Arfon Jones, 12 Lon Isaf, Menai Bridge, Anglesey LL59 5LN • Tel/Fax: 01248 712045
hajones@northwales-chalet.co.uk • www.northwales-chalet.co.uk

Anglesey & Gwynedd is rich in archaeological and historical heritage, and is home to a diversity of wildlife which inhabit the cliffs, estuaries, heaths and rich farmland. Tourists love the unspoilt beaches and extensive sands, and the popular seafront at Benllech offers miles of clean golden sands, safe bathing, boating, fishing and windsurfing activities, as well as the usual ice cream kiosks, seaside shops, and food. Snowdonia to the west attracts climbers and walkers, but the less active will enjoy the 9 mile return journey on Bala Lake Railway which runs alongside Llyn Tegid, or Bala Lake as it also known, and through the beautiful Snowdonia National Park to the market town of Bala.

Enchanting Castle Apartments within a romantic Regency Castle of timeless charm, and a much-loved home. (Grade II* Listed Building of Architectural/Historic interest).
Centrally situated in gentle Snowdonian foothills for enjoying North Wales' magnificent mountains, beaches, resorts, heritage and history.
Many local restaurants and inns nearby.
(Details available in our Information Room).

A delightfully unique selection for 2-4 persons of fully self-contained, beautifully appointed, spacious, clean and peaceful accommodation, each with its own distinctive, individual character. Generously and graciously enhanced with antiques/collectables.

32 acres of truly tranquil landscaped gardens, sweeping lawns, woodland walks and panoramic hill-walk overlooking sea, Anglesey and Snowdon. The comfortable, warm and welcoming Castle in serene surroundings is open all year, including for short breaks, offering privacy and relaxation – ideal for couples. Regret children not accepted. Fully inclusive rents, including breakfast cereals etc., and much, much more...

Please contact Mrs Marita Gray-Parry directly any time for a brochure/booking
Self catering Apartments within the Castle
e.g. 2 persons for 2 nights from £195 incl "Romantic Breaks"
Inclusive Weekly Rents from £500
Llanrug, Near Caernarfon, Gwynedd LL55 4RE
Tel & Fax: (01286) 870210
e-mail: holidays@brynbrascastle.co.uk • www.brynbrascastle.co.uk

Llanberis, Pwllheli

Bryn Gwyn Cottage
Llanberis, Anglesey & Gwynedd

Tan-y-Coed
Llanrug, Caernarfon
Tel: 07887 790714

Cosy cottage at the foot of Snowdon, sleeps five.
All modern conveniences. Ideal for mountains, lakes, rivers,
castles, horse riding, fishing, climbing, watersports,
beaches, golf, sailing; private guides. Pets welcome.

Contact Mr Eaton for details.

Crugeran
Gwyliau fferm ~ Farm holidays

SB

Self-catering holiday accommodation in a farmhouse and converted barn in beautiful North Wales.

Three cottages (sleep 4-7), very tastefully decorated in keeping with their character with antique furniture throughout, providing spacious, comfortable and well equipped accommodation.

The cottages have separate patios with picnic tables, and ample parking areas in a large communal lawned garden with fruit trees, making them ideal for individual parties or a larger split party.

Also comfortable large farmhouse one mile away (sleeps 12). It has been lovingly furnished and decorated throughout, with some original furniture auction finds, quality reproduction pieces and welcoming colours on a neutral background. Pets welcome in this property only.

Abersoch, Aberdaron, Nefyn and all the beautiful sandy beaches of the peninsula are all close at hand. Walking, golf, sea fishing trips and plenty of water sport facilities are available. The market town of Pwllheli, the resorts of Criccieth and Porthmadog as well as numerous historic and scenic attractions such as the Snowdonia National Park , Ffestiniog Railway, castles and the Italianate village of Portmeirion are all easily reached from Crugeran Farm Holidays.

Cymru Wales

Mrs Rhian Parry, Crugeran, Sarn Mellteyrn, Pwllheli, Gwynedd LL53 8DT
Tel: 01758 730 375 • e-mail: post@crugeran.com
www.crugeran.com

symbols

 Totally non-smoking   *Pets Welcome*

 Children Welcome   **SB** *Short Breaks available*

 Suitable for Disabled Guests   *Licensed*

North Wales

In North Wales there are charming towns and villages to explore, soft sandy beaches and
rugged coastline, and as many castles, stately homes, gardens, parks, craft centres, museums and
steam trains as anyone could desire. Better book a long holiday to start the grand tour, and then
come back again to catch up with all that you will surely have missed. Betws-y-Coed, North Wales'
most popular inland resort, houses The Snowdonia National Visitor Centre with its craft units and
thrilling video presentations – always worth a visit. For fun filled family holidays try Llandudno,
where a whole host of summer events and activities can be enjoyed, or Rhyl with its Children's
Village on the Promenade, plus amusements, boating ponds and fairground. Walkers and
cyclists will revel in the breathtaking scenery of the Prestatyn hillside and the Clwydian Range
and will find all the information that they need at Offa's Dyke Visitor Centre. Most people would
enjoy a break in Llangollen with its variety of attractions.

SB

Llandeilo

Carmarthenshire

SB

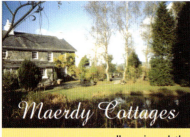

Located in one of the loveliest valleys in Wales and surrounded by woods and farmland, this 300-year-old farm and its original stone buildings have been beautifully converted into six cottages sleeping between 3 and 10. The cottages enjoy a tranquil setting, are furnished with many antiques and are well equipped throughout. They are warm, welcoming and cosy retreats, ideal for a holiday at any time of the year. From this idyllic centre enjoy local walks and famous gardens and discover the beautiful coast and countryside of Carmarthenshire. The grounds offer plenty of space for children and dogs. Two cottages are fully wheelchair accessible, and all are ideal for families of all ages. Home cooked evening meals available. Open all year. Enquiries:

Maerdy Cottages, Taliaris, Llandeilo, Carmarthenshire SA19 7DA • 01550 777448
e-mail: enquiries@maerdyholidaycottages.co.uk
www.maerdyholidaycottages.co.uk

Carmarthenshire is surely the best region for an activity or leisure break, with activities for everyone from cycling to bird watching, and from walking to sailing and fishing. The region also boasts many good golf courses, offering affordable golf to players of all abilities. The Millennium Coastal Park is one of the most popular tourist attractions in Britain, with breathtaking views of the Gower Peninsula, and a unique variety of attractions stretching from Pembrey Country Park with its acres of beautiful parkland, and one of the best beaches in the UK, as well as many excellent family attractions. Visitors will enjoy exploring the many interesting little villages, and there is an endless choice of places to eat and drink, including pubs, restaurants, inns and cafes.

Aberporth

Ceredigion

Penffynnon Holiday Properties

This small cluster of self-contained properties enjoys a unique and special setting in the quiet holiday village of Aberporth on Cardigan Bay. All visitors are delighted when they first arrive and find out just how close they are to the water's edge - every one of our properties is within 200 yards of the sea. It's hard to imagine a more relaxing holiday.

SB

DOLPHIN COTTAGE (pictured) is all on one level (Access Grade 2) and sleeps 6 in three bedrooms. **MORAWEL** has 5 bedrooms and 4 bathrooms, and sleeps 10. **CILGWYN** has been converted into two self-contained villas, each with 3 bedrooms. **TY BROC** is a split level house to sleep 8.

All are very well equipped, and prices include bed linen, heating and lighting. Open all year.

For details contact: **Jann Tucker, Penffynnon, Aberporth, Ceredigion SA43 2DA**
Tel: 01239 810387 • e-mail: jann@aberporth.com • www.aberporth.com

Dolphin Cottage

**Readers are requested to mention this FHG guide
when seeking accommodation**

Other British holiday guides from FHG Guides

**PUBS & INNS · 300 GREAT HOTELS
SHORT BREAK HOLIDAYS
The bestselling and original PETS WELCOME!
THE GOLF GUIDE - Where to Play, Where to Stay
SELF-CATERING HOLIDAYS · BED & BREAKFAST STOPS
CARAVAN & CAMPING HOLIDAYS · FAMILY BREAKS**

Published annually: available in all good bookshops or direct from the publisher:
**FHG Guides, Abbey Mill Business Centre, Seedhill, Paisley PA1 1TJ
Tel: 0141 887 0428 • Fax: 0141 889 7204
e-mail: admin@fhguides.co.uk • www.holidayguides.com**

Pembrokeshire

Carne Farm

Stone cottage adjoining farmhouse, sleeps six in three bedrooms, also a spacious residential caravan for six with two bedrooms, each with its own garden where children can play safely. In peaceful countryside on 350 acre dairy and sheep farm between Fishguard and Strumble Head, three miles from the sea. Within easy reach of many beaches by car, ideal for walking and bird-watching. No linen supplied. Children welcome. TV, microwave, cots, high chair. Baby sitting available. You can be sure of a warm welcome and visitors can feed calves and watch the milking.

Contact: Mrs Rosemary Johns

**Goodwick,
Pembrokeshire SA64 0LB
Tel: 01348 891665**

Pembrokeshire's entire coastline is a designated National Park, with its sheltered coves and wooded estuaries, fine sandy beaches and some of the most dramatic cliffs in Britain. The islands of Skomer, Stokholm and Grasholm are home to thousands of seabirds, and Ramsey Island, as well as being an RSPB Reserve boasts the second largest grey seal colony in Britain. Pembrokeshire's mild climate and the many delightful towns and villages, family attractions and outdoor facilities such as surfing, water skiing, diving, pony trekking and fishing make this a favourite holiday destination. .

Keeston Hill Cottage

KEESTON, HAVERFORDWEST
PEMBROKESHIRE SA62 6EJ
Tel: 01437 710440

Two fully equipped comfortable apartments sleeping 4/5 each, in a beautifully converted cottage with garden. 2½ miles from fabulous beaches. Open all year.

enquiries@keestonhillcottage.co.uk
www.keestonhillcottage.co.uk

SB

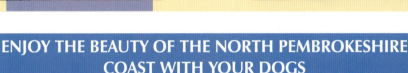

Prices from £240 to £450 per week; heating, electricity and linen incl.

Wales Cymru ★★★★

ENJOY THE BEAUTY OF THE NORTH PEMBROKESHIRE COAST WITH YOUR DOGS
Tel: 01239 881 280

Ty Newydd consists of three cottages:
• TY NEWYDD BACH (a one-bedroom cottage),
• TY NEWYDD NO. 2 (a semi-detached two-bedroom cottage),
• TY NEWYDD NO. 3 (a two-bedroom detached cottage)
in the pretty village of Moylegrove on the North Pembrokeshire Coast.

All the cottages are equipped with electric cookers, microwaves, fridges and washing machines. No. 3 has a multi-burning stove in the comfortable sitting room, a well equipped kitchen, and upstairs two bedrooms — one with a double bed and the other with two singles — and a shower room. Bed linen is provided but not towels.

Dogs welcome free of charge. Enclosed garden.

St Davids

Ffynnon Ddofn is situated in a quiet lane between St Davids and Fishguard, with panoramic views over 18 miles of coastline. The cottage is warm, comfortable and very well equipped, with 3 bedrooms sleeping 6 (double, twin and bunks). Attractive lounge/ diner with exposed natural stone wall and beams, television, DVD and CD players. Bath/shower room, new fitted kitchen with dishwasher, and central heating. Washing machine, tumble dryer, freezer. There is a large games room with table tennis and snooker, also a barbecue and pleasant, secure garden. Footpath from lane to beach and coast path. Parking beside cottage. For more information and photographs please visit the website:

www.ffynnonddofn.co.uk

For details contact: Mrs B. Rees White, Brickhouse Farm, Burnham Road, Woodham Mortimer, Maldon, Essex CM9 6SR Tel: 01245 224611

❖ Porthiddy Farm ❖
HOLIDAY COTTAGES

Near St Davids, two attractive stone and slate self-catering cottages with two bedrooms each. Sleep 4 and 5. Wales Tourist Board's 5-star rating confirms the quality and comfort. Set within sight of the sea in Pembrokeshire's National Park, 500 yards from the beach and coast path. Prices include heating, electricity and linen. Pets by arrangement.

Contact: Mrs M.Pike,
Porthiddy Farm West, Abereiddy,
Pembrokeshire SA62 6DR
Tel: 01348 831004
e-mail: m.pike@porthiddy.com
www.porthiddy.com

Wales
Cymru
★★★★★

Whitland

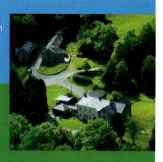
Powys

Llanfair Caereinion

Powys is situated right on England's doorstep and boasts some of most spectacular scenery in Europe. It is ideal for an action-packed holiday with fishing, golf, pony trekking, sailing and canal cruising readily available, and walkers have a choice of everything from riverside trails to mountain hikes. Offa's Dyke Path runs for 177 miles through Border country, often following the ancient earthworks, while Glyndwr's Way takes in some of the finest landscape features in Wales on its journey from Knighton to Machynlleth and back to the borders at Welshpool. There are border towns with Georgian architecture and half-timbered black and white houses to visit, or wander round the wonderful shops in the book town of Hay, famous for its Literary Festival each May. There are Victorian spa towns too, with even the smallest of places holding festivals and events throughout the year.

Presteigne

Cosy cottage in lovely Border countryside, two miles from Offa's Dyke, ideal centre for touring Mid Wales, its beautiful borderland, South Shropshire and Herefordshire.

• Central heating, washing machine, dishwasher, microwave, colour TV, inglenook fireplace, woodburner, linen included • Power shower over bath
• Two light and airy bedrooms – twin and double • Sleeps 4 plus cot
• Ample parking • Private secure sun-trap garden
• On working farm in peaceful hamlet • Children and pets welcome

**MRS R. L. JONES, UPPER HOUSE, KINNERTON,
NEAR PRESTEIGNE LD8 2PE • Tel: 01547 560207**

PENLLWYN LODGES
– MID WALES SELF CATERING HOLIDAYS –

Welcome to our Self Catering Holiday Park ...

Situated in the heart of Montgomeryshire, Mid Wales.

Penllwyn Lodges is the setting for a superb holiday for all seasons.

19 individually architect designed lodges set in 30 acres of unspoilt woodland teeming with an abundance of wildlife, offering the charming beauty of the Shropshire borders to the east and the rugged Welsh mountains and Cardigan Bay to the west.

On your arrival you will be delighted by the welcome given by Noddy the donkey, Tilley the llama, two Kune Kune pigs, Shetland ponies and Sam the parrot.

For the coarse angler we have a large pool stocked with Carp, Tench, Roach, Bream and Rudd and we also have fishing rights along the River Severn.

We have now opened a 9-hole golf course adjacent to Penllwyn Lodges with a pay and play system.
The clubhouse is open all day every day serving breakfasts, lunches and evening restaurant meals.

Well behaved pets are most welcome in specified lodges.

Week and Short Breaks available throughout the year.

Ideal for those seeking a peaceful and relaxing holiday.

**Phillip, Daphne & Emma Jones,
Penllwyn Lodges
Garthmyl, Powys SY15 6SB
Tel/Fax: 01686 640269
www.penllwynlodges.co.uk
e-mail: daphne.jones@onetel.net**

South Wales

As well as being an ideal holiday destination in its own right Swansea Bay is a perfect base for touring the rest of South Wales. A great place for all sorts of watersports such as sailing canoeing, fishing and waterskiing, or you may prefer such land based activities as walking, cycling and horse riding. Just a short journey from the City you will find the beautiful Glamorgan Heritage Coast, overlooked by dramatic cliffs. Especially popular with walkers and hikers this area is also ideal for long, leisurely strolls in the secluded coves and inlets along the coast. There are more than 15 golf courses here including the famous Royal Porthcawl. For something different visit the Wye Valley and the Vale of Usk with awesome castles, breathtaking scenery and a rich and colourful history.

Stunningly beautiful beaches...

... are right on your doorstep when you stay with us.

We are the agency with the widest range of affordable self-catering holiday cottages, houses and apartments in Gower, Mumbles and the Maritime Quarter of Swansea.

Whether you want to experience the sheer beauty and breathtaking scenery of the area, partake in some of the activities on offer or visit one of the many attractions there is so much to do and see come rain or shine.

Designated as Britain's first area of outstanding natural beauty – and deservedly so, Gower offers a great variety of beaches and coves which attract everyone from surfers and sailors, to the bucket and spade brigade.

Visit Wales
Croeso Cymru

homefromhome.com
relax unwind enjoy...

42 Queens Rd, Mumbles, Swansea, SA3 4AN
Telephone +44 (0) 1792 360624
Email enquiries@homefromhome.com
Website www.homefromhome.com

Self Catering Holiday Accommodation in Swansea Bay, Mumbles, Gower & South West Wales

Dolgellau, Snowdonia

SB

Llwyn-Yr-Helm Farm

- Caravans, Dormobiles and tents; electric hook-ups. • Pets welcome. • Facilities for the disabled.
- • Toilet block • Laundry
- • Self-catering camping lodge available.

Mrs Helen Rowlands
Llwyn-Yr-Helm Farm, Brithdir, Dolgellau LL40 2SA
Tel: 01341 450254
e-mail: info@llwynyrhelmcaravanpark.co.uk
www.llwynyrhelmcaravanpark.co.uk

Situated on a minor road half a mile off B4416 which is a loop road between A470 and A494, this is a quiet, small working farm site, four miles from Dolgellau in beautiful countryside, ideal for walking and mountain biking.

Many places of interest in the area including slate mines, narrow gauge railways, lakes and mountains and nine miles from sandy beaches.

SB

BrynGloch
CAMPING & CARAVANNING PARK

Nestled in a picturesque valley on the banks of the River Gwyrfai at the foot of Snowdon. Bryn Gloch boasts level all-weather Super Pitches, Touring Pitches, Tent Pitches, Motorhome Pitches, Static Caravans and bunkhouse also for hire.

- • Electric Hook-ups
- • Luxury Toilet-Shower Blocks
- • Mother & Baby Room
- • Disabled Facilities
- • Fishing • Games Room
- • Shop/Off Licence
- • Pub & Restaurant within 1 mile
- • Free Wi-Fi

www.campwales.co.uk • Tel: 01286 650216

Killorglin (Co Kerry)   **IRELAND**

Bodmin Moor, St Mawgan

Colliford Tavern   "AN OASIS ON BODMIN MOOR"

Colliford Lake, Near St Neot, Liskeard, Cornwall PL14 6PZ • Tel: 01208 821335
e-mail: info@colliford.com • www.colliford.com

SB

Set in attractive grounds which include a children's play area, ponds and a working waterwheel, this delightfully furnished free house offers good food and bar snacks. Sprucely-appointed guest rooms are spacious and have en suite shower, colour television, radio alarm, beverage maker and numerous thoughtful extras.

An unusual feature of the tavern is a 37' deep granite well. In the midst of the scenic splendour of Bodmin Moor, this is a relaxing country retreat only a few minutes' walk from Colliford Lake, so popular with fly fishermen. Both north and south coasts are within easy driving distance and terms are most reasonable.

Campsite for touring caravans, motorhomes and tents - full electric hook-up etc available.

The Falcon Inn

Sarah and David would like to welcome you to The Falcon Inn, St Mawgan. We hope that you will enjoy a visit with us, whether it is just for a meal and a drink, or for a longer stay. The Inn comprises a bar area and separate restaurant. Outside there is a large well-kept garden.
There are also covered areas outside for eating alfresco.
The Falcon Inn has two luxury letting rooms: one double room and one twin room. The rooms are furnished to the highest standard and we pride ourselves on providing value for money. Each room contains tea/coffee making facilities, colour TV and telephone. Guide dogs only.

The Falcon Inn,
St Mawgan TR8 4EP
Tel: 01637 860225

AA
★★★★
Guest
Accommodation

e-mail: info@thefalconinn-stmawgan.co.uk
www.thefalconinn-stmawgan.co.uk

Parkend

Fordingbridge

Winterton-on-Sea

Market Drayton

Bury St Edmunds

Hindon

The Fox & Hounds Inn

Former 16th century coaching inn, now a high quality residential Country Inn & Restaurant set amidst the beautiful North York Moors. Freshly prepared dishes, using finest local produce, are served every lunchtime and evening, with selected quality wines and a choice of cask ales.
Excellent en suite accommodation is available.
Open all year. Winter Breaks available November to March.

For bookings please Tel: 01287 660218
Ainthorpe, Danby, Yorkshire YO21 2LD
e-mail: info@foxandhounds-ainthorpe.com
www.foxandhounds-ainthorpe.com

THE **FORRESTERS ARMS** HOTEL
Kilburn, North Yorkshire YO61 4AH

Dating from the 12th century, this is one of England's oldest inns. The Henry Dee Bar still retains evidence of the days when it was the stable and the cosy lower bar has an unusual rounded stone chimney breast where log fires exude cheer in chilly weather. Both bars are furnished with the work of Robert Thompson (the 'Mouseman') who carved a tiny mouse on every piece of furniture produced. Real ale is available in convivial surroundings and ample and well-presented Yorkshire fare will more than satisfy the healthiest appetite.
This is the heart of James Herriot Country, within the North York Moors National Park, and the hotel is well recommended as a touring base, having outstanding accommodation.

Tel: 01347 868386 • e-mail: admin@forrestersarms.com • www.forrestersarms.com

symbols

 Totally non-smoking

 Children Welcome

 Suitable for Disabled Guests

 Pets Welcome

SB *Short Breaks available*

℔ *Licensed*